**CHRONICLING POVERTY**

*Also by Tim Hitchcock*

ENGLISH SEXUALITIES, 1700–1800


*Also by Pamela Sharpe*

ADAPTING TO CAPITALISM: Working Women in the English Economy, 1700–1800

# Chronicling Poverty

## The Voices and Strategies of the English Poor, 1640–1840

Edited by

### Tim Hitchcock
*Senior Lecturer in Early Modern Social and Economic History*
*University of North London*

### Peter King
*Professor of Social History*
*Nene College*
*Northampton*

and

### Pamela Sharpe
*Lecturer in Economic and Social History*
*University of Bristol*

First published in Great Britain 1997 by
**MACMILLAN PRESS LTD**
Houndmills, Basingstoke, Hampshire RG21 6XS and London
Companies and representatives throughout the world

A catalogue record for this book is available from the British Library.

ISBN 0-333-64495-6 hardcover
ISBN 0-333-67891-5 paperback

First published in the United States of America 1997 by
**ST. MARTIN'S PRESS, INC.,**
Scholarly and Reference Division,
175 Fifth Avenue, New York, N.Y. 10010

ISBN 0-312-17293-1

Library of Congress Cataloging-in-Publication Data
Chronicling poverty : the voices and strategies of the English poor,
1640–1840 / edited by Tim Hitchcock, Peter King and Pamela Sharpe.
p.   cm.
Includes bibliographical references and index.
ISBN 0-312-17293-1 (cloth)
1. Poor—England—History.  2. Poverty—England—History.
3. England—Social conditions.  I. Hitchcock, Tim, 1957–   .
II. King, Peter, 1949–   .  III. Sharpe, Pamela.
HC260.P6C4   1997
362.5'0942—dc21                                              96–48417
                                                                CIP

© Tim Hitchcock, Peter King and Pamela Sharpe 1997

All rights reserved. No reproduction, copy or transmission of this publication may be made without written permission.

No paragraph of this publication may be reproduced, copied or transmitted save with written permission or in accordance with the provisions of the Copyright, Designs and Patents Act 1988, or under the terms of any licence permitting limited copying issued by the Copyright Licensing Agency, 90 Tottenham Court Road, London W1P 9HE.

Any person who does any unauthorised act in relation to this publication may be liable to criminal prosecution and civil claims for damages.

The authors have asserted their rights to be identified as the authors of this work in accordance with the Copyright, Designs and Patents Act 1988.

This book is printed on paper suitable for recycling and made from fully managed and sustained forest sources.

10  9  8  7  6  5  4  3  2  1
06  05  04  03  02  01  00  99  98  97

Printed and bound in Great Britain by
Antony Rowe Ltd, Chippenham, Wiltshire

# Contents

| | | |
|---|---|---|
| *List of Tables* | | vii |
| *List of Figures* | | viii |
| *List of Abbreviations* | | ix |
| *Notes on the Contributors* | | x |
| | Introduction: Chronicling Poverty – The Voices and Strategies of the English Poor, 1640–1840<br>*Tim Hitchcock, Peter King and Pamela Sharpe* | 1 |
| 1 | Going on the Parish: The Parish Pension and its Meaning in the London Suburbs, 1640–1724<br>*Jeremy Boulton* | 19 |
| 2 | London Domestic Servants from Depositional Evidence, 1660–1750: Servant–Employer Sexuality in the Patriarchal Household<br>*Tim Meldrum* | 47 |
| 3 | 'Unlawfully begotten on her body': Illegitimacy and the Parish Poor in St Luke's Chelsea<br>*Tim Hitchcock* | 70 |
| 4 | 'The bowels of compation': A Labouring Family and the Law, c.1790–1834<br>*Pamela Sharpe* | 87 |
| 5 | Voices in the Crowd: The Kirkby Lonsdale Township Letters, 1809–36<br>*James Stephen Taylor* | 109 |
| 6 | Old Age in Poverty: The Record of Essex Pauper Letters, 1780–1834<br>*Thomas Sokoll* | 127 |
| 7 | Pauper Inventories and the Material Lives of the Poor in the Eighteenth and Early Nineteenth Centuries<br>*Peter King* | 155 |

| | | |
|---|---|---|
| 8 | 'An old offender tho' so young in years': The Criminal Careers of Juvenile Offenders in Middlesex in the 1830s<br>*Heather Shore* | 192 |
| 9 | 'The poor in blindnes': Letters from Mildenhall, Wiltshire, 1835–6<br>*Gregory C. Smith* | 211 |
| *Index* | | 239 |

# List of Tables

| | | |
|---|---|---|
| 7.1 | Essex probate and pauper inventories, later seventeenth to early nineteenth centuries: percentages containing selected goods | 162 |
| 7.2 | Essex probate and pauper inventories, later seventeenth to early nineteenth centuries: bedding, linen, bedroom-heating and fire equipment | 164 |
| 7.3 | Essex pauper inventories: analysis of subsamples | 179 |

# List of Figures

| | | |
|---|---|---|
| 1.1 | Number of ratepayers in St Martin's parish, 1640–1721 | 23 |
| 1.2 | Average poor rate assessment, St Martin's, 1640–1721 | 23 |
| 1.3 | Number of parish pensioners, excluding orphans, St Martin's, 1640–1724 | 23 |
| 1.4 | Yield of poor rate in St Martin's 1640–1721 | 24 |
| 1.5 | Proportion of total expenditure on the extraordinary poor, by decade, St Martin's, 1641–1724 | 25 |
| 1.6 | Average pension in pence per week, St Martin's, 1640–1724 | 25 |
| 1.7 | Number of petitions recorded in vestry minutes, St Martin's, 1640–1721 | 29 |
| 1.8 | Five-year moving average of all new pensioners in St Martin's, 1640–1720 | 31 |
| 4.1 | The Hall family genealogy | 90 |
| 7.1 | Family earnings distribution, Ashdon labourers, 1801 | 168 |
| 7.2 | Family earnings distribution, Ashdon artisans and widows, 1801 | 168 |
| 7.3 | Household size in Ashdon, 1801 census | 169 |
| 7.4 | Ages at death, Ashdon, 1795–1820 | 169 |

# List of Abbreviations

| | |
|---|---|
| CRO/K | Cumbria Record Office, Kendal |
| DL/C | London Consistory Court Records |
| ERO | Essex Record Office |
| GLRO | Greater London Record Office |
| HO | Home Office |
| OAT | Archives Office of Tasmania |
| OBSP | Old Bailey Sessions Papers |
| *OED* | *Oxford English Dictionary* |
| PRO | Public Record Office |
| *VCH* | *Victoria County History* |
| WAC | City of Westminster Archives Centre |
| WPL | Westminster Public Library |
| WRO | Wiltshire Record Office |

# Notes on the Contributors

**Jeremy Boulton** obtained his first degree from St Andrews, Scotland, and completed his PhD at the University of Cambridge in 1983. He was a Junior Research Fellow at New Hall, Cambridge, between 1982 and 1985. He was a Research Associate at the Cambridge Group for the History of Population and Social Structure, and a Fellow of New Hall, Cambridge, from 1985 until 1990. Since 1990 he has been Lecturer in Social History at Newcastle. His published work includes *Neighbourhood and Society: A London Suburb in the Seventeenth Century* (1987) and articles on marriage customs, wages and prices and aspects of urban society in early modern London. He can be contacted by e-mail: J.P.Boulton@newcastle.ac.uk. Further information can be found on his homepage: http://www.ncl.ac.uk/~njpb/.

**Tim Hitchcock** is Senior Lecturer in Early Modern Social and Economic History at the University of North London. His previous work has included articles on eighteenth-century social policy, radical religion and sexuality. His most recent book is *English Sexualities, 1700–1800* (1996)

**Peter King** is Professor of Social History, Nene College, Northampton. He has published a wide variety of articles on crime, law and society in the eighteenth and nineteenth centuries, including work on customary right and on changing attitudes to interpersonal violence, 1750–1820. He is currently completing a monograph entitled *Crime, Justice and Discretion: Law and Society in Essex and South-east England, 1740–1820* and leading an ESRC project on 'Youth, Crime and the Coming of Modernity, 1780–1840'.

**Tim Meldrum** has just completed a London School of Economics doctoral thesis on domestic service in late-seventeenth- and early-eighteenth-century London. He is a former Scouloudi Research Fellow at the Institute of Historical Research and is currently a Lecturer in History at Nene College, Northampton.

**Pamela Sharpe** is Lecturer in Social and Economic History at the University of Bristol. Her doctoral thesis was on the demographic and economic history of early modern Colyton, Devon. She recently completed *Adapting to Capitalism: Working Women in the English Economy, 1700–1850* (1966), based on her research as Essex County Council Research Fellow in Local History, 1990–3.

**Heather Shore** is a student at Royal Holloway University of London, where she is currently completing her doctoral thesis on the social history of juvenile crime in early-nineteenth-century London. She is also convenor of the postgraduate seminar on theory and methodology, which is held at the Institute of Historical Research, University of London.

**Gregory C. Smith** completed his PhD at the Ontario Institute for Studies in Education (University of Toronto) in 1992. Since then he has been raising four children and revising his thesis for publication. While completing the doctorate he taught at Scarborough College, University of Toronto, for four years.

**Thomas Sokoll** is Lecturer in Early Modern History at the FernUniversität, Hagen, Germany. He has published *Household and Family among the Poor* (1993), *Bergbau im Ubergang zur Neuzeit* (1994) and numerous articles in the field of early modern social history, historical demography and historical anthropology. He is currently working on the history of merchant-capitalist mining in central Europe and completing an edition of the Essex Pauper Letters for the British Academy's *Records of Social and Economic History*.

**James Stephen Taylor** is Professor and Chair of the Department of History of West Georgia College. He is the author of *Jonas Hanway, Founder of the Marine Society: Charity and Policy in Eighteenth Century Britain* (1985); *Poverty, Migration and Settlement in the Industrial Revolution: Sojourners' Narratives* (1989), and a number of articles on British Social welfare history.

# Introduction: Chronicling Poverty – The Voices and Strategies of the English Poor, 1640–1840
Tim Hitchcock, Peter King and Pamela Sharpe

This volume is intended to illuminate the lives and strategies, circumstances and frustrations of the majority population, 'the poor', in the long eighteenth century. By bringing together the work of a number of historians whose writing is based on a hitherto largely neglected set of sources it will explore an important and little-regarded aspect of social history, contributing to a fuller and more nuanced 'history from below'.

Recent research on the period from the later seventeenth to the early nineteenth centuries has deepened our understanding of social formations and social relations in myriad ways. In particular, the relationships between the labouring poor and those in positions of authority over them (who overwhelmingly, of course, were men of considerable property in this period) has been explored in three clusters of historical work – on the changing nature of the state, on propertied Englishmen of the middling sort and above, and on plebeian culture and collective action. The development of the military-fiscal state and its ramifications for domestic policy are now being subjected to detailed scrutiny.[1] Along with the wide-ranging debates already available on the role of the criminal law and on the various levels of government and surveillance in rural England,[2] this work has considerably advanced our awareness of the nature and impact of the various interconnected networks of authority in this period. Similarly, the polite culture and increasingly abundant material lives of those who exercised that authority, along with the mushrooming of institutional forms through which the propertied involved themselves in public life, are now much better understood.[3] And finally, counterbalancing much of this work, a long tradition of research on various aspects of plebeian culture has developed among social historians, greatly advancing our knowledge of topics such as popular recreations, labour relations, social conflict, riot and customary rights.[4] However, these bodies of work have largely neglected two important and related components of the history of the long eighteenth century – the material resources available to labouring men and women and the strategies they developed, at an individual rather than a collective level, in order to obtain the help they required from the various networks of authority that shaped their lives.

Social historians have been markedly successful in uncovering the 'social control' strategies and ideological edifices of the propertied, and the ways they used their positions as employers, poor law officials, magistrates, social investigators or MPs to make and justify policies that furthered their diverse interests. These perspectives are clearly important. Policies in relation to both the poor laws and the criminal laws were, in the first instance, largely constructed by the propertied and most of the key decisions at the local level were made by these same groups. Moreover, with rare exceptions, employers usually held the upper hand in negotiations with their employees. However, an equally deep and nuanced historical analysis of these policies as they were experienced from below has yet to materialise. As Peter Mandler has recently pointed out, while it seems logical to assume that the poor will understand the rich better than the rich understand the poor (because for the rich, social knowledge is a luxury while for the poor it is often essential to survival), this is not a perspective that appears to have informed most historical scholarship.[5] Historians have been frequently led by the abundance of readily available sources to look exclusively at the attitudes of the rich towards the poor.[6] And despite the best efforts of those who have stressed the need to write history from below, there has not developed a counterbalancing analysis of the individual strategies and social knowledge of the poor. Edward Thompson and many of those he inspired to write about plebeian culture in the eighteenth century uncovered a rich tradition of collective action, a vibrant popular culture which encouraged people to act together to fix the price of bread, to defend customary rights and to achieve a variety of other joint goals. Similarly, historians (again partly in response to Thompson's work) have developed a complex history of popular movements and popular politics from the later eighteenth century to the 1830s.[7] However, most of this work has focused on collective consciousness, and when it has analysed the everyday interactions of rich and poor on an individual level, it has tended to portray the poor mainly as passive objects, victims of the actions of the rich.[8]

Having said this, various aspects of the lives of the poor at a more individual level have been investigated by historians. But this research has been mainly confined to sources that can be subjected to quantitative analysis, the only qualitative sources quoted at any length being those written by elite observers of the poor. Historians of crime, for example, have expended considerable energy in making quantitative links between rising indictment rates and either high prices or rising post-war unemployment – implying (as some contemporaries also did) that the poor used illegal appropriation more often as a strategy in times of greater need.[9] Quantitative work on changing family earnings has also been possible, using wage series and the family earnings schedules collected by elite observers such as Sir Frederick Eden. Sterile and regionally undifferentiated though it may sometimes have been, the long-running standard-of-living debate has also added something to our understanding of the experiences of the poor.[10] More inventively, settlement examinations have recently been subjected to large-scale quantification and have yielded fresh insights into the changing seasonality of employment, the declining position of women in the rural labour market, the impact of enclosure and a number of other questions.[11] And likewise, historical demography has yielded quantitative evidence on matters such as age at marriage, family size and bastardy rates, each of which provide further narrow shafts of light, illuminating the lives of the labouring poor and the impact upon them of changing economic and social conditions.[12] Most recently, charity doles have been used in conjunction with family reconstitution to investigate, at a quantitative level, changing patterns of poverty and lifecycle-related vulnerability – thus complementing work already done by Thomas Sokoll using pre-1841 parish listings.[13]

This is not to imply that all research on the lives of the poor in the period before the early nineteenth century, when a substantial number of working-class autobiographies become available for the first time, has relied solely on elite commentators and quantitative data. Two recent works focusing mainly on the tiny proportion of the labouring poor who ended up on the gallows – Peter Linebaugh's *The London Hanged* and Victor Gattrell's *The Hanging Tree* – make innovative, if in the former case rather problematic, use of sources such as Ordinary of Newgate's accounts, ballads, broadsides, and the petitions of convicted felons in which, to quote Gattrell, 'we hear the voices of the common people'.[14] And there are excellent monographs, such as John Gillis', *For Better, For Worse* and Margaret Spufford's *Small Books and Pleasant Histories* which make imaginative use of sources created by and for the poor.[15] Moreover, the authors of the only wide-ranging general texts on the eighteenth-century labouring poor – Robert Malcolmson and John Rule – also quote occasionally from sources that are neither elite commentaries nor quantitative abstractions, such as songs, ballads and newspaper advertisements.[16] However, almost the only sources, apart from the very occasional early autobiography, that bring what might loosely be called the words of the poor into these general texts in any substantial way are the anonymous threatening letters written in times of acute conflict and so beautifully analysed by Edward Thompson in his contribution to *Albion's Fatal Tree*. Even Thompson did not, however, hold out much hope that historians would be able to uncover other sources, created in less polarised and conflictual contexts, that might enable them to analyse the strategies, experiences and attitudes towards authority of the labouring poor. He wrote:

> The letters are in many cases – and over many decades – the *only* literate expression of the 'inarticulate' which has survived. The 'dark figure' of the crime itself is dwarfed by the even darker figure of the plebeian consciousness through much of the eighteenth century and, in rural areas, well into the nineteenth. How did a society whose manifest ideology was that of paternalism feel from below?[17]

Thompson wrote these words over twenty years ago. The main purpose of this volume is to suggest that how it felt 'from below' is at least partly recoverable, using sources which had hardly been touched in 1975. In particular, the main focus here is on forms of written evidence created when the poor confronted, and were confronted by, the hierarchies and institutions of authority they were forced to deal with on a day-to-day basis – the Old Poor Law and its siblings the settlements laws, the New Poor Law of 1834, the institution of domestic service, the social investigators of the early nineteenth century, the many parish or charity-run residential institutions that were set up to employ, cure, shelter or reform the poor. Researchers have not been slow to write the history of many of these institutions. We have, for example, many detailed studies of pre-1834 poor law administration, of the coming of the New Poor Law, of the charitable institutions of the metropolis, of changing perceptions of (and institutional provision for) juvenile offenders, and, to a lesser extent, of domestic service.[18] Yet these histories, based as they are, on the records created by the institutions themselves, and on the pamphlets, books, newspapers and periodicals in which contemporaries discussed the nature and treatment of poverty, youth, bastardy and service, contain a very one-sided view, and give little space to the strategies of those who relied on these institutions. Thus, as Peter Mandler has pointed out, the places where rich and poor interacted – where social knowledge was acquired and deployed – remain little understood and difficult to penetrate.

It could be argued that the illiteracy of most labouring men and women, and their lack of the material resources or incentive needed to write about their experiences, makes this difficulty insurmountable. However, as the essays in this volume indicate, there are sources which recorded both the material lives and what may be loosely termed 'the words' of the poor. Bastardy and settlement examinations; court depositions; petitions and letters written by paupers to overseers, vestries or the poor law commissioners; pauper inventories; criminal autobiographies – all offer opportunities to gain insights into the strategies and experiences of the poor. That these sources are problematic goes without saying. A servant giving evidence in a matrimonial dispute involving a master or mistress, a 'bastard-bearer' being examined on her sexual history, a pauper attempting to describe his or her circumstances in a letter to the local vestry or to the poor law commissioners, a juvenile delinquent telling his life story to a curious investigator – all these result in documents requiring a finely tuned understanding of the often complex interactions between the poor and those in authority, which surrounded their creation. In each case, questions need to be asked about who was writing what, for and to whom; about the precise strategic positions of the writer and the receiver; and about the underlying beliefs both groups had concerning their rights and obligations in the precise social location where the document was created.

In one sense, almost all the documents just listed were, in James Scott's words, 'public transcripts' of the powerless to the powerful.[19] Yet powerless/powerful is too easy a dichotomy in many of these contexts. The domestic servant who observed her master's sexual practices, although possibly a victim of those practices, was not entirely without power. Nor were paupers threatening to make an expensive journey home if relief was not forthcoming. Nor were newly registered receivers of relief, whose often fairly considerable material possessions were part of the bargaining process which might result in the granting of a regular pension. What these documents cry out for is not simply quantification – useful though it may be to raise questions, provide context and look at differences over time or between various subgroups – but rather, a contextualised investigation of particular documents, negotiations and strategic ploys.

Not all the core documents used here contain, even in the broadest sense, the 'words of the poor'. Overseers' accounts and the records of the residential institutions to which the poor had access have both been used to trace individual careers, and to define more precisely the contexts in which other core documents were created. Pauper inventories, in which the parish overseers described the material possessions of the poor, do not, by any definition, contain the words of the poor. However, they have been given detailed treatment because they offer a glimpse, albeit through a dark, sometimes half-closed door, into the dwellings of the poor. In the process, they offer an opportunity to develop the other core theme of this volume: the need to deepen our understanding of labouring men's and women's experience of poverty in the long eighteenth century. This theme runs through almost all the other essays. The three chapters on pauper letters, those by Pam Sharpe, Tom Sokoll and James Taylor, for example, not only highlight the crises that could hit the poor at any time due to accidents, sickness or unemployment but also offer many insights into the long-term problems many inevitably experienced as their lives unfolded. As parents in their late twenties, thirties and forties, increasingly burdened by children who were either too young to work or unable to find suitable employment, the poor struggled to overcome the endemic problems of under-employment, lack of women's work, low wages, job insecurity, price fluctuations, lack of cheap housing and the seasonal nature of many forms of employment. After their children had grown up, old age, permanent disability and widowhood might quickly bring potential destitution to their door.[20] Despite their obvious problems as a source, pauper letters offer a unique opportunity to study the ways these and other problems (such as debt, rent arrears, clothing costs, family breakdown and the failure of migration strategies) were experienced by the poor in the middle and later stages of the lifecycle.

By contrast, three other chapters in this volume, those by Tim Meldrum, Tim Hitchcock and Heather Shore, focus on the problems, choices and strategies of those who were young and single. One group, London servants, were following a relatively 'normal' career path – domestic service, with all its constraints, opportunities and access (in the short-term at least) to relatively secure material conditions. The other two groups were following what most contemporaries would have regarded as 'deviant' careers. The young men and young women who chose to become, or found themselves forced to become, thieves or the bearers of illegitimate children generally came from backgrounds that were slightly closer to the naked edge of poverty than those of the majority of their contemporaries, but they were not a race apart. Their lives interlocked with, and illustrate, the more general problems of young single members of the labouring poor and the range of (often highly gender-specific) career options available to them.[21]

The chapters in this volume do not pretend to cover all the sources in which the words of the poor have come down to us. Many such sources remain largely unexploited at the qualitative level. The potential of vagrancy and settlement examinations has been indicated by James Stephen Taylor's *Sojourners' Narratives*, but their possibilities remain huge, especially in those rare places and times when the magistrates' clerk who took them down did not, for whatever reason, confine the pauper's narrative to events specifically relevant to the establishment of his or her settlement. Recent doctoral work on pauper emigrants and their negotiations with the early nineteenth-century poor law authorities (who were increasingly willing to countenance assisted emigration for some subsections of the poor) has shown that these processes sometimes created letters and petitions that are rich in detail about the strategies, attitudes and experiences of the poor. Similarly, research on the papers of the Charity Commissioners suggests that petitions from the poor in relation to lost or illegally appropriated charities may be equally useful.[22]

Other types of archive have yet to be subjected to serious scrutiny. The petty sessions examinations of paupers claiming relief, or of labourers demanding payment of wages, offer insights 'from below' into overseer/pauper and employer/employee relations. Similar examinations in relation to borrowed goods or debts open up the possibility of analysing the darker side of reciprocity and neighbourliness. The examination of members of friendly societies before the same courts after the 1793 Act provide clues about the workings of those societies and about how their members felt about the ways they were run. Moreover, the often elaborate printed rules of many eighteenth-century friendly societies, although they were sometimes stereotyped, borrowed from elsewhere or influenced by elite benefactors, should not be ruled out as potentially authentic expressions of the co-operative initiatives and organised conviviality of working people. The selective use of quarter sessions or assize depositions in relation to property-crime accusations likewise offers a range of potential sources, since in some jurisdictions nearly a quarter of such cases involved victims who were members of the labouring poor.[23] Depositions in rape cases have recently proved equally fruitful,[24] while those made at petty or quarter sessions levels in cases of general assault could also be very useful since plebeian prosecutors form an even higher proportion in such cases. A parallel source which is rarely available outside the London area – detailed printed trial reports – again offers evidence of the words of the poor, although these sources are only of use when the victim was a labouring man or woman since the defence put up by the accused was usually very brief or went unreported.

The variety of insights these records may eventually yield into the everyday lives, material problems, survival strategies, reciprocities and enmities of the poor cannot be adequately analysed at this early stage of research, but their potential is huge. There is also much further work to be done on the material lives of the poor. Even relatively cryptic documents such as property-crime indictments and recognisances can be used, along with depositions, for this purpose. The range, and changing nature, of the goods stolen from the poor can be studied in considerable detail from these records, as John Styles has demonstrated in his recent work.[25]

This volume does not therefore offer either a comprehensive survey or a typical cross-section of the types of sources that can be used to discuss the words of the poor, the strategies they developed or the material worlds they inhabited. Indeed, it will be clear by now that court records alone could be used to produce a completely different volume focusing on these very same issues. Nevertheless, this collection offers an introduction to what can be done to illuminate both the experience of poverty and the strategies of the poor. As a result, six of the nine chapters focus almost exclusively on sources created by the poor-relief system itself, while a seventh, on illegitimacy and the parish poor, uses a combination of charity and poor-relief records. That chapter, along with those on the life stories of juvenile offenders and on the strategies and problems of domestic servants, provide a balance in terms of lifecycle experience. All the other chapters deal almost exclusively with men and women who either had families or had reached a state of 'old age in poverty'.

Since research on these sources is still in its infancy, the choice of chapters for this volume has inevitably been determined partly by the availability of completed work rather than by other criteria such as the need for geographical or chronological spread. More than this, the volume itself necessarily reflects areas within the history of the Old Poor Law and of poverty which have, in the past, held particular interest for historians. Jeremy Boulton's piece, for example, looks at a period associated with the rise of a bureaucratic relief system, characterised by increasing generosity and what Paul Slack has described as widespread but 'shallow' poverty.[26] The pieces by Tim Hitchcock and Tim Meldrum look at a period and place (London) which has been of long-standing interest because of its association with the growing anonymity of the urban public sphere. Equally, the themes emphasised within the five chapters on the rural poor in the late eighteenth and early nineteenth centuries in part reflect the extent to which this period and these particular paupers have been subject to extensive analysis by historians interested in the genesis of the New Poor Law and the economic and political crises that surrounded it.

In many ways these largely unintentional foci within the volume help to create an appropriate intellectual balance within the work as a whole. Jeremy Boulton's chapter, for example, reflects the process of creation which resulted in the power relationships experienced by the poor and described in the other chapters. Its urban bias, and that of the pieces dealing with the period before the last quarter of the eighteenth century, likewise reflect the extent to which new forms of relief and of organisation were essentially urban phenomena. Workhouses, new types of institutional charities, professional overseers and paid clerks – all experiments and bureaucratic solutions which would later impact on the rural poor – could be found in London and the major provincial capitals by mid-century.[27] The chapters by both Tim Hitchcock and Tim Meldrum, while in some ways suggesting contradictory conclusions, reflect the extent to which metropolitan and, more broadly, urban life was creating a new and different set of relationships between figures of authority and the poor, and a new set of ideas about the framework within which to think about those relationships. Moreover the London-based nature of all three of the studies focusing on the young and single poor, including the piece by Heather Shore, is in part a reflection of the unique capacity of the capital to offer employment opportunities to domestic servants, institutional care to those with illegitimate children and criminal opportunities and safe areas in which juvenile offenders could thrive, and hence should not be seen as a source of significant imbalance.

Finally, the fact that five of the poor-law-related studies are not only rural but also focus primarily, although not exclusively in the case of the pauper inventories, on the late eighteenth and nineteenth centuries gives appropriate weight to an important period in the history of the poor law. In the late eighteenth and early nineteenth centuries rising panic about the inadequacy, expense and potentially pernicious effects of the poor-relief system produced an atmosphere of crisis. Broader ideological shifts had brought the poor laws under increasingly critical scrutiny and their abolition was seriously considered and indeed partially achieved in 1834. 'Benevolence, moral reform and economy marched together throughout the eighteenth century', Paul Slack concluded in his recent book on the period up to 1782.[28] However, in the half-century that followed, the latter two increasingly outweighed the former as select vestries and other pre-1834 experiments worked to keep the rates down, as a large-scale reformation of manners movement rolled into motion and as finally, in 1834, the full-blown spectres of a universal workhouse test and 'less eligibility' were imposed at a national level. In this context, the minor victories (or at least truces) achieved by the out-parish poor and described in the three chapters on pauper letters, are firm reminders of the effectiveness of some pauper strategies.

What factors governed the range and effectiveness of the strategies available to paupers in this period? Despite the considerable amount of work done on the administration of relief, on the cost of relief and on the make-up of the pauper host, we do not yet have an adequate history of the processes, customary practices and variety of attitudes that provided the context in which pauper–parish negotiations took place during the long eighteenth century.[29] However, several of the foundations which strengthened or shaped pauper strategies can be tentatively analysed.

Perhaps the poor's greatest strength was the depth and emotional power of their own belief in their right to relief, or more correctly in their right to a wide range of different kinds of relief in specific situations. As the provision of poor relief in various forms – regular doles, clothes, fuel, rent, medical relief, institutional provision – was increasingly accepted as an obligation by the propertied in the last half of the seventeenth century, so a structure of customary expectations solidified within both urban and rural plebeian culture. Moreover, despite the protestations of elite observers, those expectations grew to encompass, from the poor's point of view at least, a whole network of customary rights.[30] By the beginning of the eighteenth century, the poor-relief system in many parishes can perhaps best be characterised as a rough and ready welfare state in miniature,[31] with all the advantages and disadvantages of a system in which those who made the decisions and those who requested help frequently still knew each other intimately as neighbours, employers/employees and co-religionists. The sheer solidity and strength of the poor's belief in their right to relief was reinforced by three related factors. First, there was a considerable overlap between those groups who were small ratepayers (and might therefore also serve as overseers) and those who received relief. Many ratepayers and overseers knew that they, or more frequently their widows, would in their turn possess insufficient landholdings or other resources to support themselves in old age or prolonged sickness. Their attitudes to those requesting relief were inevitably affected by this. Indeed, the tradition upheld in most parishes, described in Peter King's chapter, which ensured that elderly recipients of regular relief were allowed to continue living in their own dwellings with their household possessions, may well have reinforced the sense amongst small ratepayers that their poor rates represented a contribution to what amounted to a state-guaranteed insurance scheme at a local level.[32] Such a scheme would have many advantages in an era when alternatives such as friendly societies were either non-existent or financially insecure. The parish was not, of course, legally bound to come up with this package of a regular pension and a physical environment similar to that experienced before their parishioner became incapacitated by old age, but customary expectations did support such a claim, and if smallholders and minor ratepayers came to believe that their hopes of future security lay in upholding such rights, they would be less likely as vestry members or overseers earlier in life to refute the legitimacy of many paupers' claims. The fully developed context for beliefs about payments and entitlements can be seen in those pauper letters requesting relief which referred to the individual's past history as a ratepayer, while the starting-point for this belief can be seen in the petitions described by Jeremy Boulton.

More crucially, perhaps, a second factor, which also affected the great majority of paupers who had never paid poor rates, also reinforced the poor's customary expectations that they were entitled to relief. As Gregory Smith's analysis of the poor's naive belief in 1834–6 that the higher authorities would save them from the tyrannical attempts of the local vestry to cut their out-relief shows, there was a deep, almost unconscious link between the entitlements the poor believed were their due under the poor law and their deferential attitudes towards those in authority over them. Poor-relief systems may be partly about maintenance – at the least possible expense – of seasonally surplus labour, about avoiding public disorder, and about creating forms of leverage which will enable the rich to reform the morals of the poor, but they are also about legitimacy.[33] To some extent the hegemony of the propertied, and in particular the rhetoric of paternalism adhered to by many gentry magistrates, relied heavily for its legitimacy on the willingness of the middling and gentry elite to suffer a compulsory tax on property in order to create a fund that was sufficient to meet a range of the basic needs of the poor. This process of legitimation and exchange created a powerful basis for the poor's sense that relief was indeed a customary right.

This sense was reinforced by a third factor – the behaviour of a considerable number of magistrates who, when faced by well-rehearsed pauper appeals at petty sessions, frequently made orders to relieve the supplicant, in stark contradiction to the opinion of overseers and vestrymen. The complex local triangles of negotiation between magistracy, vestry and labouring poor still await their historian, but while magistrates were by no means always on the side of the poor, there is no doubt that some practised a rather distanced form of paternalism which could be actively and usefully influenced by the labouring sort.[34] Many overseers complained to early nineteenth-century investigators, for example, that paupers made skilful use of their right to choose which local magistrate to go to, preferring those who had, in the past, made judgements in their favour. Joseph Mayett's autobiography, a rare jewel from a labouring man of this period, records at least two occasions on which he defeated the parish overseers by appealing to the local magistrates or petty sessions. But he also gives details of another occasion when he came off decidedly the worst from an interview with the 'old squire ... and Chief Justice in this part of the country', who had 'reduced every man's pay two shillings per week'.[35] Many magistrates were by no means automatic allies to the poor in their battles with the increasingly austere, farmer-dominated, vestries of southern England, but the fact that the propertied did not present a united face on matters of poor relief policy, and that many petty sessions courts situated well outside their parishes offered the poor a form of supplementary benefits tribunal which quite frequently decided in their favour, reinforced the poor's belief in their right to relief.

The role played by formal poor relief in the makeshift family economies of most labouring families was, of course, itself merely a facet of a broader set of relationships. Formal and informal charity could play a vital role in sustaining a family through times of crisis. Credit networks among the poor, whether based on the loaning of money or on the exchange of different services, could be quite sophisticated. Reciprocity and neighbourliness were crucial. Although they lacked the real capital which enabled the better-off to weather difficult times without outside help, the poor could and did accumulate 'social capital'. By lending tools and possessions, and by offering physical and psychological assistance to neighbours and kin in times of need, they invested in the future, being able to draw on the resources of others when they in turn hit difficult times. Moreover, depending on the availability of employment opportunities, commonable land and woodlands, women and children could engage in a wide variety of paid and unpaid work which could reduce the vulnerability of the family economy and its dependence on male wages and employment prospects.[36] Especially at the latter end of our period, between the 1780s and the 1830s, these supports were put under particular strain. The decline of cottage industry (and particularly of spinning work), the collapse of service in husbandry, the decreasing availability of small pieces of cultivable land, and the erosion of access to pasture and to various customary rights (especially after enclosure), all increased dependence on the male wage.[37] While, in southern and eastern counties at least, population growth and the increasingly seasonal nature of the demand for labour both increased the vulnerability of labouring men to under-employment, and depressed real wages. These changes inevitably led to a substantial increase in the proportion of labouring families who received relief in the late eighteenth and early nineteenth centuries. It also lowered the average age of poor relief recipients as more and more men with young families to support found it impossible to do so in an era of falling real wages and rising job insecurity.[38] Thus, the final half-century of the Old Poor Law, the period on which many of the poor law studies in this volume focuses, was a period when maintaining and maximising their right to relief became an increasingly central plank in the survival strategies of the rural poor. The anger and disbelief with which many labouring men and women greeted the coming of the New Poor Law in 1834 was not unrelated to the fact that out-relief had become increasingly vital to the maintenance of their household economies. The workhouse test and the demands of the central authorities that out-relief be abolished were seen by many of the poor as the destruction of the one remaining set of substantial customary rights that they could use to keep their economy of makeshifts together. The reality did not always prove as harsh as the rhetoric, but the disbelief and horror of the Wiltshire labourers seen in Gregory Smith's chapter on '"The poor in blindnes"' reflects the vital role played by out-relief in the period during which many of the key documents studied in these essays were created.

The volume as a whole, stretching as it does from the mid-seventeenth century to the 1840s, from one of the biggest cities in the world to some of the smallest parishes in England, from the sexual vulnerabilities and activities of the young to the aching joints, material problems and varied strategies of the elderly, is essentially a path-breaking exercise. Although it offers substantial studies of a number of areas and archives, and opens up new ways of writing a 'history from below', it also points the way to many as yet unexplored avenues and questions. For example, there is virtually nothing here about the dialogues that took place within plebeian culture – about the mutualities expressed in institutions such as friendly societies or other self-regulating groups, or about the enmities surfacing in the disputes between working people that created court hearings relating to assaults, debts, marital relations, etc. Equally, we have not attempted to develop an over-arching analysis of the ways elite-generated discourses influenced, or failed to influence, the poor. Several of the chapters suggest that the languages of the philanthropists and elite commentators did not automatically reshape the foundations of plebeian attitudes or discourses. For example, while the propertied increasingly attacked the notion that poor relief was a right in the late eighteenth and early nineteenth centuries, the chapters by King, Sharpe, Sokoll and Taylor show that the poor continued to use a very different language about out-relief. For the poor studied in these pieces, the language of the wage, the salary and the pension continued to dominate. Equally, despite the fact that the institutions set up to deal with such groups as bastard-bearers and women with sexually transmitted diseases were heavily laden with moral agendas and a desire to discourage pre-marital sexual activity, Tim Hitchcock's chapter suggests that these institutions may frequently have enabled women to survive more easily the consequences of precisely the forms of behaviour that those who set them up wanted to discourage.

Another issue inevitably raised by these studies is the extent to which the intensification of disciplinary agendas associated with what Vic Gattrell has called 'the rise of the policeman state',[39] changed the strategic possibilities open to the poor or reshaped the languages they used after 1750. Greg Smith's chapter certainly highlights discontinuities and the seismic shock of 1834 as it was experienced by the poor. However, the chapters of Sharpe, Sokoll and Taylor on pauper letters suggest many substantial continuities in the final half-century of the Old Poor Law. Questions such as these cannot be answered at a general level without further work. Here our aim has primarily been to use new sources to get as close as possible to the words and worlds of the poor, and thus to open up fresh avenues through which such questions can be explored.

## NOTES

Place of publication is London unless otherwise indicated.

1. L. Stone, 'Introduction'; J. Brewer, 'The Eighteenth Century British State: Contexts and Issues'; J. Innes, 'The Domestic Face of the Military-Fiscal State. Government and Society in Eighteenth-Century Britain', in L. Stone (ed.), *An Imperial State at War. Britain from 1689–1815* (1994); J. Brewer, *The Sinews of Power. War, Money and the English State, 1688–1783* (1989); J. Innes, 'The State and the Poor: Eighteenth-Century England in a European Perspective' (forthcoming); P. Harling and P. Mandler, 'From "Fiscal-Military" State to Laissez-faire State, 1760–1850', *Journal of British Studies* 32 (1993), 44–70.
2. D. Hay, 'Property, Authority and the Criminal Law' in D. Hay *et al.* (eds), *Albion's Fatal Tree* (1975); D. Eastwood, *Governing Rural England. Tradition and Transformation in Local Government, 1780–1840* (Oxford, 1994); see also the debate over the degree of parish-level surveillance in N. Landau, 'The Laws of Settlement and Surveillance of Immigration in Eighteenth-Century Kent', *Continuity and Change* 3 (1988), 391–420; N. Landau, 'The Regulation of Immigration, Economic Structures and Definitions of the Poor in Eighteenth-Century England', *Historical Journal* 33 (1990), 541–72; K. Snell, 'Pauper Settlement and the Right to Poor Relief in England and Wales', *Continuity and Change* 6 (1991), 375–415 (and Landau's reply in the same volume, 417–39; K. Snell, 'Settlement, Poor Law and the Rural Historian: New Approaches and Opportunities', *Rural History* 3 (1992), 145–72; J. Kent, 'The Centre and the Localities: State Formation and Parish Government in England c.1640–1740', *Historical Journal* 38 (1995), 363–404.

3. J. Brewer and R. Porter (eds), *Consumption and the World of Goods* (1993); L. Weatherall, *Consumer Behaviour and Material Culture in Britain, 1660–1760* (1988); P. Langford, *A Polite and Commercial People, England, 1727–1783* (Oxford, 1989); P. Langford, *Public Life and Propertied Englishmen, 1689–1798* (Oxford, 1991).
4. For example, E.P. Thompson, *Customs in Common* (1991); R. Malcolmson, *Popular Recreations in English Society, 1700–1850* (Cambridge, 1973); J. Rule, *The Experience of Labour in Eighteenth-Century Industry* (1981); J. Neeson, *Commoners, Common Right, Enclosure and Social Change, 1700–1820* (Cambridge, 1993); J. Brewer and J. Styles, *An Ungovernable People. The English and the Law in the Seventeenth and Eighteenth Centuries* (1980); and from a perspective which takes appropriate cognisance of issues associated with gender, see A. Clark, *The Struggle for the Breeches: Gender and the Making of the British Working Class* (Berkeley, CA, 1995).
5. P. Mandler (ed.), *The Uses of Charity: The Poor on Relief in the Nineteenth-Century Metropolis* (Philadelphia, Penn., 1990).
6. For a good example see G. Himmelfarb, *The Idea of Poverty. England in the Early Industrial Age* (1984).
7. Thompson, *Customs*, and E.P. Thompson, *The Making of the English Working Class* (1963) inspired a huge historiography that cannot be reviewed here. For general texts that have attempted an overview of these movements and of the changing experiences of the poor see, for example, J. Rule, *The Labouring Classes in Early Industrial England, 1750–1850* (1986); J. Belchem, *Industrialisation and the Working Class. The English Experience, 1750–1850* (Aldershot, 1990).
8. E. Hobsbaum and G. Rudé, *Captain Swing* (1969), for example, offers a relatively brief discussion of 'the rural poor' using such phrases as 'the traditional social order degenerated into a universal pauperism of demoralised men ... everything contrived to impoverish and to demoralise them', before going on to provide a vibrant analysis of the collective responses these conditions eventually created in 1830–1. The argument here is not with the notion that the rural labouring poor were suffering increasing impoverishment and deprivation in this period, although their lack of material possessions can be exaggerated, but rather that a detailed analysis of their individual strategies (as well as their collective actions) to some extent calls into question the assumption that they were also demoralised.
9. D. Hay, 'War, Death and Theft in the Eighteenth Century: The Record of the English Courts', *Past and Present* 95 (1982), 117–60.
10. S. Horrell and J. Humphries, 'Old Questions, New Data, and Alternative Perspectives: Families' Living Standards in the Industrial Revolution', *Journal of Economic History* 52 (1992), 849–80; T. Sokoll, 'Early Attempts at Accounting the Unaccountable: Davies' and Eden's Budgets of Agricultural Labouring Families in Late Eighteenth-Century England' in E. Pierenkemper (ed.), *Sur Ökonomik des Private-Haushalts* (Frankfurt, 1991). For a recent review of the massive standard of living debate see P. Lindert, 'Unequal Living Standards' in R. Floud and D. McCloskey (eds), *The Economic History of Britain since 1700. Volume I: 1700–1800* (2nd edn, Cambridge, 1994) pp.357–86.

11. K.D.M. Snell, *Annals of the Labouring Poor: Social Change and Agrarian England, 1660-1900* (Cambridge, 1985).
12. R. Schofield and E. Wrigley, *The Population History of England, 1541-1871. A Reconstruction* (1981); P. Laslett, *Family Life and Illicit Love in Earlier Generations* (Cambridge, 1977); J. Henderson and R. Wall (eds), *Poor Women and Children in the European Past* (1994).
13. B. Stapleton, 'Inherited Poverty and Life-cycle Poverty: Odiham, Hampshire, 1650-1850', *Social History* 18 (1993), 339-55; T. Sokoll, *Household and Family among the Poor* (Bochum, 1993).
14. P. Linebaugh, *The London Hanged: Crime and Civil Society in the Eighteenth Century* (1991); V. Gattrell, *The Hanging Tree, Execution and the English People, 1770-1868* (Oxford, 1994), especially p.198.
15. J. Gillis, *For Better, For Worse: British Marriages, 1600 to the Present* (Oxford, 1985); M. Spufford, *Small Books and Pleasant Histories: Popular Fiction and its Readership in Seventeenth-Century England* (Cambridge, 1981).
16. J. Rule, *Albion's People, English Society, 1714-1815* (1992); R. Malcolmson, *Life and Labour in England, 1700-1780* (1981).
17. E.P. Thompson, 'The Crime of Anonymity' in D. Hay *et al.* (eds), *Albion's Fatal Tree: Crime and Society in Eighteenth-Century England* (1975), p.304.
18. For example, G. Oxley, *Poor Relief in England and Wales, 1601-1834* (Newton Abbot, 1974); A. Digby, *Pauper Palaces* (1978); D. Fraser (ed.), *The New Poor Law in the Nineteenth Century* (1976); D. Andrew, *Philanthrophy and Police. London Charity in the Eighteenth Century* (Princeton, NJ, 1989); J. Hecht, *The Domestic Servant in Eighteenth-Century England* (1980).
19. J. Scott, *Domination and the Arts of Resistance. Hidden Transcripts* (Yale, 1990).
20. On lifecycle-related patterns of poverty see, for example, Stapleton, 'Inherited Poverty'; T. Wales, 'Poverty, Poor Relief and the Life-cycle: Some Evidence from Seventeenth-Century Norfolk' in R. Smith (ed.), *Land, Kinship and Life-cycle* (Cambridge, 1984).
21. On the range of occupations available to young men and women in eighteenth-century London, see P. Earle, *A City Full of People: Men and Women in London, 1650-1750* (1994). For female 'deviant careers', see P. King, 'Female Offenders, Work and Lifecycle Changes in Late Eighteenth-Century London', *Continuity and Change* (forthcoming, May 1996). Aspects of these issues are also discussed in two recently completed London University PhD theses: H. Shore, 'The Social History of Juvenile Offenders in Middlesex, 1790-1850' and T. Meldrum, 'Domestic Service in London, 1660-1750: Gender, Lifecycle, Work and Household Relations'.
22. J. Taylor, *Poverty, Migration and Settlement in the Industrial Revolution. Sojourners' Narratives* (Palo Alto, CA, 1989). At a quantitative level, of course, the outstanding work is Snell, *Annals*. The work on pauper emigrants and charity commissioner petitions is being done by two PhD students at Nene College: G. Howell, whose provisional thesis title is 'Assisted Emigration from Rural England, *c.*1820-1860' and B. Lewis,

whose title is 'Poverty, Power and Provision. A Case Study of Rural Charities in Northamptonshire'.
23. P. King, 'Decision-Makers and Decision-Making in the English Criminal Law, 1750–1800', *Historical Journal* 27 (1984), 25–58.
24. Miranda Chaytor, 'Husband(ry): Narratives of Rape in the Seventeenth Century', *Gender & History* VII, 3 (1995), 378–407.
25. J. Styles, 'Clothing the North: The Supply of Non-Elite Clothing in the Eighteenth-century North of England', *Textile History* 25 (1994), 139–66.
26. P. Slack, *Poverty & Policy in Tudor & Stuart England* (1988), see Chaps 8 and 9.
27. For a clear survey of the charitable innovations of eighteenth-century London, see Andrew, *Philanthropy and Police*.
28. P. Slack, *The English Poor Law, 1531–1782* (Basingstoke, 1990), p.44.
29. Slack, *The English*; Oxley, *Poor Relief*; J. Marshall, *The Old Poor Law, 1795–1834* (1968); Digby, *Pauper*; for older texts, see D. Marshall, *English Poor in the Eighteenth Century* (1926); and S. and B. Webb, *English Local Government: English Poor Law: Part I. The Old Poor Law* (London, 1927).
30. This theme of the poor's view of relief as a customary right is briefly discussed in J. Archer, *By a Flash and a Scare: Arson, Animal Maiming and Poaching in East Anglia, 1815–1870* (Oxford, 1990), p.50; P. Solar, 'Poor Relief and English Economic Development before the Industrial Revolution', *Economic History Review* 48 (1995), 6; Snell, 'Pauper Settlement', 400–1, and is a central theme of the essays by Taylor, Sharpe and Sokoll in this volume.
31. J. Rule, 'Land of Lost Content? The Eighteenth-Century Poor Law', *Revue Française de Civilisation Britannique* 6 (1991); Snell, *Annals*, pp.104–8.
32. Poor relief viewed as a form of insurance is interestingly discussed in Solar, 'Poor Relief', 7–12.
33. M. Van Leeuwen, 'Logic of Charity: Poor Relief in Preindustrial Europe', *Journal of Interdisciplinary History* 24 (1994), 589–613.
34. The triangular nature of local social relations is discussed in P. King, 'Edward Thompson's Contribution to Eighteenth-century Studies. The Patrician–Plebeian Model Re-examined', *Social History* 21 (1996), 215–28.
35. A. Kussmaul (ed.), *The Autobiography of Joseph Mayett of Quainton, 1783–1839* (Buckinghamshire Record Society, 1986), pp.72–93.
36. J. Walter, 'The Social Economy of Death in Early Modern England' in J. Walter and R. Schofield (eds), *Famine, Disease and the Social Order in Early Modern Society* (Cambridge, 1989); K. Wrightson, *English Society, 1580–1680* (1982) pp.39–65; Van Leeuwen, 'Logic of Charity', 603; N. Reed, 'Gnawing it Out: A New Look at Economic Relations in Nineteenth-Century Rural England', *Rural History* I (1990), 83–94.
37. J. Humphries, 'Enclosures, Common Rights and Women: The Proletarianisation of Families in the Late Eighteenth and Early Nineteenth Centuries', *Journal of Economic History* 50 (1990), 117–42; D. Valenze, *The First Industrial Women* (Oxford, 1995).
38. G. Boyer, *An Economic History of the English Poor Law, 1750–1850* (Cambridge, 1990) pp.31–43; Snell, *Annals*; Stapleton, 'Inherited Poverty'; T. Richardson, 'Agricultural Labourers' Wages and the Cost of Living in

Essex, 1790–1840: A Contribution to the Standard of Living Debate' in B. Holderness and M. Turner (eds), *Land, Labour and Agriculture, 1700–1920* (1991), pp.69–96.

39. V. Gattrell, 'Crime, Authority and the Policeman-State' in F.M.L. Thompson, *The Cambridge Social History of Britain, 1750–1950, Vol. 3, Social Agencies and Institutions*, pp.244–52 (Cambridge, 1990).

# 1 Going on the Parish: The Parish Pension and its Meaning in the London Suburbs, 1640–1724[1]

Jeremy Boulton

What weight and significance ought to be attached to the late seventeenth-century poor law? Such questions need to be asked because they are implicit in the recent elevation of the significance of the English poor law by its recent historians. Paul Slack, as is well known, has identified 'the growth of social welfare' in the seventeenth and early eighteenth centuries as 'a general phenomenon of major importance'.[2] His evidence for this statement was the significant increase in poor relief expenditure, found especially in towns and cities, much of which was generated by the increase in the size of parish pensions, some expansion in the numbers of those so relieved, and also by increased spending on 'casual', 'discretionary' poor relief.[3] In the countryside as well, poor relief seems to have become markedly more generous and comprehensive after the middle of the seventeenth century. Pensions paid seem to have been significantly higher after that date and the law itself was increasingly implemented, so that ever larger proportions of English villagers became enmeshed in its machinery, as parish officers or, more often, as recipients.[4]

If there is an emerging consensus as to the growth of this social welfare[5] there is more caution as to the social consequences of the English poor law. It is frequently asserted, however, that the pensions paid under the English poor law were part and parcel of those means of controlling and identifying the poor. The poor law became, in other words, integral to the social structure of Restoration England. Particularly frequently cited is Keith Wrightson's remark relating to the later seventeenth century concerning that 'mixture of relief and control represented by the poor laws, providing in its balance of communal identification and social differentiation a powerful reinforcement of habits of deference and subordination'.[6] The poor law, he continued, became a weapon of local social policy in many communities: 'the coupling of generosity in relief with the demand for social conformity to new canons of respectability and the badging of the poor (which became national policy following an Act of 1697) enshrined and symbolised the social transition of the age'.[7] Running the poor law machinery helped to shape the identity of that growing 'middling sort' and mirrored the widening social distance which separated them from the increasingly numerous ranks of the labouring poor, a process of social realignment partly revealed 'in the manipulation of the poor laws as instruments of social regulation'.[8]

Historians of London's[9] social policy have similarly tended to focus on the opportunities that poor relief provided for social regulation and control, albeit within a system of relief often seen as flexible and generous. Keith Wrightson himself cited with approval Valerie Pearl's assessment of parochial poor relief in the first half of the seventeenth century, namely that 'alms were often given on terms which explicitly enjoined behaviour in strict conformity to the *mores* of the ratepayers'.[10] Ian Archer has similarly emphasised the opportunities that the poor law provided of controlling and regulating the capital's poor. The operation of the late sixteenth-century poor law 'served to emphasise the dependence of the poorer members of the community on the wealthy who therefore also enjoyed greater opportunities to mould the behaviour of the poor'.[11] 'Poor relief was increasingly used as a form of social control', and pensioners exhibiting recalcitrant behaviour were removed from almshouses or saw their pensions stopped. Overseers, appointed under the terms of the 1598 Act and of higher social status than the collectors they replaced, also seemingly acted as 'correctors of the poor'.[12] The historian of later seventeenth-century London acquiesces in this tradition when he, too, discusses the 'considerable authority over their poor' which city parishes exercised, imposing, for example, badging as a condition of relief even before the 1697 Act.[13]

This emphasis on the operation of the poor law, both as a means of social differentiation and social control, has not, however, gone without some qualification. Valerie Pearl has remarked, in the context of a discussion of the generosity and flexibility of poor relief in the early modern capital, that there appear to be few cases, in practice, where relief was denied to those exhibiting irreligious or immoral behaviour.[14] Similarly, Paul Slack, although arguing that the drive 'to use new methods of social welfare to achieve a moral and social reformation was powerful throughout' the sixteenth and seventeenth centuries, noted that there were countervailing tendencies. Overseers had less freedom of action than they may have liked to reduce or cut pensions. He found little sign in ruling vestries, even when expenditure was rising steadily, of a strong sense of cost restraint and argued that the local basis of poor relief prevented the creation of 'a wholly impersonal disciplinary machine'.[15] He suggested too that the extent to which the machinery of poor relief provided a means of clear social differentiation should also be qualified, since there were cases where individuals might qualify for relief and also pay the poor rate, and because ratepayers too, might in time use the system as a potential safety-net.[16] Levine and Wrightson, similarly, have qualified that earlier emphasis on control and differentiation. In Whickham, although poor relief might have imposed a specific public identity on the parish poor and possibly 'enshrined a social cleavage between those who paid and administered the rate and those who were at risk of becoming a charge upon it',[17] it was also noted that the daily operation of the law helped to *bridge* social divides: such a process 'could involve a recognition of obligations and rights which could lay a bridge of sorts across the realities of social distance – the more so perhaps when the overseers, some of them also vestry men, were personally involved in the investigation of cases and the granting and payment of relief to those in their charge in their respective quarters'.[18]

Related to questions of social control is the extent to which the poor possessed or recognised any *right* to relief under the poor law since clearly, if there was such a right, or if one was perceived in the late seventeenth century, then the imposition of social controls and the refusal of pensions to individuals deemed undeserving, would have been very much more difficult to justify for those running local administrations. Archer argues that, in late-sixteenth-century London, 'there is little sense in which the poor were able to regard relief as a right', whilst Pearl stated that 'the dole ... provided a modest, means-tested subsistence provision which was given not of right like today's payments but out of the statutory obligation of the parish to provide for the indigent'.[19] By contrast, Slack has argued that the daily operation of the poor law after the Restoration and its expansion, meant that those in need 'naturally began to assume that they were entitled to relief. Practice taught them their rights under the statutes.'[20]

To appreciate the extent to which the parish poor law acted as a means of social control and as a means of social differentiation and identification, we need then to focus closely on how the law was administered and how it operated. What did it actually mean to be a parish pensioner in the seventeenth century? How was a parish pension achieved, increased or lost? What, if anything, can we infer about the attitudes of those who ran the poor law or about the attitudes of the poor themselves? To answer such questions this chapter presents some provisional material deriving from a study of poor relief in seventeenth and early eighteenth-century London.[21]

## THE CONTEXT OF PAROCHIAL POOR RELIEF IN LATER SEVENTEENTH-CENTURY LONDON: THE PARISH OF ST MARTIN-IN-THE-FIELDS

This study is concerned chiefly with the mechanics of the parish poor law as it operated primarily in London's West End, with some supplementary material taken from those parts of London in the county of Middlesex. It excludes from consideration the City and its liberties, partly because the system of poor relief may have been significantly different there, and partly because much work has already been done on aspects of relief in the area.[22] Its main focus is on documentation pertaining to the parish of St Martin-in-the-Fields and its adjacent parishes.[23]

The parish of St Martin's experienced a massive increase in population during the seventeenth century. The population of the parish, according to rough estimates, was around 3500 in the early seventeenth century, and had reached 18 600 by 1641. Even after the loss of the small parish of St Paul Covent Garden, carved out in the 1640s, the parish probably numbered around 20 000 people at the Restoration. This expansion continued until 1680 when the parish boundary may have contained about 52 000 people. Thereafter, growth was restricted by further administrative division. After the administrative defection of St James Westminster and St Anne Soho the population of St Martin's probably hovered around 30–35 000 until the second decade of the eighteenth century and may have been about 45 000 by 1721.[24] The parish then saw a massive expansion in its tax base. Initially, this alone funded increases in poor relief payments. Not until the 1680s did the average poor rate contribution actually rise significantly (see Figures 1.1 and 1.2). The parish, as befitted a wealthy fashionable West End location, always contained an exceptional number of titled inhabitants and Hearth Tax evidence indicates that only about 25 per cent of its households would have been exempt on the grounds of poverty in 1664.[25]

Unsurprisingly, given the population increase, the number of pensioners relieved by the parish increased considerably over the period (Figure 1.3). From just under one hundred pensioners in the 1640s, numbers had reached over 400 before the division of the parish in 1678. Thereafter the parish usually relieved between 350 and 400 on the pension books.

Not unnaturally, therefore, the total expenditure on the poor made by the overseers increased massively in the parish over the seventeenth century. In money terms, poor relief became big business by the Restoration. Poor relief expenditure per year came to £822 2s 8d on the eve of the Civil War. At the Restoration the overseers were spending over £1140 per year on their poor; by 1680 this had reached the huge total of

*Going on the Parish* 23

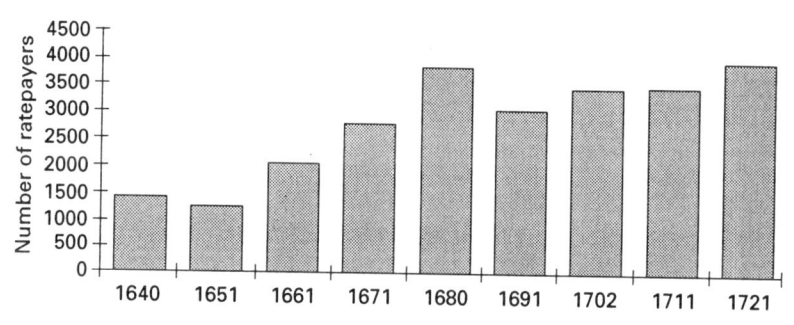

*Figure* 1.1  Number of ratepayers in St Martin's parish, 1640–1721

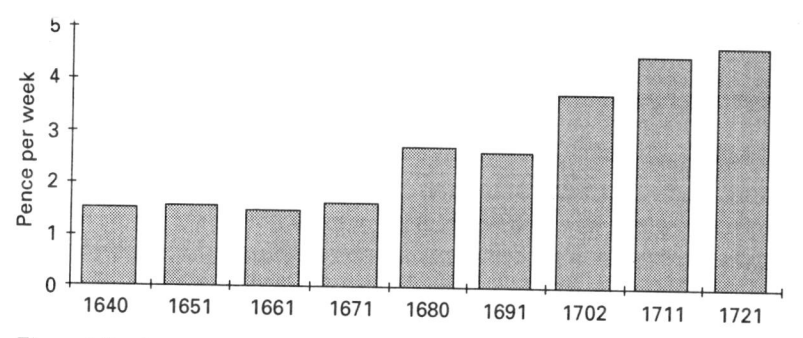

*Figure* 1.2  Average poor rate assessment, St Martin's, 1640–1721

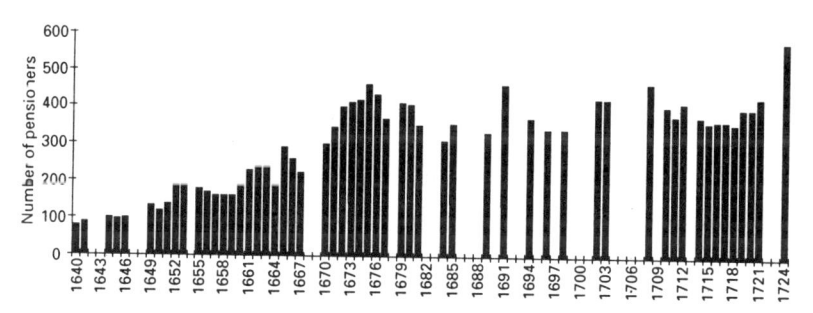

*Figure* 1.3  Number of parish pensioners, excluding orphans, St Martin's, 1640–1724

£2682 9s 0d. By 1707 expenditure was running at around £3700 per year and about £4500 by 1721. Most of this money increasingly seems to have derived from the poor rate (Figure 1.4) set annually by the vestry men and ratified by local justices.[26]

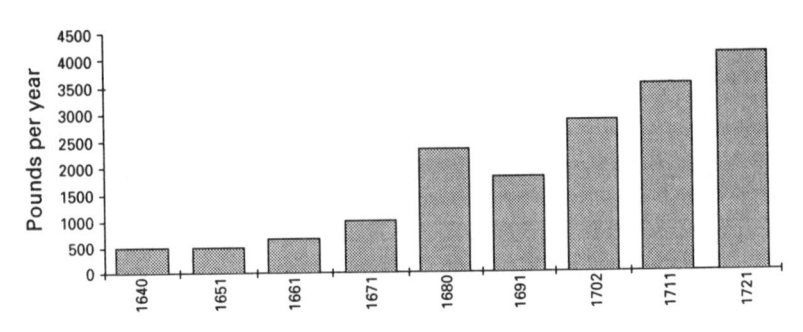

*Figure* 1.4   Yield of poor rate in St Martin's, 1640–1721

Such revenue-raising was, of course, exceptional by national standards. Investigation by the Board of Trade in 1695 indicated that the average yield of the poor rate nationally came to just £41 14s 0d per year. Even London parishes collected only £186 on average.[27] The parish of St Martin's was probably collecting between 4.25 and 7.4 per cent of the total poor rate raised in the capital.[28] It should be noted that the churchwardens, too, dispensed money to the parish poor. They often disbursed a portion of the money raised from rents and legacies detailed in the 'poor's account', and in addition they sometimes distributed money taken from the collections in church.[29]

Throughout the seventeenth and early eighteenth century, the bulk of parish spending on the poor took the form of cash pensions rather than payments to the casual so-called *extraordinary poor*. Until the last two decades of the period such pensions absorbed around three-quarters of all expenditure. The proportions allocated to the two categories of pauper did, however, vary over time. Pensioners absorbed over half of all parish spending until the 1630s; thereafter orphans seem to have comprised an increasing share of expenditure. Orphans absorbed 44 per cent of all parish spending in the 1640s, a figure not exceeded thereafter.

Over time, the proportion of money spent by the overseers on the casual or extraordinary poor increased markedly until the last two decades of the period when it became, for the first time, one of the major categories of expenditure for the parish. In 1691, spending on the extraordinary poor comprised 38 per cent of total parish expenditure and was actually the biggest single category. As Figure 1.5 shows, by the early eighteenth century nearly half of all parish spending on the poor went to the so-called casual or extraordinary poor. The substantial increase in parish spending therefore, derived partly, as we shall see below, on the payment of

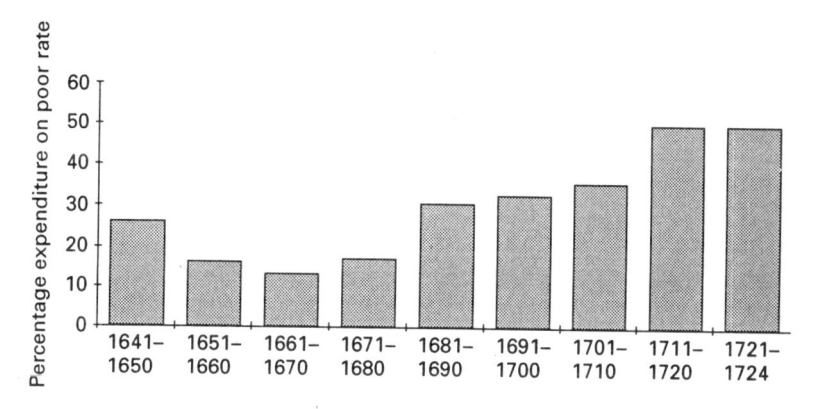

*Figure* 1.5  Proportion of total expenditure on the extraordinary poor, by decade, St Martin's, 1641–1724

increased pensions to parish pensioners, and also to fund an increase in the individual payments (running into several thousand per year by the end of the seventeenth century) to the casual poor.

Figure 1.6 presents the average value of pensions paid by the overseers to parish pensioners. Pensioners saw the money value of their pensions increase, in fits and starts, over the whole period, from fourteen and a half pence in 1641, experiencing a slump in the 1640s which recovered to about fourteen pence again by 1660 and a steady increase from that point to reach about eighteen pence by 1703 and approximately twenty pence per week by 1720.

The facts and figures relating to this parish's poor relief expenditure are important since they provide the vital context to the way in which poor

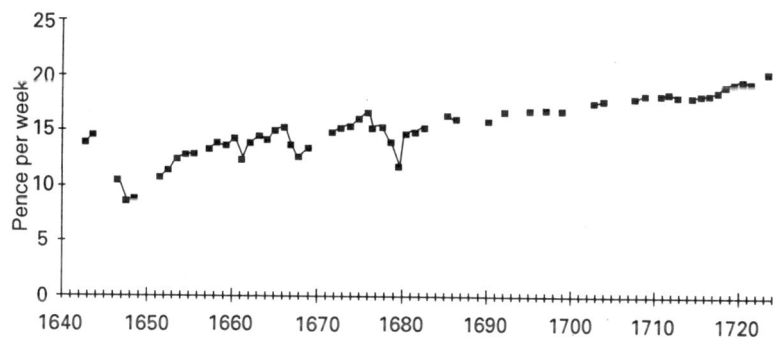

*Figure* 1.6  Average pension in pence per week, St Martin's, 1640–1724

relief could be delivered. Clearly, this was a parish where numbers of pensioners and paupers increased rapidly, to the extent that the burden of the rates began to increase from the 1670s. Monitoring the growing pensioner population must have become increasingly difficult, and it should be considered as a possibility that the poor became, therefore, increasingly remote from those running the parochial administration. The burden of the casual poor also seems to have increased. The voices of the poor were, therefore, heard increasingly frequently in St Martin's as the century progressed. To attempt answers to the questions raised in the introduction, however, we need to begin by discovering how access to poor relief was achieved. How visible were the needs of the poor and how responsive was the system in its operation?

As other historians have noted, it seems likely that the poor had to *apply* to those who operated the system for relief. Only then would some form of investigation or judgement be used to determine their fitness for relief. The form of such an application depended a great deal on the identity of those to whom the poor person was applying. Generally, the more remote the person or body, the more likely it was that an application would be made on a formal petition.

Pauper petitions, then, were directed to those supervising the distribution of relief in the parish. As far as one knows, such petitions were not usually made directly to local overseers, but to those occupying the next tier of parish administration, the vestry and churchwardens, or to JPs sitting either in petty sessions or at the frequent sittings of the Middlesex County Sessions.[30] It is also clear that the poor would have had to be selective in their targeting of those they were petitioning, since local interest in, and responsibility for, supervising additions to the pension lists varied according to local circumstances and the passage (and implementation) of contemporary legislation. Under the original Elizabethan poor law legislation the churchwardens and overseers were to tax the inhabitants and relieve the poor whilst JPs, acting in sessions, were allocated a supervisory and appellant role.[31] An Act of 1692, however, extended that role by ordering that no pensioner might be added to the pension list without the authority of a JP. That same Act also ordered that parish vestries should approve lists of pensioners each year.[32] It seems likely that the role of JPs in (at least formally) sanctioning additions to the parish pension lists was well established by the early eighteenth century.[33]

The vestry minutes of St Martin's provide an interesting case study in this regard, since, like many vestry minutes, they regularly record the receipt of petitions for relief.[34] Combined with the surviving overseers' accounts and some passing references found in the churchwardens' accounts, they tell us a great deal about how and with what success the poor made their voices heard in the forum of the vestry.

From 1647 the vestry of St Martin's began much closer supervision of the work of the overseers than they had ever attempted hitherto,[35] activity which mirrored the greater concern felt for the poor during the 1640s in the capital.[36] From June 1648, those admitted to pensions or submitting petitions are regularly recorded in the vestry books. The overseers were ordered in that year to bring in the names of all parish orphans and pensioners 'as they allowed without consent of the Vestry'.[37] Thereafter large numbers of applicants for relief are listed in the minutes. Some individuals' petitions were summarised, many others were either 'allowed' a pension, 'admitted penconers' or often merely 'referred to the Overseers of the Poor'. On occasion, the lists are prefixed by statements that make the existence of petitions explicit.[38] Occasionally, the overseers were ordered to investigate cases of especial need, 'widow Chency to be inquired after by the Overseers & to be releeved as they shall [see] cause'[39] or 'The Overseers of the Poore are desired to consider of the Petition of Wid [Hughes] & to releeve her & her children as they shall think fitt not admitting of her penconer without further order'.[40] It seems likely that petitions were read out aloud to the vestry; in 1655 those asking for pensions were to have their petition signed by the churchwardens and overseers before it was read.[41] These petitions were often delivered physically to the overseers, who were supposed to investigate the cases outlined therein.[42]

Although few have survived, the form and content of those petitions heard by the vestry were probably reasonably standard. Most probably began with some conventional obsequious phraseology, and then set out as desperate a case as possible. In so doing they stressed elements of their history that would seem to have been particularly telling. Previous ratepaying, long residence, age, the burden of children and physical infirmity were clearly important qualifications. Thomas Jarvis, in 1665, showed

> That your pet*itioner* hath lived in the parish of St Martin in the fields these three and Twenty yeares last past or thereabouts, and hath mainteyned himselfe by his hard labours, without being chargeable to any, But soe it is may it please your Wor*shi*pps, That by reason of Sicknesse & Lameness, & also being aged, hee is past his labour, and knowes noe further how to subsist, but must inevitably perish, unlesse your Wor*shi*pps be favourably pleased to behold him with an Eye of Compassion.[43]

Thomas Bighton, in that same year, claimed similarly

> That Your p[oore] petitioner, hat beene an inhabita[nt] in the parrish of St Martins this 40 years & upwards and now through exsess of age became very feeble, and lost his sight and soe rendered uncapeble of gettinge any waye a livelyhood, and nowe beinge in a Conditione likly to perrish & craveth your worships Charrytie.[44]

Such petitions sometimes included brief testimonials from neighbours or parochial officials.[45] Another recorded by the vestry men was from Henry Lidgould and is an example of a request for emergency and extraordinary relief:

> Upon reading the humble petition of Henry Lidgould son of Nicholas Lidgould of this parish Scrivener deceased, setting forth that he was ten yeares in Virginia and coming over in the last fleet, met with violent stormes and Tempests which much dampnified the Goods and provisions, so that the petitioner and the rest of the passengers were forced to come to short allowance: which caused a great sicknes wherewith the petitioner has been ever since afflicted and is now reduced to great want, And praying for forty shillings to pay his Doctor and buy some necessaries for his going to sea again.[46]

That from Christopher Dufton in 1679, lodging at one Mrs Butler's in New Street, set forth 'his long inhabitance in this parish, his late tedious sicknesse, and his and his Wives great age, and humbly begging A pencon' was likewise probably routine, as was that from Thomas Macham and Ann his wife 'havying byn Antient inhabitants and living well now fallen into Poverty'.[47] Too much weight, clearly, should not be attached to the deferential language employed in such petitions. So conventional, in fact, had the form of such applications become by the late seventeenth century, that the authorities running Christ's Hospital provided printed pro forma petitions, which included such conventional platitudes.[48]

As Figure 1.7 makes clear, however, after the early years of the Restoration the vestry men seem to have largely lost interest in hearing this manifestation of the voices of the poor, although they occasionally sought to impose further controls over the activities of the overseers, in ways which foreshadowed clauses of the (largely ignored) Act of 1692.[49] In 1676 they repeated their earlier insistence that churchwardens should give their consent before any more parish pensioners were admitted and in 1677, at a time of special concern for the growing costs of poor relief, set out a list of orders which included the resolution 'that noe poore whatsoever be admitted into any weekly pention or monthly reliefe without an Order of Vestrie

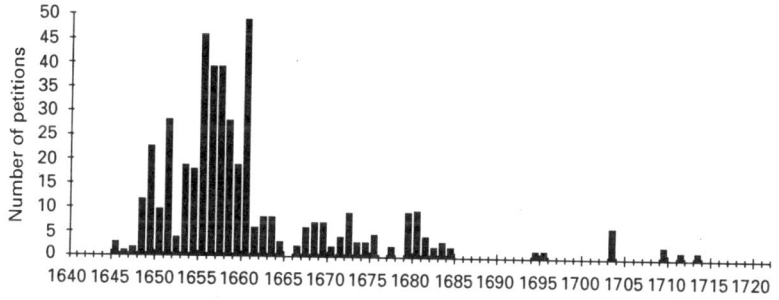

*Figure* 1.7  Number of petitions recorded in vestry minutes, St Martin's, 1640–1721

or from one Justice of the Peace & the two Churchwardens under their handes in writing which Orders to be kept by the Overseers as theire warrant for soe doeing'.[50] It is less clear, however, whether this supervision was consistently applied. It is possible, in fact, that many orders of the vestry were not always communicated effectively to the current overseers who, not being vestry members, were not normally present at their meetings.[51] Thereafter, only in 1695 and 1708 were references made to personal supervision of the pension lists by members of the vestry.[52] It is not known to what extent other local vestries sought to control access to the pension lists, but such efforts were probably commonplace.[53]

In addition to concern, only sporadically expressed, to control access to the pension books, the vestry and local JPs who often attended ex officio seem to have been increasingly concerned to oversee that growing burden of the extraordinary poor. In 1671, they ordered that no single overseer could pay any money to that category of poor without consent of the churchwardens and other overseers, and similar concern was again expressed in 1678.[54] In 1686, following objections to extraordinary expenditure by local justices, this same restriction was reiterated.[55] In 1696, overseers were supposed to give an account of the extraordinary poor to the JPs in the vestry every second Sunday in the month, after evening sermon – an order that was repeated in 1707 and 1708.[56]

In addition to the churchwardens and vestry, the poor might, of course, put their cases directly to local JPs.[57] Much of this business probably went before JPs sitting in petty sessions, often in the vestry house itself,[58] The widows in the St Martin's almshouses were forced to send a collective petition to the bench in 1704 after their pensions fell into arrears[59] but, that case apart, it appears to have been exceptional, certainly by the late seventeenth century, for many poor persons to have sent petitions to the entire bench. None are referred to in the printed calendar of sessions orders between 1689 and 1709 as coming from St Martin's, although a few paupers, from elsewhere, did make such appeals.[60]

It is clear, however, that JPs in St Martin's occasionally did intervene in the administration of relief, presumably after petitions and complaints. The vestry in 1675 noted the case of David Merritt, 'a poore aged old man being by the overseers put by his pention' who 'because hee appears to bee in great want' ordered that it should be restored 'or show cause to Sr William Pulteny knt why hee ought not to receive it'. Again in 1671, a pension of 12d weekly for one widow Yeates was recommended to the overseers by the vestry 'or else hew cause why the[y] ought not unto Thomas Balye Esq'.[61] The overseers' accounts themselves occasionally recorded this activity of JPs. In the year 1661–2, the overseers, in their extraordinary accounts, noted four cases of payments made 'by order' or 'at the request' of the two JPs, Bacon and Godfrey, as well as another made on the initiative of the churchwardens.[62] It also seems likely, too, that JPs came to have a closer role in admitting individuals onto the pension books, perhaps following the legislation of 1691, and it may have been commonplace to get at least formal sanction from a JP before granting a parish pension by the early eighteenth century.[63]

It seems likely that, with the exception of that period between 1647 and 1662 when the local vestry were hearing what was probably a significant proportion of all applications for pensions in the parish, the voices of the poor heard in petitions were often in the nature of appeals against unpopular decisions by the overseers of the poor. Petitioners asked, like Henry Stanley in October 1660, to be restored to his former weekly pension of eighteen pence, which the vestry sanctioned, 'it appearing that he is as necessitous as formerly', or Ann Wright in 1662, to be paid twelve pence weekly 'which shee hath usually', unless the overseers could show 'that shee is able to subsist without it'.[64]

All this is important, since the poor had the opportunity, which some of them clearly took, to play off the different branches of poor relief administration against each other. In neighbouring St Paul's, indeed, it was a matter of particular importance that the churchwardens should have the final say in who came onto the pension books.[65] Lines of communication between vestry, churchwardens, overseers and local JPs were not always very effective so that paupers, by repetitive petitioning or by selecting sympathetic individuals, might successfully overturn local decisions. In the early eighteenth century, indeed, the vestry of St Martin's made a resolution to end one of these potential loopholes. In 1708, they resolved that the Churchwardens do waite on the Justices of the Peace inhabiting in this parish, to desire them not to putt any such poor on the Extraordinary or pencon, who have been putt out upon Examinacon & Inquiry, by the Gentlemen of the Vestry and Churchwardens, and a List to be delivered to the Justices of the Peace of such poor who are so putt Out![66]

Up until the early eighteenth century, at least,[67] it was overwhelmingly the overseers of the poor who decided the bulk of relief cases in the West End. This can be demonstrated with reasonable ease. Figure 1.8 plots the average number of new parish pensioners (*excluding* both the large numbers of parish orphans and the even more numerous payments made to individuals on the extraordinary account) coming onto the books each year.

The figures given here are not precise, because of the difficulty of identifying accurately each individual from year to year and taking into account missing account books, but they indicate that between 20 and 60 new pensioners were coming onto the pension books each year from the 1640s. Clearly, when comparing such numbers to the number of petitions referred to in the vestry minutes, only in the 1640s and 1650s were a significant proportion of cases first mentioned in the vestry minutes.[68] The sheer number of individuals receiving extraordinary relief would, by itself, have rendered constant supervision by churchwardens or JPs entirely unrealistic. Even as early as 1661, over 500 individuals received over 1200 individual payments.

The evidence of petitions, therefore, shows they are normally likely to be the exceptional cases of hardship, cases which for some reason had

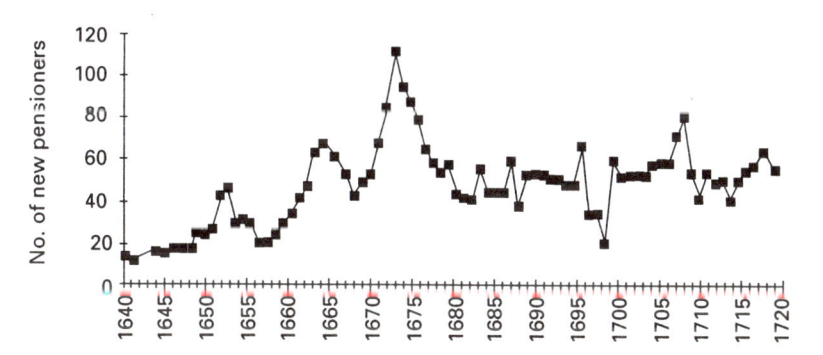

*Figure* 1.8  Five-year moving average of all new pensioners in St Martin's, 1640–1720

been rejected, ignored or perhaps simply forgotten by local overseers. It is also possible, too, that some paupers preferred, when able, to mobilise personal patronage links to members of the vestry or other local dignitaries such as the Dean of Westminster by applying for relief in this way, although such networks have left few easily recoverable traces in the records; the Dean of Westminster, for one, occasionally intervened on behalf of his tenants or clients.[69]

Most pensions and supplemental relief, therefore, must have taken place after a personal application to an overseer, a face-to-face verbal encounter, probably at an overseer's own house. It would be fascinating to know more about these doorstep encounters, but I know of no surviving notebook or diary for London that would make such a literal reconstruction of this more representative voice of the poor possible. How did pensioners and the parish poor actually behave when making their supplications, and what were the constraints over the overseer's responses? Such questions are clearly related to the extent to which overseers and their supervisors expected a standard of behaviour in return for poor relief. The verbal and physical behaviour of the poor was, after all, probably the commonest method of seeking out a pension or supplemental relief.

Vestry orders on a number of occasions made the granting of pensions, or casual relief, conditional on appropriate behaviour from recipients. The terms of these orders and their reiteration suggest, however, that such behaviour was not automatically forthcoming. When money was collected in church during service times, a disorderly crowd of local beggars and parish paupers normally gathered in the churchyard to make their own brand of verbal supplication for a share of it, which it seems was traditionally forthcoming. In 1659, 'the rude and disorderly carriage of poore that are beging in & about the Church and Churchyeard on the Saboth day, and specially on the Communion day' brought a rebuke to the parish beadles, who were ordered to 'keepe all poore from pressing on the Churchwardens & Overseers of the poore, as they stand Collecting at the Church doores'.[70] It seems likely that pensioners were not averse, apparently despite being in receipt of such money, to joining in such abusive and threatening behaviour, since in 1661 the vestry ordered that

> if any of the Poore of this parish shall on any Saboth day use any uncivill language in the Church of Churchyeard to the disturbance of the Minister Churchwardens of any Overseers of the Poore; Than then theyr pentions bee taken from them until further Order. and that noe parte of the Collection bee given to any one of the poore presente unlesse they bee very civill.[71]

Constables were later ordered to prevent beggars and common vagrants joining in hanging about in the churchyard and in lanes and streets, since they were 'greate enemyes to our impotent poore', presumably because they competed for a share in the collection money. Continuing efforts had been made for some time in St Martin's to prevent any of the collection money being given away 'at the Church doore to the poore'.[72] Begging by the parish poor was sanctioned in 1677, but only on condition that those individuals begging wore a badge.

> Who thereby have liberty to ask and receive broken meate only and not to beg of Coaches or of people going in the streets, and the hours of asking at doores allowed are from one to foure in the afternoone and noe longer, and none are to aske at doores without a badge. And if any of the said poore shalbe unruly or uncivil in their asking at doors, then the badg is to bee taken from them.[73]

Occasionally the records hint at other pauper strategies than abuse or intimidation of parish officers. One exasperated churchwarden in 1647 hinted at sheer persistence, when he noted 'Given to a poore visited man that would not goe from my doore one shilling'.[74]

The vestry did not limit their expectation of appropriate behaviour to such general orders. Their individual recommendations to overseers occasionally also carried riders setting out the expected response from the recipient. Hence, William Banbridge was to get a 12d weekly pension, 'if the Overseers finde him not for the present or for the future to bee a Common begger'.[75] In 1657, Ann Burton was to have 6d added to her pension 'if shee takes her a lodging & lives quietly'[76] and Bridget Conly, wife of one Lanhan, was to be relieved in 1670 'provided shee behave herselfe civilly'.[77] Such riders were relatively rare, however, and orders to stop payments on account of rude or abusive behaviour were similarly unusual. One case concerned one Ann Powell, in 1654, 'comonly cald by the name of Welsh Nan, being complained of for a lewd and disorderly person: shall bee payd noe more money'.[78] Not all of these few vestry orders, however, seem to have been carried out by the overseers.[79] It is certain, too, that the overseers themselves sometimes faced open abuse from parish pensioners, even as they went about their work. Those taking a census of parish pensioners in 1707 noted the names of two pensioners, one Sarah Wells of Castle Street, being 'drunken and abusive to the Overseers', as was the similarly inebriated Isabella Stanley. Both women had their pensions reduced by one shilling in that list.[80]

How much knowledge and control over the pensioner population was actually achieved in the parish? The vestry and churchwardens asked overseers routinely for reports on the parish poor, which were to be brought into the vestry.[81] Pensioners were sometimes subject to personal inspection by vestry men or churchwardens at the point when they picked their pensions up on 'pay days' in the vestry house.[82] At such inspections, pensioners were to be viewed by churchwardens or overseers, who were to 'allow of and continue such as they shall think fitt and to disallow and discontinue such as they shall think fitt'.[83] In April 1653, for example, the vestry ordered that 'the Penconers bee vewed on Munday by 10 of the Clock'.[84] This inspection was designed to facilitate vestry control over the pension lists and was, of course, designed to root out the idle or discover those fit for work; some of the particularly energetic inspections were connected to schemes to put the poor on work.[85] Interestingly, it seems that pensioners did not always appear in person to collect their pensions on pay days, perhaps to avoid this supervision. In 1656, a parish officer normally responsible for surveying inmates, was to be sent

> four or five days before theyr next pay day ... to all the Penconers and Orphants dwelling in and nere the parish to give them notice that they appear every one in theyr owne persons to rec[eive] theyr pay except such as by reason of lamnes of sicknes cannot come, and such as doe not come not haveing a lawfull excuse to hinder them are to receave noe moore pencons.[86]

It is clear, however, that notwithstanding occasional efforts made by the churchwardens and vestry men, the real responsibility for surveying the pensioners and returning their names lay with the overseers. The vestry men usually sought their recommendations as to 'who are fitt to bee continued & who not' rather than doing the work themselves.[87] In 1669 it was ordered, that to facilitate such surveys by the overseers, pensioners should not move house without giving the overseers seven days notice upon pain of having their pensions suspended.[88] In 1671, pensioners refusing to give information about the reasons for their pension were to have their money stopped.[89]

The receipt of a parish pension, too, might mean the wearing of a badge, that symbol of social identification, differentiation and perhaps humiliation.[90] To some extent, the large numbers of pensioners in the big suburban parishes enabled disorderly or immoral behaviour to go unpunished more often, and the pressure to view and survey the pauper populations must be partly understood in this context. For similar reasons, badging was peculiarly appropriate to the metropolitan environment.[91] There is some evidence, for the 1670s, that pensioners in St Martin's were wearing badges to regularise begging[92] and a general sessions order for Middlesex in 1694 prescribed the wearing of metal badges for the pension poor, again to inhibit them from begging out of the parish.[93] The clause of that 1697 Act stipulating badging of the pension poor also seems to have been implemented in St Martin's, following pressure from one of the vestry men.[94] It seems likely, however, that parish paupers left off wearing the badges after a few years and that the badging of the poor was done, at best, sporadically and might be evaded easily, sometimes with the connivance of sympathetic JPs.[95]

The meaning of being a parish pensioner, however, did not turn simply on questions of crude social control and differentiation like badging, even if imposed successfully. It was, arguably, possibly the loss of personal property rights as much as the possibility of social regulation which made the difference between the parish pensioner and the ordinary parishioner. Parish pensioners, of course, might receive additional material support from the parish in times of sickness, injury and at their deaths, but it is not generally appreciated that in return for the financial aid represented by parish relief, paupers lost all control over what little property they possessed.[96] Throughout the seventeenth century, overseers' accounts of most of the West End parishes in London demonstrate that parish authorities, as was commonplace in early modern England, took possession of the goods of parish pensioners, as well as those who left orphans on the parish at their deaths, which were either passed onto other paupers or sold to raise money.[97] Those applying for pensions, then, were implicitly surrendering what property they had to the parish in return for a pension.

This surrender became increasingly explicit over time, as the parish sought to avoid the legal implications represented by this confiscation, and to avoid being taken to court by angry heirs of the deceased paupers.[98] The sale of the goods of deceased paupers is noted throughout the seventeenth and early eighteenth century in St Martin's, but only in 1655 did the vestry begin a series of orders to the effect that in future all those petitioning for a pension should have their 'goods and estate both reall and personal' inventoried by the churchwardens and overseers and that the petitioner should 'signe the inventory promising to leave all that hee or shee shall dyth possessed of to the poore of the parish'.[99] The parish also took steps to indemnify the overseers and churchwardens against legal action in the event that letters of administration of pensioners' goods were challenged.[100] In 1678, however, one of the overseers was arrested by the administrator of the goods of Jane Owen, a deceased pensioner, after seizing her goods for the use of the poor. This persuaded the vestry to insist on further safeguards, namely that all hopeful would-be applicants for a parish pension should have their goods inventoried, 'and in consideracon of the pencon or allowance they desire to have, they shall also make a Bill of Sale of all their said goods and Chattells to the present Overseers', which assignment should with other parish documentation 'be hung upp in the Vestry for the publick view', with the names listed alphabetically.[101]

Lastly, what of the overseers? Until we have more evidence as to the attitudes of these all-important officials, and much more information at our disposal about their reasons for giving, and particularly for reducing or cancelling relief to the parish poor, then the meaning of the parish pension must remain arguable. Given that such offices were rotated annually, and that most overseers were local tradesmen, we must assume that they were as susceptible to local and neighbourly pressures as were other strands of the local administration in early modern London.[102] The poor were not only neighbours; they were, perhaps more importantly, potential customers, able to channel their cash relief and other income back into the local economy and we must assume that denials could be met with the threat of a local trade boycott. Unfortunately, by their nature, overseers' accounts detail only successful appeals for relief but we can surmise something more about the constraints under which overseers operated and which determined the level and number of pensions paid.

Overwhelmingly, however, it was the financial burden of the local poor which informed overseers' payments. Indeed, the office of overseer of the poor could only be borne by individuals capable of bearing the financial burden it imposed, since the interval between the collection of the poor rate and expenditure on the poor, as well as a failure for revenue to meet current expenditure, meant that such officials met the shortfalls out of their own pocket.[103] They might wait some years before reimbursement from the parish and, not unnaturally, many individuals paid a fine rather than serve.[104] Overseers then were as careful as possible to match expenditure to income, since it might entail personal financial loss and difficulties if they failed.[105] It is known that, as a consequence, the overseers reacted swiftly when parish income was failing to match current expenditure, to *reduce* the pensions of the parish poor.[106]

In sum, then, what did receiving a pension mean to the recipient? Would-be pensioners might, if turned out of their pensions or if the ruling vestry was intent on monitoring pensions lists closely, have to petition direct to the ruling elite or to local JPs for new pensions, restitution or additions, although this would entail both personal financial cost[107] and the possibility of rejection on moral or behavioural grounds and might still mean a wait until overseers could investigate their cases. Many applicants in the 1640s and 1650s clearly had to reapply.[108] Pensions, too, might be arbitrarily reduced across the board if parish finances so dictated. Those receiving parish pay might be 'viewed' as they picked it up at the vestry house, and might on such occasions be interrogated so that, again in theory, changing circumstances, the ability to work or various social and moral lapses, might be detected. They would have expected to be included in occasional censuses made by overseers. At various times pensions might, in theory, be stopped if badges were not worn, if paupers were rude to parish officers, if pensioners moved house without telling the overseers or failed to collect doles in person without good reason. When paupers died, their property was subject to seizure and sale by the parish authorities, although the number of cases recorded in the accounts suggest that by no means all of those pensioners dying whilst on relief had their property confiscated successfully.[109]

Any conclusion as to the actual meaning of those thousands of payments made under the parish poor law must remain tentative. Whether pensions could ever be demanded as of 'right' remains questionable, since many applications for relief were probably rejected,[110] and pensions could be cancelled on grounds other than purely objective material deprivation or physical infirmity. Moreover, those paupers taking up their supposed 'right' surrendered, in theory and sometimes in practice, their own right to dispose of their own property. We need to recognise then, that dismissal from a pension might come at any point for a variety of moral and behavioural reasons and not simply out of a recognition of changed need or circumstances. However, the evidence discussed here suggests that we must doubt whether parish pensioners, at least in large and populous London parishes, were as amenable to social control as some historians might expect. Perhaps most London parishes failed, in practice, to use parish poor relief to discipline the poor, as some interested parties complained.[111] It may be significant that when contemporaries sought new means of social control after the middle of the seventeenth century, they looked to indoor, institutional means of controlling and disciplining the pauper population rather than seeking to manipulate and exploit already existing structures of parochial relief for that purpose.[112]

NOTES

1. This chapter is based on research, currently in progress, on the reconstruction of the biographies of those receiving parish pensions from the parishes of seventeenth- and early eighteenth century Westminster. This project

focuses on the parish of St Martins-in-the-Fields, and those derived from it subsequently, to 1724. That cut-off date is determined by the erection of a parish workhouse under the 1723 Workhouse Test Act, which significantly altered the size and composition of the pensioner population in St Martin's, as it also radically changed the local system of poor relief there. I would like to thank my former research assistant, Jean Hosking, who was employed to work on this project for a year on money generously provided by the Research Committee of Newcastle University, 1992–3. The full details of this research are to appear in *The Making of the London Poor*, to be published by Manchester University Press.

2. P. Slack, *Poverty and Policy in Tudor and Stuart England* (London, 1988), p.182.
3. Ibid., pp.178–82.
4. For the growth of the poor law in rural areas after the middle of the century, see ibid., passim and also, T.C. Wales, 'Poor Relief and Life-Cycle', in R.M. Smith (ed.), *Land, Kinship and Life-Cycle* (Cambridge, 1984), pp.356–7; D. Levine and K. Wrightson, *The Making of an Industrial Society: Whickham, 1560–1765*, (Oxford, 1991), pp.346–56; K. Wrightson, *English Society 1580–1680* (London, 1982), p.154. See also for some recent research into rural poor relief, T. Arkell, 'The Incidence of Poverty in England in the Later Seventeenth Century', *Social History* 12 (1), (1987), 23–48; B. Stapleton, 'Inherited Poverty and Life-cycle Poverty: Odiham, Hampshire, 1650–1850', *Social History* 18, 3 (1993) 339–55; Mary Barker-Read, 'The Treatment of the Aged Poor in Five Selected West Kent Parishes From Settlement to Speenhamland (1662–1797)' (Open University, 1988. PhD, thesis).
5. It should be noted that, notwithstanding the research done thus far, the extent of this growth may be overstated. No authors have deflated pensions paid over time to take account of monetary inflation. We really need, too, more local studies, especially from rural areas, to appreciate the huge regional variation in the ways in which the English poor law was implemented on the ground. Not all the evidence collected thus far, either, points in the same direction: see some of the cautionary remarks in the discussion in Slack, *Poverty and Policy*, pp.173–82.
6. Wrightson, *English Society*, p.181. Most of this sentence has been quoted by Slack, *Poverty and Policy*, p.208 and also by I. Archer, *The Pursuit of Stability. Social Relations in Elizabethan London* (Cambridge, 1991), p.99.
7. Wrightson, *English Society*, p.182.
8. Ibid., p.226. See also A. Fletcher, *Reform in the Provinces. The Government of Stuart England* (London, 1986), pp.227 and 279.
9. In what follows, 'London' refers to all that area within the Bills of Mortality.
10. V. Pearl, 'Puritans and Poor Relief. The London Workhouse, 1649–1660', in D. Pennington and K. Thomas (eds), *Puritans and Revolutionaries: Essays in Seventeenth-Century History Presented to Christopher Hill* (Oxford, 1978), p.209; Wrightson, *English Society*, p.181.
11. Archer, *Pursuit of Stability*, p.96.
12. Ibid., pp.97–8.
13. S. Macfarlane, 'Social Policy and the Poor in the Later Seventeenth Century', in A.L. Beier and R. Finlay (eds), *The Making of the Metropolis: London 1500–1700* (London, 1986), pp.256 and 273.

14. V. Pearl, 'Social Policy in Early Modern London', in H. Lloyd-Jones, V. Pearl and B. Worden (eds), *History and Imagination: Essays in Honour of H.R. Trevor-Roper* (London, 1981), p.130, notes that some rich city parishes gave relief even to 'transgressors and malefactors'.
15. Slack, *Poverty and Policy*, pp.190–205.
16. Ibid., pp.178–9, 208.
17. Levine and Wrightson, *Making of an Industrial Society*, pp.348–52.
18. Ibid., p.353.
19. Archer, *Pursuit of Stability*, p.97; Pearl, 'Puritans and Poor Relief', p.209.
20. Slack, *Poverty and Policy*, p.192. He cites the remarks of the MP Richard Cockes, 1698, who exclaimed that 'the poor ... thinks the parish is obliged in old age, extremities, and necessities to provide for him', ibid. Such attitudes were hardly new, however, since similar sentiments were expressed in the early seventeenth century; see J. Boulton, *Neighbourhood and Society: A London Suburb in the Seventeenth Century* (Cambridge, 1987), p.95. See also, Fletcher, *Reform in the Provinces*, pp.188, 227.
21. See above, note 1.
22. In particular, vestrymen and churchwardens administered relief with 'considerable independence from higher authorities', whilst overseers of the poor in the city parishes were seemingly 'seldom more than collectors of the poor rates, while effective decision making was left to churchwardens', Macfarlane, 'Social Policy and the Poor', pp.255, 272. For other work done on poor relief in the City of London after 1640 see also, in addition to the work of Valerie Pearl cited above, R.W. Herlan, 'Poor Relief in the London Parish of Antholin's Budge Row 1638–1664', *Guildhall Studies in London History* 2, 4 (1977); R.W. Herlan, 'Poor Relief in London during the English Revolution', *Journal of British Studies* 18 (1979); R.W. Herlan, 'London's Poor during the Puritan Revolution: the Parish of St Dunstan's in the West', *Guildhall Studies in London History* 3, 1 (1977); R.W. Herlan, 'Social Articulation and Parochial Poverty on the Eve of the Restoration', *Guildhall Studies in London History* 2, 2 (1976). See also, S.M. Macfarlane, 'Studies in Poverty and Poor Relief in London at the End of the Seventeenth Century' (unpublished D.Phil. thesis, Oxford, 1983).
23. The other West End parishes in question are, St Margaret's Westminster, St Clement Danes, St Paul's Covent Garden (carved out of St Martin's in 1647), St James Westminster (carved out of St Martin's in 1686?), St Anne Soho (carved out of St Martin's in 1678): these together possess some of the richest poor law material surviving for seventeenth-century London. The material is now housed in the City of Westminster Archives Centre (hereafter WAC). This chapter is based on only a small fraction of the surviving documentation. For a fuller treatment, see *The Making of the London Poor* (forthcoming).
24. There appears to be some disagreement about the course of population growth in St Martin's. Shoemaker, using figures for numbers of households and houses, gives figures that are considerably less than those derived from average totals of baptisms: Shoemaker, *Prosecution and Punishment*, p.327. One possible reason for the substantial disagreement is that Shoemaker's method under-estimates the large lodging population. One source reported a

population of 40 000 in 1680, which seems a reasonable guess and certainly not exaggerated following the eccentric reference to it in T.R. Forbes, 'The Changing Face of Death in London', in C. Webster (ed.), *Health, Medicine and Mortality in the Sixteenth Century* (1979), p.118. Forbes states that the parish was 'one of London's smallest', ibid.

25. M. Power, 'The Social Topography of Restoration London', in A.L. Beier and R. Finlay (eds), *The Making of the Metropolis: London 1500–1700* (1986), p.205. Some sources suggest that the parish of St Martin's lost status after the division of the parish in the 1680s, although some of this information derives from special pleading from the parish vestry themselves.
26. In 1696, out of £3212 6s 6d collected by the parish, no less than £2791 7s 1d derived from the poor rate. WAC/F425A.
27. For the Board of Trade returns, see Public Record Office (hereafter PRO) CO 388/5/2/f.209r–211v.
28. The Board of Trade estimated that £40 000 was raised from London, although the surviving returns from the London and Middlesex archdeaconries, from 123 parishes, yielded just £22 920: see PRO CO 388/5/2/f.209r–211v and Slack, *Poverty and Policy*, p.171.
29. See the surviving churchwardens' accounts, WAC/F2–F82 passim.
30. The General Sessions for the County of Middlesex, which included Westminster and the West End parishes outside the liberties of the City of London, met eight times a year. In the early eighteenth century, petty sessions met outside the general sessions for each division of the county, and also in each parish, depending on the availability of local justices, For discussions of procedure, see R. Paley (ed.), *Justice in Eighteenth-Century Hackney*, London Record Society 28, 1991, p.xv. JPs were supposed to exercise close supervision over long-term relief in the 1730s and 1740s, p.xxiv. JPs were given extra responsibility to sanction additions to poor relief lists under the 1723 Workhouse Test Act, 9 Geo. I c. 7: see P. Slack, *The English Poor Law 1531–1782* (Basingstoke, 1990), p.63.
31. JPs were to hear appeals against unfair rating, or requests for amendments to pensions in sessions, appoint overseers and confirm their accounts, 39 Elizabeth I c. 40, 43 Eliz. I c. 2.
32. 3 William & Mary c. 11; for later extensions see above, n.30.
33. See the parish examination books, dating from 1708, which regularly include lists of pensioners and orphans to be added or returned to the pension lists, in addition to the voluminous material relating to settlement disputes, WAC, F5001-13, passim. Detailed work on these books is currently in progress by the author. It is possible that the lists of approved pensions were a mere formality since, unlike the settlement cases, no examination was actually recorded. F5001/f.27, 1708, an examination by Justice Negus, records 'These persons following haveing been examined and entered, to be put on the Book', a list containing five pensioners (all of whom began their pensions in that year) follow, 'let these be entered accordingly'. No case history is appended. Occasional extra information derived from previous settlement history, so that Ann Clancy, a parish pensioner from 1708 until 1721, had been, recorded Justice Negus, 'past from St Giles' [in the Fields?]. F5001/f.27.
34. See the discussion in Macfarlane, 'Social Policy and the Poor', pp.255–6.

## Going on the Parish

35. Earlier, the ruling vestry were constrained to remind themselves in 1635 that 'the peticons of the poor concerning pencons are to be read and answered'. WAC/F2002/f.104r.
36. Pearl, 'Puritans and Poor Relief', pp.215–18.
37. WAC/F2002/f.266. The order was repeated in 1649, f.273, in 1655, F2003/f.80.
38. WAC/F2003/f.127, 27 April 1657, noted that 'the present Overseers ... do consider of these [list of ten] peticoners ... and to take an inventory of the goods of such as they shall thinke fitt to bee allowed pencons'. For a similar order, see F2003/f.293, 28 Aug 1662.
39. WAC/F2003/f.47, 9 Aug. 1654.
40. WAC/F2003/f.53, 15 Nov. 1654.
41. WAC/F2003/f.73, 18 May 1655.
42. WAC/F2003/f.160, 10 May 1658, ordered that nine petitions were to be 'delyered to present Overseers ... who are desired to vew the peticoners at theyr habitacons & to take an Inventory of their goods ... And to Certefy the Vestry at theyr next sitting, how & who are fitt to bee releaved & who not'; for similar orders see F2003/f.221, 19 April 1660.
43. WAC F6039/7.
44. WAC F6039/8.
45. WAC F6039/7, that from Thomas Jarvis, was signed by parishioners, attesting 'that the substance of this peticon is true, and that the pet*itioner* hath beene a great paines taker, & is a man of honest life, & wee humbly conceive him a fitt object of Charity, & therefore humbly reco*m*mend him to your Wor*shi*pps to grant him Reliefe'.
46. WAC F2005/f.88, 13 April 1691.
47. WAC F2003/f.112, 6/1/1657. See also that from Ann Roger, which reported her ex-ratepaying status, five small children and no means, 21/2/1650.
48. Guildhall Library 12818A/passim. Petitions were, naturally 'Humble Petitions', from individuals who invariably 'humbly beseeches your Worships, in your usual Pity and Charity to distressed men, poor widows, and Fatherless Children' and ended with the printed promise that the applicant 'shall ever Pray etc' for the governors.
49. WAC/F2004/f.45, 8 Dec. 1669. They noticed that churchwardens and overseers had neglected to meet monthly to 'inquire after the necessitye of the poore', as required under 43 of Elizabeth. For the Act of 1692, see above, p. 26. Slack does not classify the 1692 Act as one that had 'the greatest impact on local practice', *The English Poor Law*, pp.59, 62.
50. WAC/F2004/f.190v, 3 May 1677. A copy of these orders can also be found in ff.191–2.
51. WAC/F2004, f.190v included a proviso 'that the present Overseers may not be ignorant of these Orders that soe much thereof as concernes them may be entered into their grand booke'.
52. WAC/F2005/f.154, 2 April 1695. Two gentlemen of the vestry were supposed to meet the overseers every month. In 1700, to discuss the poor, F2005/f.395 and f.396.
53. WAC/H802/f.3.
54. WAC/F2004/f.79, 30 Nov. 1671. A similar order was made in October 1678, F2004/f.236, wherein overseers were to 'give a particular Accompt in

Writing to the Churchwarden of their Extraordinary Disbursements of the Month then last past, and to whom they dispose the same, and for what. And the Churchwarden to present the same to the Vestry then next following.'
55. WAC/F2005/ff.42 and 45., 2 March and 5 April 1686.
56. WAC/F2005/f.179, 6 Oct. 1696. F2005/f.383, 29 June 1707, the justice was the 'active' Justice Negus, for whose energetic caseloads, see Shoemaker, *Prosecution and Punishment*, p.323. The possibility is that there was *increasing* supervision of the extraordinary poor from local JPs in the later seventeenth century.
57. Paley, *Justice in Hackney*, has a representative selection of such activity, although taken from a later period and thus, possibly, not typical of earlier practice: see above, note 30.
58. The notebook of one JP, not yet consulted, does survive: see the reference to it in Shoemaker, *Prosecution and Punishment*, p.332. For an example of Middlesex Petty Sessions in Hackney, see Paley, *Justice in Hackney*, passim. Justices regularly attended the St Martin's vestry, seemingly as ex officio members. St Martin's justices meeting in 'private sessions' in the vestry were particularly active in committing loose, idle and disorderly persons to the House of Correction in 1693: Shoemaker, *Prosecution and Punishment*, p.325. Petty sessions were held in this area. It was ordered in July 1696 at the general sessions, for example, that petty sessions should be held 'monthly to consult how the poor may be relieved, and how to suppress unlawful meetings of numbers of persons which may be dangerous to the public peace': W. le Hardy (ed.), *Calendar of Middlesex Sessions Orders, 1689–1709*, p.156.
59. Ibid., p.272. Their pensions had, seemingly, fallen into arrears before, in 1674, see WAC/F2004/f.166.
60. For petitions for pensions, or extra allowances, see for example, ibid., pp.18–19, 164.
61. WAC/F2004/f.55.
62. Widow Polcat was paid 3s 'in great want by Order of Justice Bacon'; Edward Clarke 5s 'at the request of Just. Bacon and Just. Godfrye'; Hannah Wood 4s 'by order of Just. Bacon being turned out of her lodging'; Thomas Mason 5s 'by order of the Justices & Churchwardens being in greate wante', WAC F389, passim. George Atwater got 5s 'by the desire of the churchwardens being in greate wante' whilst Mary Smyth 2s 6d 'at the Deane's request'. Atwater's payment is not mentioned in the vestry minutes, so that the latter presumably understate the amount of their intervention in poor relief administration.
63. See above, note 33.
64. WAC F2003/f.238; f.303, 17/12/1662 (Ann Wright). See also the case of Sarah Browne, September 1656, to 'be continued in her pencon ... or Overseers ... to shew cause why shee ought not to have it towards the reliefe of her selfe and childe', F2003/f.107.
65. The vestry minutes of St Paul's Covent Garden in 1681 recorded, 'It was the same Day Resolved that the Overseers of the Poore have noe power to add to or deminish any Pension without the Consent of the Churchwardens and

that what was abated from the widdow Thorowgoods pension shall be restored to her', WAC/H802/f.3.
66. WAC F2005/f.396, 3 Oct. 1708.
67. For a proviso, following the 1723 Workhouse Test Act, see above, note 30.
68. These vestry minutes figures, of course, record some orphans, individuals put onto the extraordinary account and also those rejected, so that even the number of petitions overstates the number which concern only applications for parish pensions proper.
69. See, for example, note 58.
70. WAC F2003/f.213, 14 Nov. 1659.
71. WAC F2003/f.242, 14 Jan. 1660/1.
72. WAC F2003/f.309, 18 Feb. 1662/3. In 1669, JPs were asked to grant warrants to two constables to prevent beggars from thronging in and about the church and churchyard on Sundays, F2004/ff.39–40, 20 April 1669. For further orders against these beggars, see F2004, f.190v. For other fruitless efforts to stop this largesse, see WAC F2003/f.11, 15 Nov. 1652; F2003/f.182, 23 Dec. 1658.
73. WAC F2004, f.198, 17 Oct. 1677.
74. WAC F4/f.26.
75. WAC F2003/f.205. Banbridge never appeared on the pension books.
76. WAC F2003/f.131.
77. 21 March 1670. WAC F2004/f.48.
78. 13 June 1654. WAC F2003/f.43.
79. Ann Powell, for example, received 32 payments in 1655, notwithstanding the earlier order, WAC F383/f.37. Ann Burton's pension was not increased by six pence a week. According to the parish books she received two pence more a week in 1657 than she had in 1656, although this was reduced again to eighteen pence in 1658, WAC F384/33, F385, F387/41.
80. WAC F4509. Their individual biographies suggest that their behaviour in 1707, if that was the sole reason, had a lasting, if small, impact on the subsequent size of their parish pensions. The drunken Sarah Wells continued to receive a pension until 1711. Her pension fell after 1707, from twenty-one pence a week to nineteen pence in 1708, and eighteen pence until 1711. Likewise, Isabella Stanley, receiving a pension of seventeen pence in 1707, received only fifteen pence thereafter until 1715 when her pension payments cease. WAC F437/ff.192, 196; F438/ff.190, 192; F440/ff.236, 241; F441/ff.160, 163; F442/f.173; F444/f.156; F445/f.151.
81. See, for example, WAC, F2003/f.120, 30 March 1657.
82. WAC F2004/f.79, 30 Nov 1671. The vestry ordered that pay days were to be held in the new 'house built for the poors Work house, and noe more to bee paid in the Church'. In 1685, pensions were to be paid to the poor outside whenever possible, in the ground under the parish library 'from Lady Day to Michaelmas in every yeare and at other times as often as the Weather will permitt', WAC F2005/f.31. F2005/f.201, 27 Sept. 1697, notes that the poor were to be paid for the future, as formerly, in the room under the vestry also used as a parish school. The schoolhouse was to be converted to a sessions house in 1707, WAC 2005/f.372, 16 Feb. 1707.
83. WAC F2003/f.99, 23 April 1656.

84. WAC F2003/f.11, 7 April 1653; F2003, f.149, 16 Feb. 1658, asked the overseers 'strictly to vew all the Penconers and Orphants & to certefy the gentlemen of the Vestry at theyr next sitting'.
85. WAC F2003/f.97, 7 April 1656, ordered the overseers to present to two dignatories, 'the names of all such poor people pencons of this parish, that are able to worke' to go to the sessions. For similar anxieties about work schemes for the poor, see in particular the measures proposed in 1677, F2004/ff.190v–195. The gentlemen of the vestry were to meet in 1700 on Thursday at nine in the morning in the schoolhouse under the vestry 'to view and examine the poor' in connection with renewed attempts to set them on work, WAC F2005/f.236. The last order was repeated in 1704, F2005/f.338. In 1708 two vestrymen were merely to meet with the overseers to discuss matters relating to the poor, ibid. f.395.
86. WAC F2003/f.99, 23 April 1656.
87. WAC F2003/f.159, 29 April 1658. See also, F2003/ff.149, 160, 205, 18 July 1659 (when vestrymen and overseers were to 'vew all the penconers on the next pay day being Fryday next ... and to examine theyr Condicons'). Proposals made by a vestry committee in September 1662 placed the responsibility for surveying the parish poor on the overseers, WAC F2003/f.294. Note, too, that order which found that churchwardens and overseers were neglecting to meet every month 'to inquire after the necessity of the poore' as the 43 Eliz. c. 2, I directed, F2004, f.45, 8 Dec. 1669.
88. WAC F2004/f.46. For the extensive residential mobility common in early modern London, see Boulton, *Neighbourhood and Society*, pp.206–27.
89. WAC F2004/f.70, 20 June 1671. For references to the returning of lists of the parish poor, see also WAC F2005, f.154, 2 April 1695; f.179 (verbal report to JPs). For two surviving lists of parish pensioners taken in 1707 and 1716, see WAC F4508, F4539.
90. For badging, see also Fletcher, *Reform in the Provinces*, pp. 227, 278–9; K. Wrightson and D. Levine, *Poverty and Piety in an English Village: Terling, 1525–1700* (London, 1979), p. 179 writes of the practice of badging paupers in Terling under the terms of the charity set up by Henry Smith (a London merchant) 'seventy yearas before the final humiliation of wearing badged clothing was inflicted upon the paupers of the nation at large'.
91. Boulton, *Neighbourhood and Society*, p.148. For badging in Restoration London, see, also, Macfarlane, 'Social Policy', pp.256 and 273, n.29.
92. The senior churchwarden had been orderd to buy 'new brass badges for the poore' by the vestry in 1677, possibly to facilitate parish begging, WAC F2004, f.195, 6 June 1677.
93. Le Hardy, *Middlesex County Records*, p.124. These badges were to be of metal bearing the name of the parish or hamlet, and were to be fixed at the end of the left sleeve of the pensioner's outermost garment.
94. WAC F2005/f.195. It was left to the discretion of the churchwardens and overseers to provide the badges.
95. WAC F2006/f.84, 22 Aug. 1722 ordered that the overseers should not pay pensioners in future 'if they do not constantly wear their Badges. And that such poor who shall neglect to wear their badges shall be struck of the pention.' Five months later, beadles seeing such neglect were to take the offending pensioners to a JP, while overseers were to be fined for every

omission detected as the 1697 Act directed (20s for every offence), ibid., f.93, 24 Jan 1723. For the 1697 clause, see 8 & 9 William III, c. 30, II. Badges seem to have been worn in Hackney, in the 1730s and 1740s, see Paley, *Justice in Hackney*, p.xxiv. For a successful petition in 1705 that sought the restitution of a pension for a child, stopped after the mother refused to wear a badge as well, see le Hardy, *Middlesex County Records*, p.291.

96. For this topic, see Peter King's chapter in this volume, Chapter 7.
97. For references to this common practice, see Barker-Read, 'The Treatment of the Aged Poor', p.92. For an example of a pauper's goods given to the parish beadle, to cover his costs in keeping a crippled boy, see F2003/f.220, 20 March 1659. In St Martin's, pauper goods were sometimes sold to brokers and others at what was termed an 'outcry' in the parish churchyard.
98. For an explicit surrender of property in return for a pension, see a case from St Clement Dane's, 'Rec of Alice Banford (a poore aged woman of this parish) five pounds, being all shee had left to maintayne her; In liew whereof the Anncients of the vestrey (uppon her humble peticon) have bene pleased to give her a weekly pencon.', WAC B24, 21 May 1646.
99. WAC F2003/f.73, 18 May 1655. This order was repeated in 1657, F2003/f.120 and in 1658 it was ordered that petitions were to be sent to overseers 'who are desired to vew the peticoners at their habitacons & to take an Inventory of their goods', F2003/f.160. For repeated orders see F2003/f.293, 6 Aug. 1662; F2004/f.190v, 3 May 1677.
100. WAC F2003/f.86, 25 Sept. 1655.
101. WAC F2004/f.218r–v. Overseers neglecting this order were not to be indemnified against any relief given to such paupers. The overseer in this case had his legal costs paid, but, presumably reflecting the dubious legality of the practice, was 'to compound and agree the matter asoone as may be'.
102. For a discussion of the constraints imposed by locality in Restoration London, see T. Harris, *London Crowds in the Reign of Charles II. Propaganda and Politics from the Restoration until the Exclusion Crisis* (Cambridge, 1987), pp.20–1.
103. The parish sometimes sanctioned borrowing at interest to get overseers out of this particular financial hole, WAC F2003/f.9. For Thomas Lee, tallow chandler, excused service as overseer of the poor, 'by reason of his poverty is not fitt to serve the said Office', F2003/f.346, 9 May 1666. See also the resignation of Roger Philpott from that office, 'who served a short time ... finding it very troublesome and uneasy to him by reason of this Trade', F2005, f.47, 5 May 1686. See also F2005/f.186, 26 Jan. 1697 for a dispute between the overseers about the payment of 'little moneys'.
104. See, for example, WAC f2004/fl.152:016/4/1675, a list of persons fining for the office of overseer.
105. Note the vestry order limiting new pensioners until 'it is certainely knowne wt the weekly charge of the penconers & Orphants is', F2003/f.162, 26 May 1658.
106. This happened on a number of occasions after 1640, notably in 1644, in 1662 and again in 1677.
107. In 1661, the overseers' accounts show that the cost of petitions prepared by the parish was one shilling each.

108. During the 1640s and 1650s many individuals repeatedly petitioned the vestry, indicating that initial appeals were turned down. Thus, for example, Robert Ashdowne petitioned the vestry three times in 1657 for relief, on each occasion being referred to the overseers for consideration, but was apparently never successful. Thomas Busby apparently tried four times between 1657 and 1658, getting a 12d pension on his last attempt. WAC F2003/ff.112, 116, 127, 160, 167. Busby was on the overseers' books from 1658 until 1663, WAC F386/f.31; F387/f.41; F388/f.39; F389; F390/f.20b; F391.

109. The parish rewarded those who informed it of the existence of such property and sometimes put such goods under lock and key, both of which lead one to suppose that nurses, family and neighbours often took such goods before the parish could confiscate them.

110. At least this follows from the repeated petitions sent into the vestry in the 1640s and 1650s, see above, note 108.

111. See the claim by the Clerk of London Corporation of the Poor, who argued that London parishes cared only for material provision of the poor so that their children were brought up 'like Atheists, after a sordid, loose and undisciplined manner ... by meanes whereof, so much dissoluteness, idleness, thefts, whoredomes, prophane cursing, swearing, and almost all kinds of wickedness do generally abound in that sort of people', quoted in Pearl, 'Puritans and Poor Relief', p.224.

112. For efforts to discipline the poor, which of course increased with the impetus provided by the Societies for the Reformation of Manners, and the SPCK, see Shoemaker, *Prosecution and Punishment*, esp. pp.238–72; T. Hitchcock, 'Paupers and Preachers: The SPCK and the Parochial Workhouse Movement', in L. Davison *et al.* (eds), *Stilling the Grumbling Hive. The Response to Social and Economic Problems in England, 1689–1750* (Stroud, 1992), pp.145–66.

# 2 London Domestic Servants from Depositional Evidence, 1660–1750: Servant–Employer Sexuality in the Patriarchal Household[1]

Tim Meldrum

Around the year 1591, a maidservant named Alice Periar became pregnant by her master, Mr Medcalf of Great Hallingsbury in Essex. Her mistress tried to bribe her to lay the paternity on a former servant but, when Alice refused, her mistress hired a man to take her to London and she gave birth in the porch of the church of St Botolph's Aldgate. Her mistress sent her money and came to see her, telling her to carry the child into the City and leave it at a certain door. Alice complied with these instructions, after which her mistress found her another service in London.[2] A century later, the matrimonial dispute of *Harrington c. Harrington*[3] came before the London consistory court. The wife of the Earl of Warrington's steward demanded a separation from her husband on the grounds of adultery, because he had got their maid Jane Burton pregnant. It seems that Burton's mistress had discovered this when she returned from the country, whereupon Burton promptly left the house and her service to go to a midwife's where she gave birth to a male child.[4]

While Periar's mistress had enough compassion to find her another place, we have no record of what happened to Burton thereafter. In both cases, the role played by the wife and mistress was crucial in the servant's experience: Periar's mistress was determined to mend the torn fabric of her family while not abandoning her maid, whereas Burton's mistress had been absent (possibly facilitating the liaison in the first place) and her return signalled the break-up of their family. We do not know if Burton resigned her post or was sacked; nor do we know whether either servant remonstrated with her master as recommended by advice manuals, whether the sexual liaisons were the result of coercion or seduction by their masters, or whether they arose from mutual attraction and/or consent. What is clear, however, is that the servants who had been made pregnant had to leave their jobs in a relatively sheltered environment in which they may well have formed bonds of friendship. These cases are not cited as typical of sexual relations between servant and master, nor as illustrations emblematic of changes over time, nor even of transhistorical continuity in households' responses to breaches of the patriarchal order. But Burton's and Periar's experiences do throw up themes which recur in female servants' accounts of sexual relations with their masters: the tensions that were created within households, the breaking of bonds that resulted, and the almost inevitable loss of place for the servant who conceived.

This chapter will focus on servant–employer sexual relations, and the implications they have for an understanding of household patriarchy in late seventeenth- and early eighteenth-century London.[5] This is not to deny the importance of servants' other household and extra-household relations, sexual or otherwise, to the servant her or himself, nor to an enquiry about the nature of their social relations. Sexual conduct and marriage between fellow-servants, for example, did not have to result in departure from employers' households.[6] In a number of cases, servants were permitted to stay on by masters and mistresses who displayed flexibility and understanding, and a high degree of affection, for these contractual members of the family.[7] Yet servant–employer relations are central to contemporary and historiographical conceptions of early modern patriarchy,[8] and the written transcriptions of testimony by servants themselves from church court depositions[9] allow the historian to tell this story in servants' own words.

There is a pressing need for such accounts to be brought to light, since the study of domestic service has been surprisingly slow to emerge from the historiographical gloom one expects when the lives and experiences of a subordinate group are described and judged – in diaries, letters and prescriptive literature – by their employers.[10] The broader history of sexuality is also littered with lacunae,[11] and though the examples cited above help to establish the importance of context in this subject, we still know very little, for instance, about contemporary women's attitudes to vital issues like conception and contraception.[12] Knowledge of abortifacients appears to have been common among women, and *coitus interruptus* may have been widely practised,[13] certainly, those with a medical education were aware that amenorrhoea would have prevented conception.[14] But contemporary motivation for sexual behaviour, and especially young women's decisions regarding sex and pregnancy, are still very much matters for debate among historians, and are discussed elsewhere in this volume.[15]

Before taking up the subject of domestic servants and their sexual relations with their employers, two final words of introduction are required. The present chapter deals with some of the strategies that members of the lower orders in eighteenth-century England employed to 'get a living' under precarious conditions. Those domestic servants who came before the London church courts to testify in defamation or matrimonial disputes clearly grasped the opportunity to ensure their own voices and concerns were heard. The following account is particularly concerned with power relations and their negotiation conducted around employer–employee sex within the household, but it is vital to recognise the role of the forum in which these narratives were told. As will be demonstrated below, the servants whose depositions were bound into the records of the 'bawdy courts' of London bore witness to their own and their fellow household members' desires and experiences, as well as to those of the litigants at whose behest they deposed.

Secondly, London domestic servants were sometimes slightly ill-fitting members of the stratum of English society who form the subject of this volume, the 'labouring poor'.[16] Many will have lived on the interstices of the labour market, slipping from service to the workhouse and back to service again; some might be better described as members of the lifecycle poor, with episodes of unemployment or under-employment interspersed with adequately remunerated service until marriage took them out of circulation. But some London domestic servants' social origins were decisively middling (clergyman diarist Ralph Josselin's daughters, for instance, were sent to service in London in the later seventeenth century); and some had opportunities for saving, which meant upward mobility in time. Hecht's use of the term 'servant class'[17] has lent domestic service the misleading appearance of homogeneity, when in fact there were vast differences in the experience and remuneration between the smallest tradesman's household and a West End mansion house. This chapter will attempt to highlight differences between domestic servants in the simplest manner possible, by discussing firstly female servants' sexual relations with their masters, and secondly male servants' (far rarer) liaisons with their mistresses.

## FEMALE SERVANTS' SEXUAL RELATIONS WITH THEIR MASTERS

Advice literature directed at servant employers in the late sixteenth or early seventeenth century did not problematise mastery, in terms of household patriarchal power and paternal obligation, in any significant way. It was the husband–wife relationship that caused difficulties, whereas those of parent–child and master–servant were far less problematic.[18] There was a reciprocal element – Dod and Cleaver, for instance, wrote in 1612: 'The householder is called *Pater familias*, that is father of a family, because he should have a fatherly care over his servants as if they were his children.'[19] In other words, all family members were entitled to the care and protection of the heads of families, and all were equally subject to their correction and guidance. But there was also a clear line of authority: writers relied on scripture, elaborating upon the fifth commandment to 'honour thy father and thy mother'; and, as Susan Amussen has pointed out, many authors used the simile of kingly government for household mastery.[20] Even as late as 1725, the author of one domestic manual asserted that 'as a family is a contracted government, a kingdom is an extended family'.[21]

However, a few manuals from the late seventeenth- and early eighteenth-century sub-genre of advice literature aimed at women as mistresses or servants displayed some ambivalence in their representation of ideal relations between master and maid, even if they sometimes reflected the earlier period's injunctions to reciprocity. 'In servitude, which is a subjection to the will of another, difficulties may be expected by those that must be subjected not only to the good and gentle, but (as it may happen) even to the froward[22] masters, who will sometimes punish them (though it be a hard case) even for doing well', wrote the author of *The Servants Calling* with uncharacteristic candour. But as readers of these manuals would expect in the wake of such admissions, the solution to the problem was better on hope than redress: 'it more generally happens that a servant who is careful to discharge a good conscience, will be valued even by bad masters'.[23]

The earliest edition of Eliza Haywood's *Present for a Servant-Maid* of 1743 discussed the sexual threats posed to female servants in a seven-page section entitled 'Chastity'.[24] Predatory male sexuality was a danger posed by male servants, lodgers and apprentices, but the manual was most forcefully direct about the threat contemporaries found most alarming, 'temptations from your master'. Haywood put the dilemma succinctly: 'Being so much under his command, and obliged to attend him at any hour ... will lay you under difficulties to avoid his importunities, which it must be confessed, are not easy to surmount.' His marital status might affect the manner of seduction but not the nature of the threat. 'If he happens to be a single man and is consequently under less restraint, be as careful as you can, opportunities will not be wanting to prosecute his aim.' But the prescriptions for repelling his advances cannot have inspired too much confidence since Haywood conceded that 'a vigorous resistance is less to be expected in your station'. She advised servants 'to keep as much as possible out of his way', and employ a 'steady resolution' which, by 'persevering, may perhaps, in time, oblige him to desist'; she had enough sympathy for her readership to add, 'it is a duty, however, owing to yourself, to endeavour it'. In an echo of Richardson's *Pamela*,[25] she gushed 'How great will be your glory if, by your behaviour, you convert [the single master's] base design he had upon you, into an esteem for your virtue!' But, failing miracles, she averred that 'it is much better you should lose a month's wages, than continue a moment longer in the power of such a one'.[26]

The lascivious attentions of married masters had particular ways of disrupting household order by overturning the strict division of household labour characterised by Filmer as, on the one hand, the housewife's 'generation', and on the other, the servant's 'preservation'.[27] If, once the servant had become aware of her master's lewd advances, the tactic of avoidance (nearly impossible in most households, one would have thought) had failed to work, 'you must remonstrate the way he would do his wife, and how much he demeans both himself and her by making such an offer to his own servant'. Again, the servant was expected to practise a self-effacement that gave no space (at least in Haywood's mind) for the servant to assert her own sexual autonomy against her master. This is reinforced by the defeatist advice, conceivably in some cases sensible, that if these measures proved ineffective, 'your only way is to give warning' to leave the job. In a manner inconsistent with a manual which characterised mistress–servant relations with the aphorism, 'the eye of the handmaid looks up to her mistress', another route of redress was explicitly closed:

> be very careful not to let your mistress know the motive of [your departure]. That is a point too tender to be touched upon even in the most distant manner, much less plainly told: such a discovery would not only give her an infinite uneasiness (for in such cases the innocent suffer for the crimes of the guilty) but turn the inclination your master had for you into the extremest hatred. He may endeavour to clear himself by throwing the odium on you.[28]

In denying intimacy between mistress and maid and putting the husband–wife relationship above that of master–servant, Haywood was highlighting a cruel aspect of the double standard. She recognised that the master's account of events would be believed much more readily than that of a mere servant, and that tearful confessions or brave accusations could not profit the wronged party. Such a conclusion was rammed home in her stock, but nevertheless evocative, cautionary observation: 'Every street affords you instances of poor, unhappy creatures who once were innocent till seduced by the deceitful promises of their undoer; and then ungratefully thrown off, they become incapable of earning their bread in an honest way.'[29]

Historians of eighteenth-century sexuality have been less reticent than the household manuals in their discussion of this subject. Edward Shorter's provocative advocacy of an eighteenth-century 'sexual revolution' placed master–servant sexual relations centre-stage. His thesis was based on a transition from 'manipulative sexuality' and 'master–servant exploitation',[30] to modern 'expressive sexuality'.[31] Not surprisingly, the response to Shorter's original arguments (which he admitted were of a 'speculative character') were swift, and critical of his chronology and/or his thesis on the liberation of individual desire, particularly for women.[32] The publication of studies based on research into French *déclarations de grossesse* and their English equivalent, bastardy examinations before justices of the peace, supplemented by those on applications to the London Foundling Hospital, have demonstrated the centrality of household and neighbourhood relations to illicit unions in the eighteenth-century metropolis, and that female domestic servants formed the vast majority of women in urban centres coming to the attention of the authorities for giving birth to bastards.[33]

Yet while it may be true to say in this context, as Cissie Fairchilds has done, that 'the keynote of relationships of inequality would seem to have been the male exploitation of ... female vulnerability', most declared bastard births resulted from liaisons between people of more or less equal social status, with very few from sexual relations between master and maid.[34] Of course, all sources have their drawbacks and silences: births from liaisons between these women and higher-status men, including their masters, were more likely to be taken care of without the need for parochial assistance and with an emphasis on avoiding publicity.[35]

Nevertheless, the birth to a servant of a bastard child fathered by her master was a rare symptom of the generality of sexual relations between master and maid; yet it was the event almost guaranteed to create a breach in the fabric of the family. It was an event some manual writers tried to prevent but for which most apparently did not feel fully qualified to advise. There could be, however, ambiguous undertones to such liaisons. Michael Roberts has suggested, at least for the late sixteenth- and early seventeenth-century urban environment, that there 'was an increase in the number of "quasi-uxorial relationships" between migrant women and single male employers'. This confused status is illustrated in probate cases where a woman's place as wife or housekeeper was contested.[36] Susannah Beardsley testified in a case that came before the prorogative court of Canterbury in 1721: she had twice dined at the house of deceased bookseller Henry Rhodes, 'at which times Jane Lillington [whose role as either housewife or housekeeper was at question] sat at the upper end of the table and carved as mistress of the family, and the servants ... attended upon her and addressed themselves to her as their mistress'.[37]

A similar situation arose from a matrimonial dispute at the London consistory court – a servant reported that the housekeeper 'lived and lodged at his master's houses ... and converse and keep company with him and sat at table and managed his affairs as wives usually do', adding that 'there was a report in the neighbourhood that they ... live together in a lewd and scandalous manner'.[38] Concubinage could therefore be an act of choice rather than coercion. 'But', Roberts continues, 'these relationships were also vulnerable to exposure, particularly by an unwanted pregnancy ... for some women at least intimacy with an "employer" may have represented a high-risk strategy for the acquisition of economic security.'[39] In a more forthright manner, Fairchilds alleges that 'force [in master–servant sexual relationships] was rarely needed; in most cases the economic power of the master sufficed'.[40]

The realms of emotional choice for female servants would appear to have been circumscribed, both by the ideology of mastery within the parameters of a relatively clear social order, and by the real vulnerability of subordinate young women in other men's households. A regulatory 'office' case before the London consistory court in 1716 (an infrequent procedure in this period)[41] helps to illustrate the pressures under which some of London's servants might have found themselves working. Spinster Elizabeth Wade served at the house of a widower and salesman, a 'substantial man' who, according to other witnesses, was 'of good credit and reputation', and an overseer of the poor in the parish of St Giles in the Fields. It should come as no surprise that Wade had to be presented with a subpoena to give evidence against him. She alleged, nonetheless, that he had 'several times attempted her chastity'. On one occasion, finding Wade to be in the kitchen alone, 'he there told her he would give her a crown if she would permit him to put his hands up her coats, upon which Elizabeth in a passion [rage] went out of the kitchen and left him, asking him if he took her to be a common whore'.[42]

Wade's strength of resistance and resolve kept her out of trouble, and she explicitly contrasted her reputation and behaviour with that of her master: her appearance in these records was as a witness in a case promoted by another salesman to have him punished as a fornicator, and she declared 'that her master hath of late years been reported among his neighbourhood to be a loose and debauched man'. Martha Vose, another of this man's servants, was rumoured to have 'threatened to be revenged on him for his turning her away at an hour's warning'.[43] Her experience gives us a harrowing picture of the servant as victim of a predatory master. Repeating a pattern made familiar by Wade's account, Vose had been in his house for only three or four days when her master, 'both by words and actions several times attempted her chastity, and she opposed his unlawful desires'. After a week, in 'his lodging room behind his shop in the house', her master 'prevailed on Martha to drink some strong waters and thereby intoxicated her brains, and then taking advantage' he raped her. Thereafter she appears to have had sex with him by consent several times, and the inevitable eventually happened: in June 1715 she gave birth to a baby boy in St Giles, and 'constantly owned and acknowledged such child to be begotten on her body by her master'. She averred that it was only after she left her service that she found out he was reputed to be 'a lewd and debauched man'.[44]

It is crucial to the accounts of both these servants that there was no mistress at home, enhancing Wade's vulnerability to attacks in the kitchen and especially the bedchamber, and permitting the master to have sex with Vose 'sometimes on her bed in the kitchen and sometimes on a bed up two pairs of stairs'. Eliza Haywood's *Present for a Servant-Maid* advised caution to the servant of the single man because he was 'under less restraint ... opportunities will not be wanting to prosecute his aim'.[45] She may have had bachelors in mind, but she could well have been writing about widowers. It is also significant that we learn later on in Vose's testimony that she was a tailor's widow who had spent the previous three years in service, 'but for about four months happening within the time when she was very big with child' by her former master, when 'she maintained herself as privately as she could to avoid disgrace by working at her needle'.[46]

What remained of Vose's reputation was central to her testimony in terms of its content (that is, her experience as a servant), but also in the manner in which she gave it. She stated that 'as she has nothing else to maintain herself by but by going to service, and services are only to be had by a good character and reputation, and she having already lost two or three places by means of the knowledge and report of her having had a child by her former master, and being now in a very good service, she hopes that the court will not oblige her to set forth or discover the particular places she hath lived in within the time [asked] or where she now lives'. She had already 'performed a penance for the incontinence in the parish church of St Giles ... and performed the same to avoid being under the lash of her former master and being put in prison by him for incontinency with him and upon no other consideration ... in order to prevent further harm befalling herself'.[47] When he offered only to give her £10 to lay the child's paternity to someone else ('which she refused to do'), she said that if he 'would allow her £15 she would lie in the country in private without bringing any disgrace upon him, and if the child would die she would refund him £5'. He refused, and as he still 'took no care of her', the overseers and parish churchwardens of St James Westminster (presumably the parish with which she had her original settlement) 'took away her child from her when it was three days old and provided for it, and the parish of St Giles supported her in her lying in' (probably after coercing a lump sum from her master).[48]

Whatever her motives, however vulnerable she may have been to the advances of her master,[49] she appeared at least more willing to believe that his intentions might have been directed at a more honourable goal after he had had 'the carnal knowledge of her body'. Her behaviour thereafter, allowing her master to have repeated access to sexual favours, mirrors that of spinster women who claimed to have given in after being promised marriage.[50] It could also plausibly be the behaviour of someone feeling trapped and without alternative. She did have kin near enough to request assistance, but her tragedy was compounded by the failure of that assistance, her former master's attempt at bribery, the indignity of his insisting on checking she was pregnant, and the intervention of the parish authorities, even if she must have been grateful for the timely support at her lying-in. She had been abused by a man who in theory had a duty of care over her, and in the end, even her own body was not hers to control.

By no means all masters, however, were immune to community sanction or damage to household reputation in cases of alleged sexual harassment. One servant witness told the court clerk that her former master was bringing a case (presumably of defamation) against another maid who had claimed publicly that he had propositioned her, and put his hands up her skirts 'to know whether she was a man or a woman'. The master had brought the case to clear his name which 'is much disgraced among his neighbours', and his wife was 'much disturbed about it'.[51] On the other hand, Vose's master was not alone in serial rape or attempted rape: a certain Mr Vesey 'did attempt the chastity' of at least two of his servants, one of whom complained to her mistress, the other to her aunt (and both, when the attempts did not stop, left their jobs).[52] Jane Peareth described her master, Mr Hall, as 'a person of low, lewd and wicked life'. When attempting to rape her, he told Jane 'he had lain with all his maids and that he would lie with her, and in all appearance he did then design and with all his power then endeavour so to do'.[53]

This particular master considered he had a right to his servants' sexual favours, or at least made full use of the power his status gave him. The presence of his wife certainly did not deter, and may even have encouraged him, since this violence occurred in the context of his repeated violence towards his wife. While in his service, her master 'both in public and in private and sometimes in the presence of his wife was frequently very rude and immodest' with Jane. On one of the several occasions her mistress intervened to rescue Peareth, she told her husband 'that if he must have a whore he should go abroad for one and not meddle with her maids, for as they came honest into her house she desired they might go away so'. Again the concern with the reputation of the household arose, and the remedy here was to keep whoring beyond its bounds. Peareth, too, 'for preserving herself ... was obliged to quit her service'.[54] Mistresses were not always prepared to put their servants' concerns over and above the sexual demands of their husbands: Isabel Bagnall's master came home drunk one evening and her mistress, fearing his blows, asked Isabel to go to bed with him. She refused, so the two women shared a bed together in the parlour instead.[55]

Some attempts at rape by masters appear to have been half-hearted acts of the sexually frustrated,[56] or clumsy failures thwarted by other household members, with the ever-present threat of recourse to neighbourhood publicity.[57] A servant's fear of assault was heightened if she knew that her master had syphilis or other venereal diseases, a condition evident to anyone in close proximity with their employers or who washed their bed-linen and clothes. One servant had her sleeve torn off by her master in an attempt at rape and he promptly gave her half a crown to have it mended; she resorted to getting female friends to share her bed with her at night to discourage him because she knew he had the pox 'by his sheets'.[58] In a ghastly case from 1687, Susannah Yeareley was raped by her master when she was in the midst of an epileptic fit. She did not realise what had happened until a few weeks later when she overheard him boasting about his conquest to another woman, saying he had done it because Yeareley was too kind to her mistress, his wife; it was only then that she found out she had the pox, and her master paid the surgeon £10 to have it cured.[59]

Were either of these masters moved to pay out of remorse, as bribery for what they hoped would be silence, or as the result of blackmail by the servant's threat to inform mistress, neighbourhood or JP? It is important to note that such reports emerged *incidentally* in matrimonial disputes where a request for separation was founded on allegations of violence by the husband against the wife, as further evidence of masters' violent actions and bad characters. Servants displayed resourcefulness in employing a strategy that ensured they were heard in a public forum when the golden opportunity to speak and be listened to arose.[60] Few used the judicial routes of the bastardy examination to name masters as fathers of their bastard children, but Rogers believes that the pressure applied by community and parish on wealthier fathers to hand over lump sums for the care of the child meant that in their case, 'a bastardy deposition was often an admission of failure to secure a suitable maintenance by informal means'.[61] So the frequency of the events described here is impossible to determine, although the relative viciousness of the reported cases hints at their rarity.

These case studies do, however, give us clues to some of the preconditions for servant–master liaisons. In general terms, they occurred right at the point of elision between 'family' and 'household': for masters, sex with their female servants risked neither polygamy nor incest. In practice, there was an unspoken corollary between the 'natural rights' of mastery and the duty of servants for fidelity, trust and silence, that for some masters justified (or at least excused) such liaisons. They might risk community opprobrium or financial penalty from the local authorities, but the vulnerability of servants must have lessened that risk for many of them. The nature of vulnerability to the attentions of masters could vary in particular circumstances, especially according to the presence or absence of the mistress in the household and the assiduity of her surveillance, the degree of the master's aggression and his willingness to trick or beat his servant into submission, and the circumstances of the servant herself, which governed her strength, physical or emotional, to resist. Isolation, poverty and the threat of unemployment could all influence whether a servant risked pregnancy and the loss of reputation.

## MALE SERVANTS' SEXUAL RELATIONS WITH THEIR MISTRESSES

According to Lawrence Stone, 'the one sexual relationship that was totally outside the bounds of the moral order in eighteenth-century England was adultery between an upper-class woman and a lower-class male, especially a mere domestic servant'.[62] Yet for all the revulsion for the 'gravest of social inversions', several well-documented cases of these liaisons from the eighteenth century exist which suggest that some mistresses considered such relations to be too tempting to resist, or worth the risk of opprobrium.[63] The early eighteenth-century case of *Dormer c. Dormer*[64] came to the London consistory court when a wealthy member of the London gentry, John Dormer, Esquire, sought separation from his wife, Diana, on the grounds that she had committed adultery with her footman, Thomas Jones; she may even have begun a second affair with another male servant named Lawrence Burges.

No fewer than 21 servants were brought forward to testify in the case, and unlike most matrimonial disputes before the church courts, few if any of them were prepared to put a word forward in their mistress's defence. The evidence they gave condemned Diana Dormer by testimony of sexual encounters and pregnancy,[65] but most frequently, of the disruption caused to a relatively large family of male and female servants. Aside from these more or less direct accusations of incontinence, the Dormer family servants backed up their master's case with accusations of their mistress's favouritism towards Jones,[66] particularly over the distribution of left-over or deliberately secreted food (even after he had officially left her service),[67] by 'constantly [speaking] to him in a very smooth and soft style', and by allowing him to monopolise her time and space. Her chambermaid, Alice Hogger, was often told by Diana to send Jones upstairs to her chamber 'under pretence of making tea for her or bringing her breakfast', and her mistress became angry if Alice ever came into her room, even though to do so was the clear prerogative of the chambermaid.[68]

Jones sought to usurp other servants' roles too, particularly that of the laundrymaid, due to the intimate knowledge of their affair conveyed by the bed-linen.[69] After one encounter, the then laundrymaid complained to Diana, who replied, 'Well I don't care, if he uses you all like dogs you shall take it ... if he were a villain she should not live with a villain', and dismissed her soon after. What Jones said, as one footman observed, 'was law'.[70] However, Jones's behaviour began to get out of hand as the attention he received from his mistress, and the privileges she gave him, went to his head; news of the affair got out, and his master John Dormer dismissed him.[71] Diana Dormer had often told Alice Hogger 'that if Mr Dormer turned away Jones she would turn away all her servants', and a number of them were removed, both from the Dormers' employ and from that of their later employers when their former mistress vindictively pursued them.[72] Others 'voluntarily quitted and left their service' because they incurred Diana Dormer's displeasure in their attitudes to her affair with Jones, and she made their working for her very uncomfortable.[73]

Jones continued to visit the house, but when Diana's waiting woman informed her master that Jones 'had beat and very much abused' his wife,

John Dormer warned that any servant letting Jones into the house faced instant dismissal.[74] When Jones attempted to commence a *charivari* outside the house by hitting the window-shutters and shouting 'Room for cuckolds, here comes a company! Room for cuckolds, here comes my lord mayor!' John Dormer determined to see off this threat to his household, and set the male servants on him.[75] A large crowd gathered while the Dormers' servants caught up with Jones and beat him, but the crowd separated the antagonists and helped him to get away, possibly suggesting some sympathy for him amongst the neighbours.[76] As for Diana Dormer, her behaviour managed to alienate even the closest of her female servants, and at least one maid empathised wholeheartedly with her master, as 'she verily believes him to have been much abused' by his wife. And while one footman claimed that he was only obeying his master's orders, the servants seem to have set about Jones with a vengeance, to be justified in hindsight by their later dismissals at the hands of their mistress.[77]

At least until Diana's infatuation with a second footman,[78] Jones seems to have been in receipt of a private income. Drinking with a footman named James Webster from another household, who asked him 'after what manner he lived since he had been out of place for so long', Jones replied that 'he had no occasion to take any more places, for his Lady maintained him ... for he had debauched her' and made John Dormer 'a cuckold'. Later on in the conversation, he 'took his privy members from out his breeches and let them hang down bare and exposed for some considerable time', saying (in a pungent phrase which summarised many of his rural contemporaries' impressions of the life of the idle metropolitan footman) that 'his prick was his plough'.[79]

Male servants certainly had a reputation as sexual predators towards maidservants,[80] and the stories that examinations and *déclarations* throw up are too frequently of false promises, arm-twisting and rape for us to dismiss footmen's predatory machismo lightly.[81] Solidarity among menservants was apparent, for instance, in the matey use of the appellation 'brother-coachman';[82] while Jones may have put himself beyond group loyalties between servants (male or female) in the Dormer family, the drinking episode with Webster points to aspects of male behaviour encompassed by the metropolitan 'footman sub-culture'.[83] Patricia Seleski has written (in the context of their behaviour at theatres, but applicable more widely) about 'the male clubbiness of the footmen's fraternity', and how the 'reputation of footmen for independence and unruliness was widespread'.[84] The boasts of sexual conquest, and the bravado that led one of the Dormers' footmen to claim that 'he would break Jones's neck before he should come into the house',[85] were constituent elements of a macho creed that came with the livery. This is not to deny that Jones and the other menservants who had affairs with their mistresses did not fall in love with them, but that one way of dealing with the contradictions of such tempting, illicit relationships was to shelter behind collective norms.

The Dormer case has been quoted at length because of the insights it provides into household relations and the nature of mastery in its breach. An affair between mistress and manservant was not just a sexual but a social inversion. Theoretically, the male lover interposed himself between mistress and master by taking his master's place in the matrimonial bed in a dastardly act of disloyalty, and in so doing, usurped his power over both mistress and servants.[86] Favouritism, a minor crime committed by many masters or mistresses on their servants, was taken to its order-disrupting conclusion, with Jones himself having the audacity not just to obtain mastery over the family, transgressing work-roles and giving indirect commands, but also to exercise all the conjugal rights of the husband, including physical chastisement – and all under the eyes of the whole household.[87] The inevitable notoriety of such a relationship (heightened here by Jones's *charivari*, which ironically sought to involve the neighbourhood in a judgement on his act) threatened the reputations not just of the household heads, but of the whole family. This helps to explain the unwillingness of the female servants particularly, to offer testimony in support of their mistress, and conversely, their all-too-willing desire to appear at the consistory court to condemn her and Jones. The footman's code of collective solidarity beyond the household appears to have collapsed *within* it when predatory sexuality was directed at mistresses rather than just maids.

CONCLUSION

Recalling the two *fin de siècle* episodes from the beginning of this chapter, and the other descriptions of sexual relations between master and maid, the contrasts with Jones's experience is quite stark. The clearest impression is the relative isolation of women preyed upon by their masters, and the range of options available to footmen. It must be re-emphasised here that constraints of space have curtailed a broader account of the full range of household and extra-household relations. But it is quite apparent that illicit sexual relations for servants of either sex were problematic within the patriarchal household, since both undermined patriarchal norms. Loss of employment and a decisive breach of human bonds were risks for both male and female domestic servants in this position.

Yet the two most pressing concerns for a maidservant, the risk of pregnancy and damage to her reputation, enhanced her potential loss from the experience of an affair or rape by the man ideally endowed with a duty of fatherly care over her. As all masters knew, the penalties for publicity mainly fell on the maid; and while Haywood's portrayal of the inevitability of destitution or prostitution may have been somewhat melodramatic, it is highly unlikely that the combination of concerned civil authorities and widespread awareness of the burgeoning market for service should encourage mistresses to find their fallen maids another place in the way Alice Periar's did in the late sixteenth century.

Mrs Dormer, on the other hand, had far more to lose in the gossip-ridden world of London society (particularly if the suspicion lingered that she had initiated the affair) than had Jones the footman. Despite his complete subversion of household patriarchy, he attempted to conduct a *charivari* outside his former master's house, and the crowd ensured his escape; and he could boast of his sexual prowess with a fellow-footman under the terms of an alternative code of conduct that validated his actions. That code may not have run to offering him support within the Dormer household itself, but there were extra-household collective norms he could appeal to, and ears he could bend. Further work as a footman for the quality or nobility resident in London may well have been out of the question, for a while at least, but he had plenty of other options available to him within the metropolitan economy.

However, it is not the purpose of this chapter to paint women merely as victims, even in these heightened circumstances: Martha Vose, driven by fears for her reputation, attempted to negotiate from weakness, received the support of the parochial safety-net, and still managed to get herself what she considered to be a good service place a few months afterwards. Female domestic servants may have had their emotional choices circumscribed by the twin effects of what has been called here household patriarchy and of their relative vulnerability to predatory male sexuality. But their courage to voice their words to church court clerks has given posterity the very real opportunity to gain insight into their lives.

## NOTES

1. This work stems from my forthcoming thesis, 'Domestic Service in London, 1660–1750: Life-cycle, Gender, Work and Household Relations'. A relational database of over 1500 domestic servant biographies was constructed,

mostly taken from London consistory court depositions kept at the Greater London Record Office (hereafter GLRO), series DL/C (London Consistory Court Records) – other church court depositions have been used, and those sources are referred to when cited. I would like to express my thanks to the staff of the GLRO for their assistance, to Peter Earle and Paul Johnson for their advice and encouragement and, for help with this paper, to the editors.
2. Essex Record Office, Q/SR 126/34, 34a. I would like to thank Pamela Sharpe for this reference.
3. DL/C/245 f.416 and passim.
4. DL/C/245 f.422, Amy Robinson; f.425, 13/01/1698, Hanna Gery. Mr Harrington was nominally a servant himself, of course, though his managerial or even professional status, and the fact consistently averred by witnesses that his income was in the order of £200 a year, belied nominal servility.
5. Judith Bennett prefers the term 'familial patriarchy', but I shall substitute 'household' to avoid appearing only to be addressing husband/wife or parent/child relations: see J.M. Bennett, 'Feminism and History', *Gender and History* 1 (3) (1989), 251–72, esp. 260.
6. See the following depositions: DL/C/245 f.228, 3/5/1697, Margaret Lichfield; DL/C/632 f.337, 14/7/1712, Jane Morgan; DL/C/249 f.23, 5/2/1706, Robert Kemp; DL/C/249 f.40, 4/1/1706, Judith Hilliar. Elizabeth Newbold lent her fellow female servant a ring so that she could marry their master's male servant: DL/C/250 f.409, 15/6/1709. The matrimonial cause of *Wilson c. Wilson* was fought between a couple who had married while maid and apprentice surgeon in the same household: DL/C/631 f.28, 20/1/1700, Margaret Clay. William and Sarah Ashley married a few years after working together as coachman and laundrymaid respectively in the same household: DL/C/250 ff.461–3, 7–14/7/1709.
7. See DL/C/253 f.26, 3/11/1712, Judith Lush, and f.38, 19/11/1712, John Lush; Mary Slicer was servant in a household in which her fellow-servant married, a union recognised by their employers, and she only left to give birth to her child: DL/C/252 f.185, 19/4/1711. Also DL/C/273 f.248, 2/2/1744, Elizabeth Cole; DL/C/637 f.534, 21/2/1745, Mary Kirke; DL/C/631 f.233, Mary Dorrington.
8. Or in an earlier legalistic usage, 'patriarchalism': G.J. Schochet, *Patriarchalism in Political Thought: The Authoritarian Family and Political Speculation and Attitudes, especially in Seventeenth-Century England* (Oxford, 1975). See also the discussion below on household manuals, p. 49–52.
9. For the most comprehensive up-to-date discussion of these records, see M. Ingram, *Church Courts, Sex and Marriage in England, 1570–1640* (Cambridge, 1987); for their metropolitan peculiarities in the early eighteenth century, see T. Meldrum, 'A Women's Court in London: Defamation at the Bishop of London's Consistory Court, 1700–1745', *London Journal* 19 (1) (1994), 1–20.
10. The only extant monograph on eighteenth-century English domestic service is that by J.J. Hecht, *The Domestic Servant Class in Eighteenth-Century England* (London, 1956), which embodies a few of the virtues and all of the vices of what he terms 'the descriptive or impressionistic method' (p.xii). See also D.A. Kent's criticisms in his 'Ubiquitous but Invisible: Female

Domestic Servants in Mid-eighteenth-Century London', *History Workshop Journal* 28 (August, 1989), 111–28, esp. 112.

11. For a summary of current findings for the eighteenth century, see R. Porter and L. Hall, *The Facts of Life: The Creation of Sexual Knowledge in Britain, 1650–1950* (New Haven and London, 1995), Introduction and Chap. 1.

12. Eleanor Parsons, originally hired as a live-in wet-nurse to her master's daughter but who became a housemaid, related to a fellow-servant that her lover had told her after sexual intercourse to 'wipe her private parts with her shift and make water immediately to prevent her being with child', which she did. While this woman's age is unknown, she had been married and had already given birth to one child, whose livelihood was assured with the gifts of money the lover gave her: DL/C/637 f.204, 27/11/1746.

13. For contemporary attempts at birth limitation or prevention, see K. Thomas, *Religion and the Decline of Magic* (Harmondsworth, 1973 edn), pp.223, 760; L. Stone, *The Family, Sex and Marriage in England 1500–1800* (Harmondsworth, 1979 edn), pp.261–7, 307–8; G.R. Quaife, *Wanton Wenches and Wayward Wives: Peasants and Illicit Sex in Early Seventeenth Century England* (London, 1979), pp.133–4, 148, 151; Ingram, *Church Courts, Sex and Marriage in England, 1570–1640* (Cambridge, 1987), pp.158–9; S.D. Amussen, *An Ordered Society: Gender and Class in Early Modern England* (Oxford, 1988), pp.114–15, describing a mistress who gave her servant herbal medicine to induce her birth. E.A. Wrigley produced statistical evidence for birth limitation in 'Family Limitation in Pre-industrial England', *EcHR* 2nd ser., XIX (1966), 82–109, but toned down those findings in 'Martial Fertility in Seventeenth-century Colyton: a Note', *EcHR* 2nd ser., XXXI (3) (1978), 429–36.

14. DL/C/637 f.204 and passim. V. Fildes, *Wet Nursing: A History from Antiquity to the Present* (Oxford, 1988), p.83, showing husbands' attitudes towards the need to procreate forcing wealthier mothers to put out their children to nurse, and pp.102–4, discussing medical opinion; R. Houlbrooke, *The English Family 1450–1700* (Harlow, 1984), pp.132–4. Even when breast-feeding became fashionable in high society in the late eighteenth century, some gentry women insisted on bottle-feeding or employing wet-nurses: L. Stone, *Broken Lives: Separation and Divorce in England 1660–1857* (Oxford, 1993), p.168; Fildes, *Wet Nursing*, pp.116–22.

15. See T. Hitchcock's chapter in this volume, '"Unlawfully begotten on her body": Illegitimacy and the Parish Poor in St Luke's Chelsea'. Hitchcock utilises poor law records to great effect, demonstrating the responsiveness of parochial institutions and the ways the poor made use of them in managing their economies of makeshifts.

16. Dorothy Marshall wrote, 'as the Poor Laws had power not only over those who were actually chargeable, but over those likely to become so, their operation included the greater part of the lower working class under the designation of "The Poor"'. D. Marshall, *The English Poor in the Eighteenth Century: a Study in Administrative History* (London, 1926, 1969 edn), p.2; most servants would fall under such an all-embracing, blanket definition. But see the more recent discussions in P. Slack, *Poverty and Policy in Tudor and Stuart England* (London, 1988), Chap. 2, esp. pp.27–32;

G. Himmelfarb, *The Idea of Poverty: England in the Early Industrial Age* (London, 1984), Chap. 1.
17. The word 'class' was dropped from the 1980 reprint of his monograph, but probably due to his publisher's perception of intellectual fashion rather than a reconsideration of the adquacy of the term.
18. Amussen, *Ordered Society*, pp.38–41. Davies is sceptical about this literature's worth as a source, noting the 'monotonous similarity of highly generalised advice' by Gouge and others: K. M. Davies, 'Continuity and Change in Literary Advice on Marriage', in R.B. Outhwaite (ed.), *Marriage and Society: Studies in the Social History of Marriage* (London, 1981), pp.58–80, esp. pp.62, 78.
19. J. Dod and R. Cleaver, *A Godly Forme of Household Governement: for the Ordering of Private Families, According to the Direction of God's Word* (London, 1612). This classic statement is cited by Lawrence Stone, who noted that it 'really repeated much of the work of Robert Cawdrey published in 1562': *Family, Sex and Marriage*, p.27. See also Amussen, *Ordered Society*, pp.40–1.
20. S.D. Amussen, 'Gender, Family and the Social Order, 1560–1725', in *Order and Disorder in Early Modern England*, A. Fletcher and J. Stevenson (eds) (Cambridge, 1985), pp.196–217, and her *Ordered Society*, Chap. 2, esp. pp.36–8. For a well-known contemporary example, see R. Filmer, *Patriarcha, or the Natural Power of Kings* (London, 1685, 2nd edn), p.24. Amussen and Schochet both point out that this view was contested, most notaby by Locke: Amussen, *Ordered Society*, pp.61–6; G.J. Schochet, *Patriarchalism*, p.246.
21. [Mr Zinzano], *The Servants Calling; with some Advice to the Apprentice: designed for such as have had the benefit of a good education, or would be assisted under the disadvantage of a bad one* (1725), pp.7,11.
22. Perverse, untoward: *OED*.
23. [Zinzano], *Servants Calling*, p.11.
24. [E. Haywood], *Present for a Servant-Maid, or the Sure Means of gaining Love and Esteem* (1743 edn) pp.42–9; perhaps instructive of changing sensibilities (though of course saying nothing about changes or otherwise in predatory male behaviour within the eighteenth-century household), this section is reduced to less than one page in a later edition (between pp.16 and 17). Rather than go through the different threats, predator by predator, it ends, 'There may be some circumstances in which you will have occasion to vary your denials according to the different character of the persons who solicit you': *Present for a Servant-Maid* (1771 edn) p.17.
25. As Pamela's parents wrote early on in her employment to her bachelor master, 'what a sad hazard a poor maiden ... stands against the temptations of this world, and a designing young gentleman ... who has so much *power* to oblige, and has a kind of *authority* to command as your master' – the book's subtitle is of course 'Virtue Rewarded': S. Richardson, *Pamela* (1740–1; Penguin Classics edn, Harmondsworth, 1985), p.52, emphasis in the original.
26. [Haywood], *Present for a Servant-Maid* (1743 edn) pp.44–6.
27. Filmer, *Patriarcha*, p.39.
28. [Haywood], *Present for a Servant-Maid* (1743 edn) pp.5, 46–7.
29. [Haywood], *Present for a Servant-Maid* (1743 edn) p.44.

30. In other words, 'the coercion of women into bed by men who use their powers as employers or social superiors to wrest sexual favours from them': E. Shorter, 'Illegitimacy, Sexual Revolution and Social Change in Modern Europe', *Journal of Interdisciplinary History* II (1971), reprinted in R.I. Rotberg and T.K. Rabb (eds), *Marriage and Fertility: Studies in Interdisciplinary History* (Princeton, 1980), pp.85–120, 91.
31. Shorter, 'Illegitimacy', pp.93–4. His thesis on the modern 'surge of sentiment' is expanded in his *The Making of the Modern Family* (Glasgow, 1976 edn), p.15 and passim.
32. Shorter, 'Illegitimacy', p.89; for the debate that followed in the *Journal of Interdisciplinary History*, see many of the essays in Rotberg and Rabb (eds), *Marriage and Fertility*. Shorter's general point about the increase in the ratio of illegitimate births to all births across the eighteenth into the nineteenth centuries has, however, been supported by the historical demographers: P. Laslett, 'Introduction: Comparing Illegitimacy over Time and between Cultures', in P. Laslett, K. Oosterveen and R.M. Smith (eds), *Bastardy and its Comparative History* (London, 1980), pp.1–68.
33. J. L. Flandrin, *Les Amours Paysannes (XVI–XIXe Siècles)* (Paris, 1975); C. Fairchilds, 'Female Sexual Attitudes and the Rise of Illegitimacy: a Case Study', Journal of Interdisciplinary History VIII (4) (1978), reprinted in Rotberg and Rabb (eds), *Marriage and Fertility*, pp.163–204, esp. p.166, and Appen. I, Table 3; C. Fairchilds, *Domestic Enemies: Servants and their Masters in Old Régime France* (Baltimore, 1984), Chap. 6; N. Rogers, 'Carnal Knowledge: Illegitimacy in Eighteenth-century Westminster', *Journal of Social History* 23 (2) (1989), 355–75, esp. 358, 363; A. Wilson, 'Illegitimacy and its Implications in Mid-eighteenth Century London: the Evidence of the Foundling Hospital', *Continuity and Change* 4 (1) (1989), 103–64; J.R. Gillis, 'Servants, Sexual Relations and the Rise of Illegitimacy in London, 1801–1900', in J. Newton, M. Ryan and J. Walkowitz (eds), *Sex and Class in Women's History* (London, 1983), pp.114–45, esp. p.116; Patricia Seleski, in Chap. 4 of her thesis, concentrates on the decade 1800–9 and includes a transcript of the questions examiners asked applicants to the hospital: 'Women of the Labouring Poor: Love, Work and Poverty in London, 1750–1820', unpublished PhD thesis (Stanford, 1989), pp.15, 132–7 and n.25.
34. Fairchilds, 'Female Sexual Attitudes', p.171, Table 1 and p.185, Table 2, quote from p.175. See also S. Maza, *Servants and Masters in Eighteenth-Century France: The Uses of Loyalty* (Princeton, 1983), p.255; Rogers, 'Carnal Knowledge', 359, Table 2.
35. Rogers, 'Carnal Knowledge', 360.
36. Roberts, 'Women and Work in Sixteenth-century English Towns', 92; above, Chap. 2, part I, sect. ii.
37. Public Record Office (hereafter PRO), series PROB 24/59 f.223, *Popping c. Rhodes*, ?/11/1721.
38. DL/C/263 f.63, 26/2/1726, *Thomas Con*.
39. Roberts, 'Women and Work in Sixteenth-century English Towns', 92–3; for the decline of concubinage in France in the early modern period, see J.-L. Flandrin, *Familles: Parenté, Maison, Sexualité dans l'Ancienne Société* (Paris, 1976), pp.176–80.

40. Fairchilds, 'Female Sexual Attitudes', p.175.
41. Meldrum, 'Women's Court', 2–3.
42. DL/C/633 f.220, 15/06/1716, Elizabeth Wade.
43. DL/C/633 f.220 passim.
44. DL/C/633 f.226, 17/8/1716, Martha Vose.
45. [Haywood], *Present for a Servant-Maid* (1743 edn) p.44.
46. DL/C/633 f.226 and passim.
47. DL/C/633 f.226 passim. 'Penance' was the lesser punishment meted out by the church courts for spiritual offences, and here probably involved a formal apology at the altar before the priest and perhaps a congregation: see Ingram, *Church Courts*, pp.51–5; and Meldrum, 'Women's Court', 4, for a metropolitan example. Wade had already 'heard it said that Martha swore her child to him in St James's parish': DL/C/633 f.220 passim.
48. DL/C/633 f.226 passim. For lump sums (apparently £10 in 1720) to parishes for the care of bastards and to prevent further demands on the parents, see George, *London Life*, p.214; Rogers, 'Carnal Knowledge', 360. One of St Martins in-the-Fields' overseers of the poor served a warrant on Ann Davis' former master after she had sworn his paternity of her child, to get a promise from him to indemnify the parish for his bastard: see DL/C/258 f.88, 21/2/1719, Dorothy Catherell, and f.106 passim.
49. Fairchilds describes the French perception that master–servant sexual relations were 'socially acceptable ... part of the privileges of a patriarch' (although it is not clear if this refers to particular social strata), and dates this from Greek and Roman slavery: Fairchilds, *Domestic Enemies*, p.167; despite its probable frequency (and the anticipation of its dangers in the advice literature), it is not so clear that such 'privileges' were part of the English mode of mastery, although Stone has recently affirmed that 'élite opinion on the whole was tolerant of adultery by the male, especially with women of inferior social status such as maidservants, kept mistresses or prostitutes': L. Stone, *Broken Lives: Separation and Divorce in England, 1660–1857* (Oxford, 1993), p.242.
50. 'Once a woman had succumbed, there was no point in her further resistance; she had, in fact, every interest in allowing the relationship to continue in the hopes that it would lead to marriage': Maza, *Servants and Masters*, p.93. Getting a woman drunk was a noted seduction tactic used by men, or at least a plausible story used by women: see Fairchilds, 'Female Sexual Attitudes', p.181; Rogers, 'Carnal Knowledge', 363; and the case of *Belton or Chambers c. Chambers*, DL/C/245 f.58 and passim.
51. DL/C/241 f.92, 3/10/1684, Elizabeth Collingwood.
52. DL/C/241 f.5, 17/03/1684, Elizabeth Taverner; f.31$^v$, 8/4/1684, Elizabeth Wilcox.
53. DL/C/264 f.149, 2/2/1727, Jane Peareth.
54. DL/C/264 f.149 passim. Hall also made attempts of rape against several of his maids: f.163, 28/4/1727, Dorothy Evans, who related how 'especially when she has been warming his bed he has often endeavoured to be rude and lewd with her insomuch she was afraid to go up to warm his bed without her mistress or some other servant along with her'; and also f.177, 19/7/1727, Elizabeth Banfield.
55. DL/C/267 f.50, 15/12/1729, Isabel Bagnall.

56. DL/C/269 f.66, 15/11/1731, Elizabeth Mead: while her mistress was lying in after the birth of her son, Mead let her master in 'late at night and much in liquor', after which he 'offered to push open the door of Elizabeth's chamber in which she then was ... and she pushed on the inside of the door to keep it shut'. More ambiguously, one master told his servant to share his bed with his lover, since he would not be using it that night; but later on he burst in on both of them, so she leapt out and he got in: DL/C/244 f.256, 10/12/1694, Lucy Oates. See also DL/C/262 f.327, 5/5/1725, Mary Dodd.
57. DL/C/635 f.49, 27/6/1732, Ann Musgrave, who 'heard the cookmaid cry out murder and thereupon she opened the casement of her room and cried out thieves, and then her master came down from the garret where the cookmaid lay in his shirt and cap only, and presently after the maid came down to Ann and her mistress and told them her master had endeavoured to force into her room and to fling the door off the hinges'.
58. DL/C/244 f.78, 5/5/1693, Christianna Lovegrove.
59. DL/C/242 f.80, 2/6/1687, Susannah Yeareley. Elizabeth Benfield related how her master had left for Kensington to get cured of syphilis and her mistress was treated at home by several surgeons. She saw her master on his return pleading to his wife to stay, promising he would change his ways, but confessing that 'he had lain with the cook maid in Kensington and that he was afraid that she had given him the foul disease': DL/C/262 f.323, 4/5/1725. G. Walker and J. Kermode, in a reference to women accused of witchcraft but perhaps applicable here too, suggest that women's 'professed bodily ignorance might itself have been part of a strategy to portray themselves as good, "honest" women': G. Walker and J. Kermode, 'Introduction', in J. Kermode and G. Walker (eds), *Women, Crime and the Courts in Early Modern England* (London, 1994), pp.1–25, quote from p.15.
60. In the same way that defamation disputes allowed women to perpetuate a conflict out of the streets and into the judicial realm, see L. Gowing, 'Language, Power and the Law: Women's Slander Litigation in Early Modern London', in Kermode and Walker (eds), *Women, Crime and the Courts*, pp.26–47.
61. Rogers, 'Carnal Knowledge', 360.
62. Stone, *Broken Lives*, p.243. For the dangers of male servants' sexuality within the household, see P. Seleski, 'The Footman's Revenge: Masculinity and the "Feminisation" of Domestic Service in Late Eighteenth and Early Nineteenth-century London', paper to the Berkshire Conference on Women's History, June 1993, pp.24–7.
63. See the late-eighteenth-century case of *Middleton c. Middleton* recounted by Stone, *Broken Lives*, pp.162–247; Dorothy Marshall records the marriage of Lady Harriet Wentworth to her footman John and her consequent renunciation of finery – she appears to have been able to dispose of her own fortune, settling £100 a year on him: 'Domestic Servants of the Eighteenth Century', *Economica* 9 (25) (1929), 15–40, 34.
64. DL/C/255 f.80 passim.
65. DL/C/255 f.116, 14/3/1715, Mary Horne; f.137, 17/3/1715, Elizabeth Cotton.
66. DL/C/255 f.129, 16/3/1715, Thomas Lewin.

68    *Chronicling Poverty*

67. DL/C/255 f.151, 24/3/1715, Thomas Edwards.
68. DL/C/255 f.141, 18/3/1715, Alice Hogger.
69. DL/C/255 f.107, 12/3/1715, Alice Rigby.
70. DL/C/255 f.166, 25/3/1715, Mary Davis; f.129, 16/3/1715, Thomas Lewin.
71. DL/C/255 f.129; f.157, 24/3/1715, Charles Whiston.
72. DL/C/255 f.107; f.129; f.141; f.151; f.157; f.166.
73. DL/C/255 f.133, 17/3/1715, Robert White; f.162, 25/3/1715, Joseph Morris.
74. DL/C/255 f.181, 17/5/1715, Francis Warrington; f.162. Jones had earlier tried to embarrass her in front of some female servants, so his aggression may be seen as a need to humiliate her: DL/C/255 f.107.
75. For the *charivari* (or its English equivalents) more generally, see E.P. Thompson, 'Rough Music', in his *Customs in Common* (London, 1991), pp.467–538, a phenomenon which 'attached to the victim a lasting stigma' (p.488, see also pp.513–14); M. Ingram, 'Ridings, Rough Music and the "Reform of Popular Culture" in Early Modern England', *Past and Present* 105 (1984), 79–113; and for London specifically, R. Shoemaker, 'The London "Mob" in the Early Eighteenth Century', *Journal of British Studies* 26 (July 1987), 273–304, esp. 278, where he discusses defamatory riot and disturbance; Meldrum, 'Women's Court', 9–10.
76. DL/C/255 f.172, 17/5/1715, John Knight; f.181.
77. DL/C/255 f.107; f.181.
78. DL/C/255 f.162; f.178; f.181.
79. DL/C/255 f.168, 12/4/1715, James Webster. For the use of this phrase in a defamation case in the same period, see Meldrum, 'Women's Court', 8, where it had the same connotation of kept man.
80. [Haywood], *Present for a Servant-Maid* (1743 edn) p.35.
81. Rogers, 'Carnal Knowledge', 359, Table 2. See also pp.362–5 for servant–servant encounters. For French examples, see Fairchilds, 'Female Sexual Attitudes', 179–80, and *Domestic Enemies*, pp.88–9; Maza, *Servants and Masters*, pp.70–1, 91–2.
82. From testimony arising, appropriately enough, from storytelling about another coachman getting a maid pregnant: DL/C/638 f.45, John David; f.47, John Pidgen, both dated 10/11/1749.
83. Hecht wrote that 'servants, especially in London, where great numbers of them were concentrated in a relatively small area and where the rate of interaction was high, were animated by a strong sense of solidarity or group loyalty': *Domestic Servant Class*, p.85. He does not make it clear whether his remarks referred particularly to male servants in the West End, though he stresses Mandeville's words on insolent footmen rather than Defoe's on intriguing wenches (which Hecht reads as describing an 'informal association', p.86).
84. Seleski, 'Footman's Revenge', 21: she is also keen to stress the mutually reinforcing behaviour of master and man, and the imitative qualities of menservants' dress and behaviour.
85. DL/C/255 f.145, 19/3/1715, Richard Morris: of course, he calmed down when warned by the household's longer-standing servants to keep quiet if he wished to retain his post.
86. When an apprentice was alleged to have had an affair with his mistress, a maidservant in the household defended him by denying that he 'ever took

upon him to command [her mistress] or her servants or to domineer over them': DL/C/249 f.423, 17/10/1707, Mary Revell.

87. In the case of *Clifton c. Clifton*, maidservant Ellen Slater was forced to witness her mistress's fondling and mutual masturbation with her husband's apprentice (who nearly raped her once when he mistook her for her mistress in the dark), and eventually to their intercourse on her bed. With a more forthright fellow-servant (who had told the apprentice to his face that 'it was a shame he should keep company with her mistress and that he ought not to come near the house'), Ellen plotted 'concerning what method would be most proper to [expose the affair] to their master, but were afraid to do it lest the discovery should occasion some mischief'; their master then sued his wife for separation at the consistory court: DL/C/265 f.47, 27/6/1728; also f.55, 29/6/1728, Mary Gould, who saw their mistress 'toying and playing' with her master's footman, and 'sitting together on the bedside, and she ate ... liquorice out of his mouth and he out of hers'; and f.57, 3/7/1728, Martha Metton *née* Astbridge.

# 3 'Unlawfully begotten on her body': Illegitimacy and the Parish Poor in St Luke's Chelsea[*]

Tim Hitchcock

In 1745, when Rebecca Clement was 18, she gained a place as a servant to the parish clerk of Chelsea, Andrew Banton.[1] With meat, drink, lodging and 50 shillings a year, it was a secure place in a well-run household. Fifty years earlier she might have remained a servant until she had been able to save ten or 20 pounds, allowing her to marry in her mid-twenties. But, by the middle of the eighteenth century, she was willing to partake of courting practices which resulted in her losing her place and ending in the workhouse. At the age of 20 she met John Coustos, a jeweller, who lived in Tibal's Row, near Red Lyon Square. They conducted a courtship at several inns around London, but always a good distance from his home just south of the Foundling Hospital. They had penetrative sex for the first time at the Angel Inn, just behind St Clement's Church, and for a while the Angel became their regular rendezvous. Until, on a night in August, at the Cheshire Cheese by 'the creek adjoining to Chelsea', Rebecca became pregnant.

As the pregnancy began to show, John quietly disappeared, and it quickly became evident that he had no intention of marrying her. On 7 April 1748, Rebecca, by now nine months pregnant, was admitted to the Chelsea workhouse. She gave birth to Sarah on 13th April.

For the next three weeks Rebecca stayed in the house, nursing her child but, on 5 June, Sarah died. That night Rebecca took her clothes and what goods she could, jumped over the workhouse wall and disappeared into the night.

This chapter will examine the experience of people like Rebecca in mid-eighteenth-century London in order to ascertain the range of options open to a woman in her circumstances. It will ask what were the likely scenarios for a young unmarried mother, and speculate if these were influential in her choice of courting practices. It will look at the ways in which the crisis of an illegitimate pregnancy and birth affected the economic prospects of the women involved, asking if becoming a bastard-bearer in the mid-eighteenth century led to ruin, or else was simply a nasty interlude, the result of which could be abandoned.

Historians have traditionally tended to look to the changing positive opportunities for marriage and household formation as an explanation for changing patterns of sexual behaviour. This chapter will ask if the existence of new types of provision for bastard-bearing and a changing experience of the negative effects of illicit pregnancy might likewise have influenced the contemporary perception of the consequences of penetrative sex.

Historians of eighteenth-century demography and sexuality have long faced a conundrum. It has been obvious from the late 1970s that a fundamental transition occurred in the sexual behaviour and family-formation practices of plebeian and middling-sort people. We know that the age at marriage dropped significantly, that the percentage of bastards born increased threefold over the course of the century and that the percentage of women who gave birth within eight months of marriage increased to over a third of the total. And finally, the percentage of the population remaining unmarried and presumably celibate, dropped precipitately. In other words, the sexual practices of a portion of the population changed, resulting in an increase in population, and a transition in the nature of the demographic regime. The difficulty is to know why this transition occurred, and what changes in perception and experience on the part of individuals might have contributed to it.[2]

One explanatory strategy which has recently received a deal of attention has been adopted by Adrian Wilson and Nicholas Rogers. Both look at illegitimacy among the London poor. Adrian Wilson looks at the records of the Foundling Hospital, established in 1739, and concludes that a high proportion of all illegitimate children ended up in the Hospital, and that this reflects an extremely high level of illegitimacy in London which in turn resulted from a specific pattern of courtship. This pattern is one in which 'marriage was an act contingent on pregnancy' and upon periods of high wages and low prices. In other words, penetrative sexual activity occurred as a prerequisite to betrothal, that pregnancy was the normal cue for marriage, but that it was dependent upon both parties feeling economically secure. In the absence of this last criterion, couples simply did not marry, and women gave birth to bastards. Wilson then goes on to argue that this London pattern was spread, along with the influence of metropolitan culture, to the rest of the country, resulting in more marriages, bastards and children in general.[3]

In parallel research on the bastardy examinations for Westminster parishes, Nicholas Rogers has determined that the vast majority of illegitimate births were to women in relationships with their social equals, that penetration and pregnancy were part of courtship and that finally, the disruptions of unemployment, war and premature death were the most significant causes of illegitimacy. Rogers makes no claims about the typicality of the information he assays, but he does use it to argue for the primacy of economic factors in determining levels of illegitimacy.[4]

As a result of the work of Rogers and Wilson, the experience of London women has become increasingly significant to our understanding of one possible explanation of national trends in illegitimacy and population change. It is important, therefore, to establish what factors impinged on that experience.

In the view of most historians of the period, it is the positive attraction of giving birth to a legitimate child in the context of a secure marriage which leads young women into premature sexual activity. This framework, however, tends to exclude a wide range of possible influences – both cultural and economic. The negative experience of the possibility of bearing a bastard, the downside of the risk of sex during courting, does not fit easily into most economic models, nor does the role of peer pressure, or changing patterns of opportunity for sexual behaviour. But, each of these could easily have had a profound effect on the individual decisions which contributed to the creation of a changing birth and bastardy rate. If, for example, bearing a bastard child was likely to result in being permanently unable to find legitimate work, if it would mean the mother would be unable to marry at a later date, if the options available were likely to be prostitution and nothing else, there would exist a very strong disincentive to partaking of courting practices which would put one at risk. Likewise, if peer pressure from both women and men suggested that penetrative sex was definitely not a normal part of courting, the ability of anyone to suggest otherwise would be severely limited.

At least one body of literature would suggest that these kinds of disincentives should be in place. The work of historians such as Martin Ingram and, for the eighteenth century, Tim Meldrum, has suggested that sexual reputation, and hence peer control of sexual behaviour, was a central component in the social lives of early modern women in both the countryside and the town.[5] The lives of London bastard-bearers do not, however, entirely support this conclusion.

The lives of plebeian women are notoriously difficult to reconstruct. They left few records of their own and their circumstances can only be gleaned from a series of intractable, generally bureaucratic sources. In order to get at this material, at least for a limited sample of plebeian women, the bastardy and settlement examinations, workhouse records, and pension lists of the parish of St Luke's Chelsea have been analysed.[6] The existence of the records themselves, and the nature of the parish ensures that the sample cannot be typical – the experience of the typical bastard-bearer was simply not recorded. But these records do give us access to a wide range of eighteenth-century metropolitan paupers, whose lives delineate a diverse set of experiences.

Joan Rumbold grew up in Chelsea and was 19 years old when she met John Phillips, who lived by the river just south of the Rectory. They had sex for the first time on a bed in a house near Charing Cross, and again at various places around London over the course of the next three years.[7]

At some point during this relationship John became infected with gonorrhoea, which he then passed on to Joan. Worse, when Joan did become pregnant, he abandoned her completely.

Alone, suffering from gonorrhoea and pregnant, Joan was admitted to the workhouse at Chelsea on 24 March 1757, where she gave birth to a male bastard child. She still hoped that John Phillips would come for her. Despite his behaviour, despite the disease he had passed on to her, she named her child John, after its father.

He did not return, and Joan and her son were sent to the recently established Lock Hospital for a cure, and from there back to the workhouse.[8] The disease had, by now, gone into its latent phase, and Joan appeared reasonably healthy, and so she and John were sent out of the workhouse and back to her father's home. Her father, however, was not entirely sympathetic, and unceremoniously deposited her and John back at the workhouse a week later.

There was little left for Joan or the parish to do. In July she was sent to service at Brompton with a new pair of shoes, while her son John was left in the workhouse, where he died two years later.

Joan Rumbold did not die tragically of a fever brought on by moral turpitude. Nor did her economic circumstances become significantly worse. Indeed, while her reputation seems to have suffered, at least in her father's eyes, the parish and the Lock Hospital together provided a remarkably effective safety-net. Eighteenth-century institutions were intended for the deserving poor, for the hard-working and provident, for the moral and the obsequious. Joan Rumbold does not seem to have possessed many of these qualities in any observable measure, and yet she was in the first instance admitted to the workhouse without question, and attended through a successful birth. She was then sent to the Lock Hospital where she and her son would have received an expensive cure. In contemporary understanding of parental responsibility, her father was under a relatively strong obligation to support her and yet, when he refused, the workhouse again accepted her without question. And finally, as a bridge to the world of work, a crèche facility was provided for her child while she entered into domestic service. Two years later when the child died, she was essentially back where she began. To suggest that Joan's experience represents anything less than a tragedy would be wrong, but likewise, to suggest that it irrevocably altered the course of her life would likewise be inaccurate.

A slightly different experience is provided by the case of Elizabeth Edwards. By February 1742, when she first appears in the workhouse register, Elizabeth Edwards already had a long track record with the parish of Chelsea.[9] Elizabeth, and her daughter by a dead husband, were in the workhouse, as was her sister, Alice Gouldon. In the spring of that year, she and Alice were ordered to quit the house within a week, leaving Elizabeth's daughter behind. During that week she became dangerously ill, and the workhouse committee was forced to relent. Alice stayed behind to nurse her, while Elizabeth concentrated on getting well. By the following December, they were all living outside the house, in reduced circumstances, but independent of the parish. The week before Christmas Elizabeth asked for a pair of shoes, and was refused.

Elizabeth was a young widow of 25, whose husband, Thomas, had died of the dropsy in a charitable hospital to which he had been sent by the workhouse authorities a couple of years earlier. She had no means of support, a daughter to raise, and an improvident sister to think about. Over the next couple of years she picked up work where she could until, in 1745, she took a job nursing the wife of Richard Jones through her lying-in. Elizabeth Edwards and Richard Jones, a Chelsea waterman, began a sexual relationship. They had sex for the first time while Richard's wife recovered from giving birth in the next room.

Over the next three years they snatched what opportunities they could, making love in his house by the river and, when that became inconvenient, arranging to meet at Elizabeth's sister's apartment at Chelsea Park. The inevitable eventually happened, and Elizabeth became pregnant in July 1747. They continued their affair for as long as was practical, and Elizabeth went into the workhouse in spring 1748, giving birth to Thomas Edwards on 11 April.

From this point on, Elizabeth's life, and that of her two children, Mary and the infant Thomas, were shaken by illness and ill-luck. By November

1747, Elizabeth, with Mary and Thomas in tow, was back in the workhouse, sick and unable to work. Nine months later they were all ordered out of the house, only to be readmitted eight days later because Elizabeth could find neither lodging nor work. Elizabeth and Thomas were allowed to stay for only four days, but Mary was allowed to continue in the house.

Elizabeth's circumstances did not improve. In the middle of March 1749 she went lame and ended up back at the workhouse with Thomas, who then died in the house on 12 April. On the 23rd, Elizabeth asked permission to go out to look for work and disappeared, reappearing only a year and a half later when she came to collect Mary.

She was able to keep her daughter with her for only a month, and when Mary became ill she was sent back to the workhouse, eventually being apprenticed to a cordwainer in St Margaret's Westminster. Elizabeth continued to live in reduced circumstances and was given a little bit of support over the course of the 1750s to help ensure that she did not become too burdensome to the parish.

Elizabeth Edwards' circumstances were already profoundly complex when she first appears in the records. And, indeed, she seems just the sort of person eighteenth-century institutions were designed to discourage, and yet even she found the workhouse flexible enough to allow her to remain independent throughout most of the period during which she can be observed. It provided care for her children while she sought employment, and a ready refuge for her whole family during bouts of illness and unemployment. It may not have been comfortable, and it is certain that the poor hated these institutions, but they did provide a service suited to working women with children – allowing them to behave in the marketplace in much the same way as their unencumbered contemporaries.

Considering the horrific image eighteenth-century social policy evokes in the mind of most historians, it is significant that London's parochial and hospital provision was uniquely well designed for problems faced by unmarried, plebeian mothers. The institutions were designed for the entirely destitute and dependent, apparently set up in order to suit people without property or place. Unlike the pensions and out-relief generally associated with the Old Poor Law, the increasingly institutional care given in both parochial and charitable institutions coped best with just the sort of short-term crisis an illicit pregnancy and birth represented.

Indeed, by the 1750s, the range of institutions in London available to the indigent poor, and unmarried mothers in particular, was immense. Besides the Foundling Hospital there were several lying-in hospitals, the Magdalen Hospital for penitent prostitutes, the Lock Hospital for the treatment of venereal disease,[10] and almost 70 parish workhouses of varying sizes and degrees of sophistication. There was also a range of smaller, more specific charitable hospitals.[11] This list includes only the most prominent sites of indoor provision, designed for the totally destitute. And while it is certain that these institutions were patronising in their intent, abhorred by their users, and largely unpleasant in their overall formulation, they likewise provided a comprehensive service to a wide range of the population of London.

If we look at the numbers of babies and children involved, the likely impact of London social policy becomes apparent. The parochial workhouse movement began in the early 1720s, and by 1776 there were 86 houses in the metropolitan area, including Middlesex and Westminster, accommodating 15 180 paupers. Of these, approximately 31 per cent were children, amounting to some 4700 babies and children at any one time.[12] Most of these children would either die or be taken out of the workhouse in a matter of weeks or months (although a substantial minority would be entirely abandoned and be apprenticed by the parish), suggesting in turn that the percentage of London's children left to the parish would amount to a significant number, certainly tens of thousands over the course of the second quarter of the century.[13]

The Foundling Hospital, like the workhouses, was available as a depository for misbegotten and financially burdensome children. During the 19 years between its first opening in 1741 and the end of the General Reception of 1760, the hospital admitted over 16 000 babies. During the first year of the General Reception, 1756, 3300 children were received, most of whom were sent to the country to be nursed, in the certain knowledge that it was healthier for the children.[14]

These numbers alone suggest a remarkably open and available social service, which is the more surprising given the obvious ideological baggage carried by parish officers, the governors of charities and workhouse administrators. That these numbers were made up of the babies of women who had transgressed what was meant to be a fundamental precept for early modern society, whose very name, 'bastard-bearer', was an actionable epithet in the church courts and who had a negligible moral purchase on that society, reinforces this impression. That these women could also look to the Foundling Hospital, certain that they could reclaim their child if they wanted to, but likewise certain that no one would advertise their predicament, is equally startling. One can argue, indeed, that London social provision provided the opposite to the contemporary welfare state. Whereas today, all the rhetoric suggests a universal benefit while the reality excludes an increasing proportion of the population, in the eighteenth century the rhetoric was exclusive while the reality remarkably inclusive. In a similar mirror-image, while the modern welfare state seems determined to support marginal poverty, and has fewer and fewer provisions for the increasing number of entirely destitute, London's eighteenth-century equivalent is bristling with institutional care, while the level of out-relief and marginal support is in relative decline.

Besides their apparent openness to single mothers, however, there is one other aspect of most of these institutions of which we should be aware. They murdered babies at a tremendous rate. The three examples provided so far were not chosen because the bastard children cited in them died; their deaths were typical of the fate of most bastards who came into contact with any metropolitan institution – whether workhouse or foundling hospital.

The figures for child mortality in just one workhouse will stand for the rest. At St Margaret's Westminster between 1746 and 1750, 106 children were either born in the house or admitted to it before the age of 20 months. Of these, seven were eventually apprenticed, 16 discharged to their families and 83 died.[15]

Among the largest single contingent of abandoned babies – those left to the mercies of the Foundling Hospital – a similarly large number died. Both the Hospital and many of the better-run workhouses sent babies to the country to be nursed, but even given these prophylactic measures the majority of children died. The crude level of mortality for the Foundling Hospital, for the 16 326 babies admitted was 61.02 per cent – representing nearly 10 000 dead babies and children. Even among those sent to the supposedly more salubrious countryside, 53.28 per cent died.[16]

In a tragic twist to the literary image of bastardy, in which the mother dies and the child goes on to make good as the lost heir to a noble household, the most likely outcome of an illegitimate birth was that the child should die, while the mother went on to new employment.

It is not the point of this chapter to enter into fashionable debates about the emotional intensity experienced by past generations. It would be condescending and simply wrong to suggest that the mothers of the thousands of abandoned children who passed through the institutions of London did not feel their loss to a devastating extreme. But, it is likewise apparent that having abandoned their children, these women went on to essentially new lives. They were not in a better financial situation and their employment was as insecure as that of any London servant but they were, in the end, able to make a living and contract a future marriage. Less than 1 per cent of the children left at the Foundling Hospital were ever reclaimed by their parents – although elaborate arrangements were made to ensure that track could be kept of individual children.[17] This is reflective both of the extent to which it was impossible to be a single mother in the modern sense, and to which it was possible to actually *abandon* a child, as opposed to simply leaving it in the care of another.

The experience of these women is part and parcel of the general insecurity of the poor, and of poor women in particular. Most lesser servants in London changed jobs frequently, had a very tenuous support-system among family and friends and were prey to debilitating illness. Even if they managed to trade penetrative sex for the marginal security of marriage, there was every likelihood they would be abandoned, or their partner would turn out to be a bigamist. In reading through the settlement and bastardy examinations of women of this period, it sometimes seems they lurched from crisis to crisis, with only months or days in between. Within this economy of insecurity, pregnancy and the birth of a bastard was only one possible crisis among many, and because of the nature of institutional provision, was dealt with as such.

Elizabeth Langford's experience represents a good example of the range of things which could go wrong.[18] In the autumn of 1753 she clandestinely married Thomas Boxall in the Liberty of the Fleet.[19] She was 23 at the time and pregnant with their first daughter, Elizabeth, who was born later that same year. Unfortunately, the marriage was not a happy one. Thomas Boxall had grown up in a problem family for the parish, and the names of his father and other relatives appear numerous times in the poor law records. There seems to have been a history of promiscuity among the members of his family, and while Thomas was trained as a whitesmith and clockmaker, he does not seem to have gained regular employment. Two years after their marriage Elizabeth was pregnant again, when Thomas deserted her. Elizabeth and her daughter entered the workhouse at Chelsea on 17 October 1755, and her second child, Mary, was born on 20 December.

Two-year-old Elizabeth died in the June of the following year, and her mother was sent out to work, with the infant Mary, on the day after Boxing Day, 1756. She had five shillings in her pocket and nowhere to go. She eventually found work, but was forced to return Mary to the workhouse, where she died a year later at the age of two.

In the meantime, Thomas had removed to Chatham, where he continued for the next five years, eventually becoming temporarily reconciled to Elizabeth. By 1760 Elizabeth was pregnant again, and again found herself deserted by her husband, who by this time was keeping 'another woman', and hence expected the parish to keep his wife and infant son, James.

It is unlikely that Thomas was deeply mourned when he died the following year. But it did leave Elizabeth in the unhappy circumstance of being a widow with a small child, and forced, for the second time, to enter into courtship as one of London's ubiquitous female domestic servants. She and James found a place at a master baker's in St Paul Shadwell and for the next several years seem to have done reasonably well. Unfortunately, this situation did not last. She had sex with a fellow-servant, a journeyman baker, David Edwards, and became pregnant. A situation which had been supportable, very quickly collapsed. By the end of her second trimester she and James, now aged five, were applying for entry into the Chelsea workhouse. She had lost her place because of her pregnancy and had nowhere else to turn.

During the next two years she entered the workhouse on four separate occasions. In late April 1766 she and James entered the workhouse, Elizabeth giving birth to Lucy on 28 August. By late September she felt well enough to seek work, and disappeared with James in tow – leaving Lucy to the care of the workhouse.

A mere three days later, however, both she and James were back, having been unable to find a place. This time she stayed for a month and when she attempted to leave it was with both children. It did not work, however, and she was back in the house within a day. A week later, she again discharged herself, and sought the refuge of her late husband's family.

Sometime during the next ten months Lucy died and Elizabeth became ill. She and James returned to the workhouse in August 1767 and stayed for a couple of weeks. By now things were seemingly getting rather desperate. She re-entered the workhouse in early 1768, but this time, when she left, James stayed where he was. She was only able to collect him just after Christmas, three years later.

Of course, young women of marriageable age from the service sector of the London economy were in a difficult situation.[20] Women outnumbered men in the population of the metropolis (as they did in most cities), and the level of job insecurity was incredibly high. Wages could amount to little more than 40 or 50 shillings a year after board and lodging, if that, while many of the structural support-systems of family and friends which characterised rural societies were undermined by the impact of widespread in-migration and population growth. As London grew and its social organisation became more complex, the ability of women to form a stable household was undermined, while the necessity of doing so in order to create a supportable life increased.

At the same time, the influence of neighbours and of reputation declined. It is no accident that eighteenth-century London witnessed the development of the street sign – the increasing anonymity of urban life required these aids to navigation.[21] This period also saw the effective demise of church courts, and their only partial replacement by the expanding role of the secular courts. The general inability of plebeian women to enforce legal sanctions against sexual defamation (a common practice a century earlier) reflects a situation in which it was increasingly difficult for the peer group of these women to enforce sexual probity, if indeed they continued to seek to do so.[22]

Just as the church courts declined as a venue for the defence of sexual honour, so the secular courts became less assiduous in prosecuting bastard-bearing. What might have resulted in several months in a house of correction during the previous century, some time in the pillory, or a public whipping was now deemed a matter of social policy rather than criminal justice.[23]

If we consider these factors from the point of view of the young women of courting age in mid-eighteenth-century London, their likely impact seems self-evident. The high proportion of women in the population as a whole made contracting a marriage more difficult, while the extreme insecurity of employment made it extremely desirable. If, as is demonstrated by the work of historians such as John Gillis, eighteenth-century marriage can be seen as a process in which betrothal, penetrative sex, pregnancy, the marriage ceremony itself, and finally the birth of the first child, were all elements in the creation of a secure union, then we should not be surprised to find evidence of women attempting to collect the full jigsaw puzzle by putting together three of the pieces. More than this, the decline in defamation, and the importance of sexual reputation, would remove at least part of one disincentive to courting practices involving penetrative sex, while the changing patterns of criminal prosecution would remove a further element from the possible litany of disasters associated with too-enthusiastic courting. And finally, the existence of readymade institutional dumping grounds for the products of failed attempts at contracting a marriage, along with the provision of relatively good circumstances in which to give birth, must have removed a substantial part of the final and most severe disincentive to sex as courting.

Of course, at first sight, this conclusion seems to imply a level of self-serving calculation on the part of these women which seems unreasonable – surely the natural parental instinct of anyone would ensure that any risk leading to the death of a baby would be studiously avoided. And yet, while not denigrating in any way the emotions experienced by these women, we need to remember that modern conceptions of parenthood, in which physical bonding is deemed central, are just that: 'modern'. Ruth Perry has recently charted the rise of a more sentimental form of motherhood in which women were effectively chained to their children, and breast-feeding and the personal care of the child by its biological mother became central to the new role of mother. She has located the rise of this relationship in the late eighteenth century.[24] At mid-century, however, mothers did not necessarily expect to breast-feed their child, and certainly did not expect to be overcome by parental feelings, and whether or not they were in fact overcome does not alter their expectation of a lesser set of feelings, which would more easily allow them to contemplate abandonment as a solution to an unwanted pregnancy.

At the same time, the decision to participate in penetrative sex cannot simply be understood as a bald calculation. Peer pressure, pressure from one's partner, the assumption that penetration represented a form of sexual 'normality', as well as the creation of reasonable provisions against the possibility of becoming pregnant, all influenced the individual decision. Likewise, the expectation of pleasure and the construction of sexual desire as being associated with penetrative sex each had their part to play.[25] There can be little doubt, for example, that Elizabeth Edwards decided to have sex with Richard Jones because she expected to enjoy the experience, rather than as a calculated bid for economic security.

John Gillis has characterised the sexual regimes of urban life as celibate in the seventeenth century and conjugal in the eighteenth. He has identified, for London in particular, a transition from a regime in which all the emphasis seems to have been placed on remaining single to one, after 1700, which increasingly advertised marriage as the appropriate state for adult men and women.[26] By the second quarter of the eighteenth century, this increased emphasis on marriage and penetrative sexual activity had reached such a pitch that one author, at least, could consider it proverbial knowledge 'That a Middlesex Maidenhead is to be had for asking for'.[27] While this shift must certainly have been associated with changing patterns of employment, it must likewise have been the result of a shift in the complex inter-relationship between expectations, the social policy provision and sexual opportunity. The creation, for whatever reason, of new forms of relief for bastard-bearers was one aspect of the multifaceted transformation in which women like Rebecca Clement and Joan Rumbold participated.

Of course, most sexual activities likely to result in pregnancy generally involve two people of different sexes. This chapter has tended to ignore possible changes in the behaviour and attitudes of men, in favour of an analysis of those of women. But it is, likewise, possible that men simply came to expect penetrative sex in a new way, and that women were forced to conform to this expectation. Indeed, this whole chapter has been premised upon the assumption that women could say no, but this was, of course, not always the case. Violence, threat and economic power were all factors in the complex mix of influences that might result in the creation of a bastard child.[28]

In order to emphasise both the tragic nature of these women's lives and, likewise, some of the alternative forces at work on those lives, I want to end with a short account of the experiences of someone who did not give birth to a bastard, but who exemplifies the insecurity and horror that could engulf plebeian women.

On the Saturday night before Easter in April 1750 a reformation of manners riot took place in the Strand. The bawdy houses and bagnios were systematically looted and the prostitutes of the area attacked. While the noise and violence of the riot took place in the street, Samuel Firmin, a button-seller of St Clement Danes, sent his errandboy out of the house, and carefully locked the doors behind him. He was now alone with a 25-year-old servant – Elizabeth Bussell.[29] Samuel Firmin took out his penknife and held it to Elizabeth Bussell's throat and raped her, holding her down while she struggled. Repeatedly over the next two months, Samuel Firmin beat and raped her. By May she was covered with bruises and one eye was swollen completely shut, forcing her to seek the help of Mrs Dean, an oculist.

During the same period Samuel Firmin's father-in-law, Mr Stammers, was raping her less violently. He drugged her with warm ale laced with sleeping powders, and forced himself upon her while she was semiconscious. She became pregnant, and suffered a painful miscarriage in early June.

By mid-June Elizabeth Bussell was frantic. With no place to go to and unable to deal with the violence and horror which had been perpetrated upon her, by the very people who were responsible for her wellbeing, she lost her senses. On 16 June she was found on the street and taken to the workhouse, where she was fed and clothed and probably restrained. It took several slow months for her to recover, and it was only in October that she felt strong enough to give evidence before Justice Peter Elers. It was a further three months before she felt able to venture out of the workhouse. Seven months after she had been found on the street, lunatic, and nine months after Samuel Firmin had first raped her, she left the workhouse and went back into service on 9 January 1751.

## NOTES

\* I would like to thank Penelope Corfield and Tim Meldrum for their comments on a draft of this chapter. I hope my attempts to deal with the comments have made this a stronger piece. I would also like to thank John Black, whose work on the records of St Luke's Chelsea helped make this chapter possible.
1. Greater London Record Office (hereafter GLRO), 'St Luke's Chelsea, Workhouse Register, 1743–1766', Microfilm, X/15/37, Rebecca Clements, 7 May 1748, Sarah Clements, 13 May 1748; GLRO, 'St Luke's Chelsea, Settlement and Bastardy Examinations, 1733–1750', P74/Luk/121, Rebecca Clements, 29 April 1748.
2. For material on eighteenth-century demography see Peter Laslett, Karla Oosterveen and Richard Smith (eds), *Bastardy and Its Comparative History* (London, 1980); David Levine, *Family Formation in an Age of Nascent Capitalism* (New York, 1977); Roger Schofield, 'English Marriage Patterns Revisited', *Journal of Family History* Spring (1985), 2–20; Richard Wall, 'Leaving Home and the Process of Household Formation in Pre-Industrial England', *Continuity and Change* II, 1 (1987), 77–101; David R. Weir, 'Rather Never Than Late: Celibacy and Age at Marriage in English Cohort Fertility, 1541–1871', *Journal of Family History* Winter (1984), 340–54; E.A. Wrigley and R.S. Schofield, *The Population History of England, 1541–1871* (Cambridge, 1981); E.A. Wrigley, 'The Growth of Population in Eighteenth-Century England: A Conundrum Resolved', *Past & Present* 98 (1983), 121–50; E.A. Wrigley, 'Marriage, Fertility and Population Growth in Eighteenth-Century England' in R.B. Outhwaite (ed.), *Marriage and Society: Studies in the Social History of Marriage* (New York, 1982), pp.137–85. For a statement of the problems contained in many of the above analyses see David Levine, '"For Their Own Reasons": Individual Marriage Decisions and Family Life', *Journal of Family History* Fall (1982), 255–64. For a powerful critique of the overall methodological approach contained see Bridget Hill, 'The Marriage Age of Women and the Demographers', *History Workshop Journal* 28, Autumn (1989), 129–47.
3. Andrian Wilson, 'Illegitimacy and Its Implications in Mid Eighteenth Century London: The Evidence of the Foundling Hospital', *Continuity and Change* IV, 1 (1989), passim. While Wilson's argument is too complex to be entirely convincing, he is certainly correct to draw attention to the role of the Foundling Hospital in the demographic regime of the capital.
4. Nicholas Rogers, 'Carnal Knowledge: Illegitimacy in Eighteenth-Century Westminister', *Journal of Social History* XXIII, 2 (1989), 355–75.
5. Martin Ingram, *Church Courts, Sex and Marriage in England, 1570–1640* (Cambridge, 1987) and Tim Meldrum, 'A Woman's Court in London: Defamation at the Bishop of London's Consistory Court, 1700–1745', *The London Journal* 19, 1 (1994), 1–20.
6. Eighteenth-century Chelsea was a unique mix of the urban and the rural and its records are remarkably complete and sophisticated, all of which makes it necessarily atypical of either London or the country as a whole. For information on its economy, social make-up and population see Daniel

Lysons, *The Environs of London: Being an Historical Account of the Towns, Villages and Hamlets, Within Twelve Miles of that Capital*, vol. II (London, 1795), pp.71, 148, 174; C.G.T. Dean, *The Royal Hospital, Chelsea* (London, 1950); Thomas Faulkner, *An Historical and Topographical Description of Chelsea and Its Environs*, vol. II (London, 1829), pp.276–93. Population figures for Chelsea can be calculated from the numbers of baptisms recorded at St Luke's annually throughout the eighteenth century, and reproduced in Lysons, *Environs*, II, p.116.

7. GLRO, 'St Luke's Chelsea, Workhouse Register, 1743–1766', Microfilm, X/15/37, Joan Rumbold, 24 March 1757, 18 March 1758, 2 May 1758, John Rumbold, 20 March 1757, 18 March 1758, 2 May 1758; GLRO, 'St Luke's Chelsea, Settlement and Bastardy Examinations, 1750–1766', P74/Luk/122/RI104, Jane Rumbell, 25 April 1758.

8. For an account of the Lock Hospital see Donna Andrew, *Philanthropy and Police, London Charity in the Eighteenth Century* (Princeton, NJ, 1989), pp.69–71.

9. GLRO, 'St Luke's Chelsea, Workhouse Committee Minutes, 1735–1750', Microfilm, P74/Luk/X26/1, Thomas Edwards, 12 May 1736, 29 Dec. 1736, 16 Nov. 1737, Elizabeth Edwards, 23 Feb. 1742, 2 March 1742, Elizabeth Edwards, 21 Dec. 1742; GLRO, 'St Luke's Chelsea, Workhouse Committee Minutes, 1750–1755', Microfilm, P74/Luk/X26/1, Elizabeth Edwards, 20 Nov. 1750, 28 Nov. 1752, 15 May 1753, Mary Edwards, 6 Feb. 1753, 13 Feb. 1753; GLRO, 'St Luke's Chelsea, Workhouse Register, 1743–1766', Microfilm, X/15/37, Elizabeth Edwards, 4 Nov. 1747, 13 Sept. 1748, 15 March 1749, Mary Edwards, 13 Sept. 1748, 2 Oct. 1750, 8 April 1752, Thomas Edwards, 11 April 1748, 13 Sept. 1748, 15 March 1749; GLRO, 'St Luke's Chelsea, Settlement and Bastardy Examinations, 1733–1750', P74/Luk/121, Elizabeth Edwards, 21 May 1748.

10. For a treatment of specifically charitable institutions in London see Andrew, *Philanthropy and Police*, passim.

11. See T. Hitchcock, 'The English Workhouse: A Study in Institutional Poor Relief in Selected Counties, 1696–1750' (PhD thesis, Oxford University, 1985), pp.258–81.

12. The numbers for 1750 are based on Hitchcock, 'The English Workhouse', pp.258–81. For those for 1776, see the parliamentary enquiry of the following year, House of Lords Records Office, 'Poor Rate Returns, 1777', Parchment Collection, Box 162. The figure of 31 per cent for the number of children in these houses is calculated from GLRO, 'St Luke's Chelsea, Workhouse Register, 1743–1766', Microfilm, X/15/37. The equivalent figures for adult men and women (those over 16 years at entry) are 19 and 50 per cent respectively.

13. The average length of stay of each of the 1403 children under the age of 16 who are recorded in the workhouse registers for St Luke's Chelsea before 1800 is 325 days. This group made up 31 per cent of the total sample. GLRO, 'St Luke's Chelsea, Workhouse Register, 1743–1766', Microfilm, X/15/37.

14. For an excellent account of the early history of the hospital see Ruth McClure, *Coram's Children: The London Foundling Hospital in the Eighteenth Century* (London, 1981); for a more directed analysis of the

'Unlawfully begotten on her body'

significance of the numbers of babies going through the hospital, see Wilson, 'Illegitimacy and Its Implications', passim.

15. See Westminster City Library, 'E2420 shelf 38, 'St Margarets Westminster, Orders of Vestry, 1738–1755', pp.249–52.
16. McClure, *Coram's Children*, Appendix III, p.261.
17. Wilson, 'Illegitimacy and Its Implications', p.109.
18. GLRO, 'St Luke's Chelsea, Workhouse Register', Microfilm, X/15/37, Elizabeth Boxall, 17 Oct. 1755, Elizabeth Boxall, 17 Oct. 1755, Elizabeth Boxall, 22 April 1766, Elizabeth Boxall, 27 Sept. 1766, Elizabeth Boxall, 29 Oct. 1766, Elizabeth Boxall, 21 Aug. 1767, Elizabeth Boxall, 2 Jan. 1768, Elizabeth Boxall, 11 Jan. 1769, Mary Boxall, 20 Dec. 1755, James Boxall, 22 April 1766, James Boxall, 29 Oct. 1766, James Boxall, 21 Aug. 1767, James Boxall, 2 Jan. 1768, Lucy Boxall, 28 Aug. 1766, Lucy Boxall 29 Oct. 1766, GLRO, 'Settlement and Bastardy Examinations, 1750–1766', P74/Luk/122/RI104, Thomas Boxall, Autumn 1753, William Boxall, Autumn 1753.
19. For material on Fleet marriages see Jeremy Boulton, 'Clandestine Marriages in London: An Examination of a Neglected Urban Variable', *Urban History* XX, 2 (1993), 191–210; Roger Lee Brown, 'The Rise and Fall of the Fleet Marriages' in Outhwaite (ed.), *Marriage and Society*, pp.117–36; John Gillis, *For Better, For Worse: British Marriages 1600 to the Present* (Oxford, 1985), pp.90–8; Lawrence Stone, *Road to Divorce: England, 1530–1987* (Oxford, 1990), pp.110–20.
20. For material on the circumstances of service at this time and the difficulties faced even by married women from this class, see David A. Kent, '"Gone for a Soldier": Family Breakdown and the Demography of Desertion in a London Parish, 1750–91', *Local Population Studies* 45, Autumn (1990), 27–42; David A. Kent, 'Ubiquitous but Invisible: Female Domestic Servants in Mid-Eighteenth-Century London', *History Workshop Journal* 28, Autumn (1989), 111–28.
21. Dan Cruickshank and Neil Burton, *Life in the Georgian City* (London, 1990), p 19
22. For an account of the development of the church courts in early eighteenth-century London see Meldrum, 'A Woman's Court in London'. Meldrum argues that the Bishop of London's Consistory Court becomes a much more female-dominated court over the course of the first half of the century, but there is little doubt about the absolute decline in the court's role in defamation cases.
23. See E.J. Burford and Sandra Shulman, *Of Bridles and Burnings: The Punishment of Women* (London, 1992), pp.19–21.
24. Although Ruth Perry misconstrues the role of the Foundling Hospital she is undoubtedly correct in her depiction of the general direction of attitudinal change. Ruth Perry, 'Colonizing the Breast: Sexuality and Maternity in Eighteenth-Century England', *Journal of the History of Sexuality* II, 2 (1991), 204–34.
25. At least one historian has recently suggested that the eighteenth century witnessed a marked change in the nature of sexual desire. See Henry Abelove, 'Some Speculations on the History of Sexual Intercourse during the Long Eighteenth Century in England', *Genders* no. 6, Fall (1989), 125–30.

26. Gillis, *For Better, For Worse*, pp.161–89.
27. Anon, *Hell Upon Earth: Or the Town in an Uproar* (London, 1729), p.13.
28. According to at least one historian, rape was a normal part of family formation in rural France. Cissie Fairchilds, 'Female Sexual Attitudes and the Rise of Illegitimacy: A Case Study', *Interdisciplinary History* no. 4, Spring (1978), 627–67.
29. GLRO, 'St Luke's Chelsea, Workhouse Register, 1743–1766', Microfilm, X/15/37, Elizabeth Boswell, 16 June 1750; GLRO, 'St Luke's Chelsea, Settlement and Bastardy Examinations, 1750–1766', P74/Luk/122/RI104, Elizabeth Bussell, 13 Oct. 1750.

# 4 'The bowels of compation': A Labouring Family and the Law, c.1790–1834
Pamela Sharpe

I

The Old Poor Law was one of the first subjects explored by social historians. Yet the way in which this law was used, both by those giving and those receiving poor relief, remains little examined. The history of the eighteenth- and early-nineteenth-century poor law has been concerned with administrative or economic changes, generally at the national level. There has been considerably less attention paid to the interaction of individuals with the poor law authorities and how within the statutory system of poor relief provision, social and ideological factors came into play, aside from concepts of the 'deserving' and 'undeserving' poor. Gertrude Himmelfarb looked at the history of ideas regarding poverty, but bemoaned the lack of 'the direct testimony of the poor themselves'.[1]

The poor law determined who would and would not be relieved, through the operation of settlement provisions for example, and it is clear that individuals saw poor relief as a 'right' in ways comparable to those by which people with means safeguarded property rights in the eighteenth century. This does not preclude the possibility that overseers or magistrates, in determining the level and frequency of poor relief, were swayed more by some voices than others. Not only the criminal law, but also the machinations of the poor law can be seen as the outworking of forms of local ideology. When we start to deliberate on the decisions of parish vestries or the magistracy, we cannot lose sight of the fact that this was, as Peter Laslett put it, a 'face to face world'. Countless value judgements and the nods and winks of personal acquaintance must have affected the way in which relief was administered at a personal level. Likewise, local religious and political differences could have affected the complexion of giving within the overall structure. By looking at letters from poor relief recipients to overseers we can begin to see glimpses of a process of negotiation, which was carried out for most of the eighteenth century by the appearance of a pauper at the meeting of a group of parish officials, to beg for his or her bread, and was later sometimes replaced by written communication. After 1795, with soaring levels of poverty, the tailoring of poor relief benefits to the needs of particular paupers, within a paternalist framework, was being replaced by more standardised methods of distributing financial relief to the labouring poor in general such as the Speenhamland system, whereby wages were supplemented from the poor rates. In stating their individual needs and seeking relief for them, paupers who wrote to their settlement parishes requiring relief in the French Wars and through to 1834, were resorting to a traditional, pre-Speenhamland system.

Essex has what would appear to be a particularly large collection of letters written by poor law recipients to overseers.[2] Here, I will look at the interactions of a family called Hall with the overseers of St Botolph's parish in Colchester, in a time-period from the French Wars to the passing of the New Poor Law. Their life experiences were ordinary, except perhaps for the fact that they left behind a collection of some 40 letters to the St Botolph's overseers, written over a 20-year time-period. The Halls lived in Chelmsford and London and claimed non-resident relief from their settlement parish of St Botolph's.

By the 1820s, overseers in all of the large Essex towns were operating 'non-resident' relief schemes. They would cover the maintenance of paupers who lived elsewhere in periods of unemployment, in the belief that they still had a greater chance of finding work in the parish they had moved to. As George Boyer has shown, this policy was economically rational in an environment of both seasonal changes in employment levels and trade fluctuations.[3] The demographic conditions of the 1820s also encouraged these schemes. The average age of marriage was low and rate of marriage high, and the number of children surviving infancy was growing. Towns or cities, and London in particular, offered widening employment opportunities for women and children as well as adult men. The hope of parish overseers, often shared by the paupers, was that the job opportunities in their new situation would allow them to gain settlement, whether by a year's hiring or the rental of a house to the value of at least ten pounds a year, so that they were no longer the legal responsibility of the parish.

Overseers had no intention of giving poor people excess funds, however. Extraneous payments were to be given only in cases of absolute need and regular relief was to be kept at a level which would meet their basic needs but prevent the paupers from coming home and perhaps having to enter the workhouse. To monitor this, either the overseers or people they knew who lived near the paupers would visit them to check on their needs. For example, John Sheppey, assistant overseer at Chelmsford, visited London in December 1823 to see all the London paupers.[4] Ostensibly, the purpose of his visit was to tell them that Chelmsford was stopping all relief to non-resident paupers. In fact, he aimed to establish the minimum regular payment necessary to stop them from coming home. On the pauper's side, it was necessary to alert the overseers to the level of their needs. This could be done by word of mouth if a member of the family was travelling back to their parish, but the usual way was by letter. They would describe their unemployment, illness or other misfortune in detail and sometimes exaggerated tone. Usually the paupers were already in receipt of an allowance or trying to start one and wanted a lump-sum payment, perhaps to eliminate rent arrears, for example.

The documents left by this negotiation process for funds are a series of letters between paupers and overseers – sometimes using the same piece of paper. Stephen Taylor has looked at the large number of similar letters for Kirkby Lonsdale and the non-resident relief system operating in Manchester.[5] Survival of the letters from the 1820s was undoubtedly enhanced by the passing of Sturges Bourne's Act of 1818 (58.Geo. III. cap. 69) which ensured preservation of papers relating to parish business. The letters are of two types – those written by or for paupers on their own behalf, or, the petition. Sometimes a group of neighbours or an employer would write to the overseer giving the needs of a particular pauper and explaining why they should be relieved. It had become traditional in the seventeenth and eighteenth centuries to petition quarter sessions in this way to reverse a decision made at parish level and this became an accepted way for paupers to approach overseers. In this vein, John Hall refers to himself as a 'petitioner', signing off 'with gratitude So I Remain your Humble Petitioner'.[6]

In these letters, the details of the pauper's lives became public property and were open to common scrutiny. The family's economic standing, their claims to respectability, to honour or shame, and their right to relief were open to the community for examination and judgement. Nevertheless, the facts are put forward with an assumption of reciprocity – the poor law represented a set of rights and obligations involving the paupers and the parish in a mutually reinforcing relationship. The way in which this particular relationship evolved gives us clues to both the potential and the limitations of paternalism in the early nineteenth-century context. Here I will consider how St Botolph's overseers dealt with members of the Hall family (see Figure 4.1 for family relationship details).

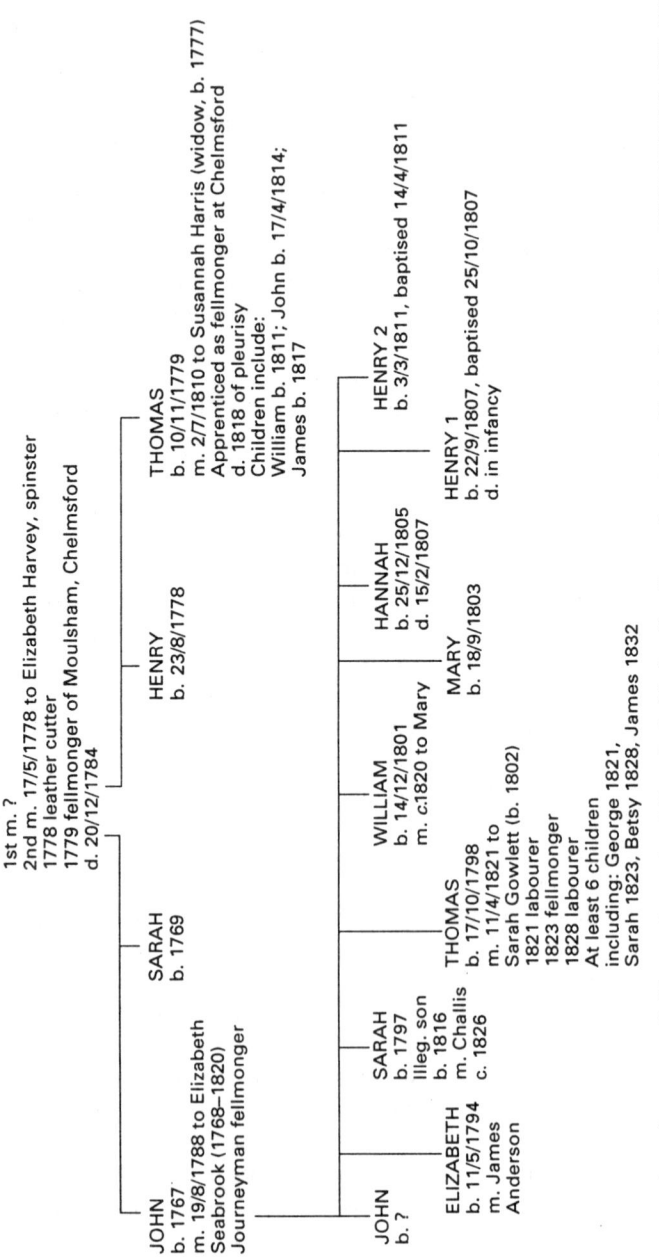

```
                            JOHN HALL
                            1st m. ?
                            2nd m. 17/5/1778 to Elizabeth Harvey, spinster
                            1778 leather cutter
                            1779 fellmonger of Moulsham, Chelmsford
                            d. 20/12/1784
   ┌────────────────────────────┼──────────────────────┐
   JOHN                         SARAH                  HENRY                  THOMAS
   b. 1767                      b. 1769                b. 23/8/1778           b. 10/11/1779
   m. 19/8/1788 to Elizabeth                                                  m. 2/7/1810 to Susannah Harris (widow, b. 1777)
   Seabrook (1768–1820)                                                       Apprenticed as fellmonger at Chelmsford
   Journeyman fellmonger                                                      d. 1818 of pleurisy
                                                                              Children include:
                                                                              William b. 1811; John b. 17/4/1814;
                                                                              James b. 1817
   ┌──────────┬─────────┐                      ┌──────────┬──────────┐
   JOHN       SARAH     Illeg. son             WILLIAM    HANNAH
   b. ?       b. 1797   b. 1816                b. 14/12/1801  b. 25/12/1805
              m. Challis                       m. c.1820 to Mary  d. 15/2/1807
              c. 1826
   ELIZABETH                                   THOMAS         MARY         HENRY 1         HENRY 2
   b. 11/5/1794                                b. 17/10/1798  b. 18/9/1803 b. 22/9/1807,   b. 3/3/1811, baptised 14/4/1811
   m. James                                    m. 11/4/1821 to             baptised 25/10/1807
   Anderson                                    Sarah Gowlett (b. 1802)     d. in infancy
                                               1821 labourer
                                               1823 fellmonger
                                               1828 labourer
                                               At least 6 children
                                               including: George 1821,
                                               Sarah 1823, Betsy 1828, James 1832
```

*Sources*  Apart from poor relief letters: International Genealogical Index; Boyd's marriage index; Chelmsford baptisms ERO D/P 94/1/9 1678–1812 (xerox 1790–7); D/P 94/1/13 1813–30; Chelmsford marriages ERO D/P 94/1/12 1754–97, 1797–1812; Chelmsford burials ERO D/P 94/1/7 1678–1812; D/P 94/1/16 1813–36; First Meeting House, Baddow Lane, Chelmsford ERO D/NC22; Colchester All Saints baptisms D/P 200/1/14.

*Figure* 4.1  The Hall family genealogy

## II

John Hall senior, a Chelmsford journeyman fellmonger (dealer in skins) died on 20 December 1784. His eldest son John, born in 1767, with whom we will mainly be concerned, went into the same business as apprentice in 1782 at the age of 15. Their masters were the firm of fellmongers, William and Thomas Johns of Baddow Lane, Chelmsford, who also owned a skin warehouse in Witham. The Johns business was not only leather-dressing but also sorting and storing wool. As such they were involved in the Essex wool textile industry, which was in decline in the late eighteenth century.[7] Nevertheless, the firm survived into the early twentieth century as one of the largest and oldest wool dealers in the county; as we will see, the Hall family's long standing as employees did not. The Halls maintained a settlement at St Botolph's parish, Colchester, one of the most commercial parts of the town, in the late eighteenth century. The family must have once lived there, and John Hall's standing must have been the same as that of his half-brother Thomas Hall, as apprentice in Chelmsford while under certificate from St Botolphs in the 1780s.[8]

The first of a long series of letters from John Hall was sent from Chelmsford to the overseers in St Botolph's in December 1811 when Hall was 44 and his wife Elizabeth was 43.[9] Hall was literate and his letters show few of the idiosyncrasies of spelling and writing found in other pauper letters. During the period from 1807 to 1814 the Hall family, along with that of John's half-brother Thomas, attended the Old Meeting House on Baddow Lane in Chelmsford. Their employers, the Johns family, were prominent non-conformists and the Halls' involvement with the chapel coincided with Thomas Johns' (John Hall's immediate employer) period as deacon from 1808 to his death in 1813. Mrs Elizabeth Hall's admittance to the chapel in April 1808 followed the establishment of the first non-conformist Sunday school in Chelmsford by the Independents. Boys met in a wool warehouse owned by the Johns family and the girls in a cottage opposite. The Independents had a reputation for promoting literacy, and this at least, is likely to be the source of some of the Halls' children's ability to read and write.[10] The Halls probably also attended Chelmsford Charity School which taught reading and writing as well as practical skills to boys and girls from the early eighteenth century.[11]

John Hall had at least nine children and most of the correspondence concerns the children born later. At the time of his first letter, on New Year's Eve 1811, he owed two pounds two shillings for rent and work was very short. His son, who lived in London, had sent for his sister (Elizabeth?). Having found her a job, she needed clothes to travel there.[12]

In March 1812 he wrote about the same matter: his son had found his sister a place in London as a servant. Another daughter also had a good place. This was Sarah, aged 15, who was probably in a domestic servant's job locally. If the overseers would send money for things, there would only be four children left in his home.[13] In the years through to 1817 Hall complained of constant debt.[14] Yet he was not on a regular allowance and he himself still paid the poor rate and into a club. Indeed, he hoped that the overseers would give him lump sums now and again to tide over short-term emergencies. While the Independent chapel also provided some alms, as the Halls slid into deepening financial problems they no longer attended.

In January 1816, Hall's 19-year-old daughter, Sarah, left her service position and gave birth to an illegitimate child.[15] She was put on regular relief of three shillings a week.[16] The birth left Sarah incapacitated for months and in May her father was still paying doctors' bills for attendance on her. At the same time, the child grew 'a Grate Boy' and Hall started to worry whether Sarah's parish allowance would suffice.[17] In March the following year the St Botolph's overseers were making attempts to track down the father of the child to secure Sarah's maintenance because she complained that she was not getting her allowance regularly from him.[18] As Sarah wrote to them, 'for what we know or Can hear he is At his fathers at Latchendon'.[19] The father was Charles Ellis ('Else' in the letters), a carpenter from Latchingdon near Purleigh in the southern agricultural hundreds of Essex. A few weeks later, Sarah wrote to the overseers in great distress as her allowance had been cut off, resulting in her father's debt.

> My parents Cannot Aford to Maintain me & the Child without my Alowance for I Can't get Anything to do I am in view of a Place in Chelmsford But I can't go to it Without the money to get me a thing or tow to go in for i am in wants of things.[20]

She was now out of contact with the father of the child who was presumably still failing to pay regular maintenance. She wrote, 'My child grows a fine Boy he only wants a Good father'.[21] She had not had any money since her brother had last been in Colchester and collected it, and if none arrived she claimed that she would have to present herself and the child to St Botolph's parish.[22] Obtaining money from St Botolph's became an endless problem for Sarah,[23] and she was frequently forced to send a note with her brother Thomas every time he went to Colchester: for example, 'i hope you will send my Childs money by the Bearer Thomas hull for i want it very bad it is next Sunday one pound 13'. On the bottom of this slip of paper the overseers had written 'pd Aug 29 1–13–0'.[24] Ellis later tried to claim the child and Sarah was forced to go to a magistrate, who underlined that the child was to be given relief, 'for he cannot demand him from me – I hope that you will inform Charles Ellis of the same'.[25] By 1821 she was still having difficulty in obtaining her regular pay.[26] Sarah's independent and almost strident tone in these letters is quite surprising; nevertheless, in financial terms, parish generosity to Sarah and her illegitimate child well exceeded that given to other members of the family.[27]

In the summer of 1818 John Hall had become ill and was unable to work.[28] His problems were compounded by having to support his daughter and the child. At the same time, work had fallen very short. When writing in September 1818, it was a Wednesday yet Hall had so far had no work to do that week.[29] Writing in thanks for the money the overseers had sent Hall he said, 'I hope I shall have my health & shant trouble you no more at Present'. He was now over 50, however, and still had a family to support. His half-brother Thomas, also a fellmonger with the Johns, had recently died of pleurisy.[30] Indeed, only three months later, Hall wrote that he had no work and neither did his two sons who were also in the fellmonger business.[31] According to the chapel minutes, an elder son, John, left for London in the second half of 1817, probably due to the bad times in fellmongering. In his letter, Hall was referring to Thomas, now 20 and to William, his 17-year-old younger brother. Indeed, some of the trips to the St Botolph's overseer made by Thomas for his sister may have been to also secure money for his father. The situation was further explained in another letter ten days later. Hall had only managed to do two days work in the week before last and three days work in the previous and present weeks, which were not sufficient to maintain his family. He was still supporting Thomas although had obviously tried to get the overseers to find him some work in his parish of settlement as he wrote, 'I have to maintain the lad that came down to you for work and but verry Little for the others to do'.[32]

Thomas Hall had been apprenticed to a tailor in Chelmsford in 1816 when he was 17. Was it a sign of the times that Thomas was not apprenticed at the Johns establishment or was it something to do with the character of Thomas? He worked for the tailor for the first year for nothing and his father gave him board and lodging. In the second year he was given seven shillings a week. With his father's financial insecurity and the support needed for his sister's illegitimate child this was obviously not considered enough and, after a year and three-quarters of the tailoring apprenticeship, Thomas had left to become a weekly labourer at W & T Johns.[33] In the winter of 1818/19 the Johns business was not flourishing, however. John Hall wrote that he had never experienced such a time of short-time working in all of his 36 years with Johns. Although Thomas worked for them, he had nothing to do.[34] Johns were experiencing the post-war downturn in the woollen industry. Hall was at a low ebb and without much money for the whole winter.[35] The following spring both John and Elizabeth his wife fell sick with fevers and would have died had they not been given medicine.[36] Hall suffered several ills in that year. In the autumn, although business seemed to have picked up, he had strained his leg and was unable to work.[37] In November, he was forced to apply for regular poor relief due to illness. He had previously been getting support from a working-man's benefit club but now explained 'my Club is shut up'.[38]

Elizabeth Hall did not survive this depressed period and died in 1820.[39] Hall negotiated with the parish for funeral expenses: 'I hope you Will not take it Amiss of my Troubling you With Letter for I have to Inform you that my Wife is no More for the Lord is been Pleasd to sepperate her from me'.[40] Thereupon his fortunes slid inexorably. Early in 1821 both John and Thomas were unemployed and had their settlements examined.[41] This was a result of a circular letter being distributed around Chelmsford stating that 'The select vestry having found that a great number of Mechanics, Labouring Men and Boys are out of employ do most earnestly recommend to all parishioners having employment for such persons will give the presence [*sic*: precedence] to their own poor'.[42] Chelmsford now urgently sought their removal to St Botolph's but this was not effected. In March of that year, John was still supporting both of his sons, one of whom was ill, and apparently Sarah and her child were back living with him again, possibly taking over the housework after the death of his wife. John Hall was now in work, however, as he tried to persuade the parish to buy him a pair of 'stout high shoes' and a pair of 'strong ancel shoes'.[43] These suggest some kind of labouring work rather than his trade as fell-monger. By now Hall was being paid regular relief by St Botolph's.[44] At the same time, possible irregularities over the payments for his wife's funeral were being investigated. One of St Botolph's overseers was sent to Chelmsford as John Hall was suspected of 'some mysterious dealings, it is thought prudent to send some person to examine into the affair'.[45] The outcome of this verbal confrontation is not recorded. However, at the end of 1821 the Halls were given more relief. John was ill, having met with an accident and broken his rib and one son had been very ill as well. The doctor's bill came to two pounds twelve shillings and again one of the overseers was dispatched to Chelmsford to see them.[46]

Following this, John Hall appears not to have applied for any more assistance until 1826. The reason for this was that he was now receiving regular relief from St Botolph's and, at the same time, had far fewer children to support.[47] In April 1821, Thomas married 19-year-old Sarah Gowlett. Twenty-two-year-old William was also married. In May 1823, he followed the path of his elder siblings and moved to London. Having found a job in London, he first applied to St Botolph's to bear his expenses of moving.[48] Shortly afterwards his wife, Mary, applied for relief for herself and their two children aged two and three, as their father had left for London to find work.[49] A few weeks later she applied for money to join him.[50] Sarah also was married, to a man called Challis, while continuing to draw relief from the parish for her son.

John Hall's letter of September 1826 was to inform St Botolph's that his youngest daughter, Mary, had been in London in a 'Verry Good Place' but had become ill and was told to return to 'her own Natural Aire'.[51] She had tried several places in Chelmsford but been told she was too ill for service. John had difficulty in accommodating her because the departure of his children from home meant he had given up housekeeping and had sold all his belongings except for his bed. 'But if you will be so Kind as to send me a Something to buy her a Bed i will get a fue things & she shall do for me or she will have to come home to you'. The case of Mary Hall was treated with great suspicion by St Botolph's who insisted on enquiring into the truth of Hall's letter, examining settlements and looking into his daughter's service.[52] Mary Gullofson of Tower Wharf wrote to certify that Mary Hall had indeed come to live with her on 24 August and suited her but she had to let her go as she was too ill to do her work. This was countersigned by a surgeon who said 'Mary Hall is afflicted with a Pulmonary complaint of a very serious Character'.[53] These letters did not have the desired effect. In January 1827, after investigations about Mary were completed, St Botolph's announced that no more relief was to be granted to John Hall.[54] Yet Hall's poverty-stricken state must have been obvious, as the Chelmsford overseer wrote to Colchester to ask whether he should relieve Hall. St Botolph's advised that he should rather be sent home.[55]

John, now aged 60, had been paid five shillings a week by St Botolph's by way of a pension.[56] This treatment did not last. The St Botolph's overseers had written in reply to those in Chelmsford to say that he had been trying to impose on the authorities by presenting Mary as dying, obtaining a certificate from a professional man and attempting to get a bed and other necessaries for her, but they had since discovered that she was married. There is no supporting evidence for this and it may be that the overseers confused Mary with Sarah. At the same time they offered to find him work in Colchester. 'As we are McAdamizing Street(s) we can find him employment'.[57] Thus did John Hall move to Colchester, the town of his settlement, a place in which there are no indications he had ever lived. His youngest son, Henry Hall, 16 in 1828, then appeared as a pauper in his own right.[58]

Some time elapsed. John was presumably kept busy by St Botolph's parish. Over three years later, at the end of 1829, John Hall was living in St Botolph's workhouse when he received a letter from his son-in-law, James Anderson, who had married his eldest daughter, Elizabeth. They lived at the end of the Essex turnpike, in Commercial Road, Whitechapel. Anderson had already written to the St Botolph's overseers about William, Hall's son who had an inflamed chest and rheumatic gout.[59] To John he said, 'at present there is no hopes of recovery'. Having no London settlement, the local parish were unable to help. Anderson had difficulty bearing the expense of his brother-in-law with his own young family and slight wages. John Hall must have a 'stony heart' not to reply. Anderson wrote to the parish that he was

> under the painfull necessity of writing to you concerning a young man named William Hall ... I am very much surprised that his Father who knows his complaint so well should neglect coming or sending to ... as it is almost a week since I wrote to him about him as his father is known to you Gentlemen he being under your care as an inmate or pensioner I fully expected that he would either have come or sent to me.[60]

Elizabeth Anderson wrote that William was 'as bad as he can be to be alive, & not able to be removed since the hour he was taken'. She said:

> for it is impossible to bear the trouble & expense out of my husband's wages only 15s Per Week & my being so ill, I am not able to do for him, therefore we are obligated to have People to be with him night & day, As this is the worst illness he ever had & as it is not my husband's brother it is so much the worse for me & I must say that both Wm & me takes it very hard that you nor marry [Mary] have not wrote ... he is so bad his speech & his sencess have left him at times & when he has come to himself all his talk has been about you ...[61]

The overseers appear to have sent no money to help William; perhaps they suspected another trick was afoot and being played by the literate members of the Hall family to goad the local authorities into giving them money. Indeed, William was still alive in 1832.[62] Realistically speaking, of course, John was in no position to go to his family, and this looks as if it could have been a tactical move on the part of his children and in-laws to reinforce their demand for relief.

## III

John Hall's removal to Colchester and final residency in the workhouse came about because he had supposedly deceived the overseers over Mary's marriage, in the autumn of 1826. Yet it may also have been a result of the problems the poor relief officials were concurrently having with his son, Thomas Hall. Whichever the reason, the implication is that the boundaries of appropriate behaviour for paupers were tightly drawn. Thomas and Sarah had started to apply for relief almost as soon as they set up house together.[63] Shortly after this, however, by the birth of their second child in 1823, Thomas' occupation was again described as 'fellmonger' rather than 'labourer'. Little was heard of the family until the summer of 1826, when Thomas and his family appeared in Colchester and put themselves into the workhouse 'in consequence of not being able to procure employ'. St Botolph's agreed to allow him twelve shillings a week on condition he supported himself, his wife and family, worked on the roads and paid his own rent.[64] This was based on a resolution passed in the parish in May 1826 that those who applied for relief and were unable to get work were to be employed by the parish surveyor of the roads. The same scheme employed his father the following winter.[65] Such disciplined work did not suit Thomas, however, and two weeks later he had not removed himself and his family from the workhouse and had refused to go and work in the parish gravel pit.[66] The overseers complained to the magistrate and at this Thomas made off.

It was harvest-time and Thomas Hall disappeared leaving his wife, Sarah, and three children in St Botolph's workhouse. Mrs Seward, the keeper of the workhouse, applied for articles for Mrs Hall who was 'quite destitute'.[67] The overseers advertised his disappearance all over the county and in London, circulating a description in three newspapers and offering a reward.[68]

> The said Thomas Halls is a native of Chelmsford, by trade a Skinner, is about 36 years of age, 5 feet 6 or 7 inches high, thin visage, light hair, and light complexion, and had on when he went away a short white woollen jacket and light canvas trowsers, and is supposed to be now working somewhere as a labourer. [He was, in fact, 27 – but poverty ages people.][69]

Just two days after the appearance of this description in the *Chelmsford Chronicle*, the overseers received a letter from James Milbanks, an officer of Great Wakering, Rochford, to say that Hall was working in his parish, 'A remote place where A many of our Essex chaps especially Runaways fly too when they desert their families'.[70] He knew Hall personally and was aware that he had previously worked for Mr Johns. Due to labour shortages, extra harvest-men were always in demand in the Essex hundreds.[71] He suggested that the St Botolph's overseer should immediately go there and arrest him: 'his wife has had a letter from him about the middle of Augst. but the man that wrote did not seal it as he said he was going to send something in it but what he did not say please to ask her if she had it'. Clearly the suspicion is, that far from making off altogether, the Halls' plan was that while Sarah and the children were kept by the parish in the workhouse, Hall would be earning harvest money. On the outside, Milbanks wrote, 'be as quick as you can after you have seen her for fear of A Letter going to him to disturb him'. One significant point to emerge from this letter is that while it appears that Thomas could read and write, he had letters written for him. Yet Thomas had signed the marriage register whereas his wife crossed it and, as we will later see, he did write letters although his standard of literacy was below that of his father and sisters. What this points to is the ability to opt in and out of the literacy process. Perhaps while working hard he simply found it too much effort: after all, Thomas had tendencies to laziness. Perhaps when earning harvest money he was even prepared to pay for a letter to be written for him.

Thus did Thomas find himself in Colchester gaol. He had no sooner been arrested than he was applying for release because he had found work to go to in London, and applied for the carriage and clothes to travel there from the parish.[72] Indeed, he would seem to have had this arranged for the end of the harvest prior to his arrest. The proof of this was a letter from a Mr Saunders, a builder in Bermondsey who, writing on Friday night, said 'i beg to inform you that I can give Th. Halls work if he can come midday as we are rather Busy an i must suit my self with another Labourer'.[73] We can imagine that Hall had negotiated this either through his employer in the Essex hundreds or perhaps through a network of communication between casual labourers. Hall was almost immediately on the coach to London, paid for by the overseers, and had been given cash to get some things to set himself up with.[74] Saunder's operations centred on New Road and the overseers clearly thought that the possibilities for work in building the new streets of Georgian London might get the Hall family off their books for ever.[75]

They were probably very disappointed then to receive a letter from Hall in December saying that, although there was plenty of work to do, he was not well enough to do it. His wife had a bad breast and was unable to look after the family, 'for my wife expects to be confined every day and I cant Get a nus [nurse] for les then 4 shilen a weak'. If the parish did not send money he would have to resort to the local overseers. Of course, they could remove him, so the St Botolph's reply, on the same piece of paper, was to send a pound to meet the costs of the confinement, remind him that he was in bad odour at home due to his former conduct and promise to send a member of the vestry around to see him next time someone was in London.[76]

Barely three weeks later, Hall requested another pound as his wife was confined and very ill due to lack of nourishment. He said that he would not have had to trouble them if he had not 'lost my time through Liven so bad in the sumer'.[77] This time his request was not granted. Four days later he was unemployed again, discharged from the building work.[78] This time he resorted to the local parish of St George's, who wanted to remove the family back to Colchester. Thomas wrote that he had 'no work to do i expets another Place of work in another fortnight and if do not want to come home if i can helpe it'.[79] He wanted non-resident poor relief on a regular basis: 'pleas to aloue us sumthng a weeak til i get sume worke to do for if [I] do not like to keep riten so every weake'. Without a regular allowance they would have to come home 'for the worke is bad in London for there is nun to be got at present'. They had no bread to give the children and 'me, and my wife never broak our fast for too Days'.[80] Hall was out of manual labour due to a bad foot, which forced him to go to Guy's Hospital as an out-patient.[81] The following month his wife applied for, and was granted, a shirt for Thomas and shoes for herself.[82]

They made it through the early summer without any further applications but at the time of year when Thomas had, the year previously, sought harvest earnings they had again to approach St Botolph's due to unemployment.[83] Indeed, Thomas must have committed some misdemeanour in the autumn as Sarah Hall was given an allowance during his imprisonment.[84] On leaving prison he was again without work, and later claimed that he was unable to support his family with his present level of earnings, a mere five shillings a week so he claimed.[85] He had to be sent more clothes and in December asked for a regular allowance.[86] He was granted four shillings a week to take them through the winter and his wife's next confinement.[87]

During the next few years, both Thomas and Sarah seem to have moved between living in Colchester and Bermondsey several times, presumably sometimes being removed. In April 1828 the overseers did not grant his application for the expenses of moving back to London.[88] In May, Sarah applied for clothing for her five children and a weekly allowance when Thomas was sent to the treadmill in Colchester.[89] She made several other similar applications through the summer of 1828 when the family were back in London.[90] A man whom the overseers knew and respected was sent to interview Thomas in the autumn of 1828. He had found Hall's lodgings with some difficulty. At this point, Thomas' wife and children were back in Colchester. The man could get little out of Thomas about his future movements except that he thought he might return to Colchester for an uncertain length of time. He had recently sent his wife ten shillings but it was not clear when he would be able to send more money as he was not always in constant work. He had also muttered something about going to New South Wales 'which I suppose you know about which I think would be the best place for him as he will always be a trouble to the Parish'.[91]

One reason for Sarah Hall's frequent trips back to Colchester may have been because the impoverished state of the family was not visible to the overseers, as she invariably returned with a new set of clothes.[92] When the poor law officials referred to the poor, their concern was often more with their clothes and external appearance than whether they had bread or not, so there are frequent references to nakedness, lack of cleanliness and whether poor people are 'decent and sweet'. This emphasis on external appearance and respectability suggests that the very invisibility of the poor who wrote letters worked to their disadvantage. The signifiers of morality, of being a member of the deserving poor, were still face-to-face. By the winter of 1832/3, Hall was still receiving varying amounts of money from the overseers, from twelve shillings and sixpence when a special need arose, to sixpence at another time.[93]

IV

Within the space of three generations the family fortunes of the Halls had sunk from John Hall senior's position as a journeyman fellmonger to his grandson Thomas being a labourer with only casual work who was seen as a habitual pauper and criminal in his twenties – a not untypical experience for those caught in the downside of the Industrial Revolution. There is no evidence that John Hall senior ever claimed poor relief. His son John did not resort to relief until he was in his forties. By then he was supporting the end of a long line of children while finding inadequate work in a declining industry. He also had to support adult children who, a generation earlier, would have been in apprenticeship or service. While John junior had been apprenticed at the age of fifteen, his son Thomas did not leave home until he married in his early twenties. It was lack of subsistence which partly lay behind the ill-health, particularly chest problems, which dogged the family. Nevertheless, the sense of family was strong (or at least, was portrayed in their letters as such). John senior supported his children into adulthood and was ready to take them back into the family home even when he had no resources. He was still seen as the patriarch to be resorted to even when he was in the workhouse. Thomas set up a household in chronically unstable economic circumstances. He and his wife and children spent much time separated in an effort to get some money together. Meanwhile, their activities were viewed as criminal by the authorities.[94]

This could be because the parish had a long memory. A late eighteenth-century court case had involved Thomas Hall, John's uncle, a labourer in some sort of wool business, who had been trying to set himself up as a fellmonger in 1792. He was prosecuted by Colchester borough quarter sessions for purchasing stolen hair from a tannery owned by William Swinborne. William Clark, Swinborne's servant, went to Hall to purchase a comb for twopence. Hall asked him 'to help him to some hair'. Clark answered 'I don't know that I can'. Hall replied that if he did he would make sure he wasn't found out, so then Clark took him some hair for which he received sixpence from Hall. Hall then said that he would give him sixpence per pound for as much as he could get. He then frequently took Hall small quantities of hair, never receiving more than ninepence in value at a time: at one time, instead of sixpence for a pound of hair, he received six small oranges.[95] It is interesting to recall this series of criminal acts when we reflect on the Halls' later connection with St Botolph's parish. The 'wheeler-dealer', Thomas Hall, was sentenced to a public whipping on market day and three months' hard labour. For the 13 weeks after his conviction, St Botoph's sent the money for Thomas' family's upkeep to Chelmsford parish.[96]

John Hall himself did not, as far as we know, ever commit any misdemeanour but his actions are nevertheless viewed as suspicious. The parish officials treated the Halls as a family collective; indeed, the actions of one member would influence the ways in which the officials treated another member. They were troublesome – a bad sort. It is no accident that John Hall was transferred to the workhouse when his son was in so much trouble. This was more than a little paradoxical when working-class lives so often involved resort to individual strategies in order to survive.[97] How did the Halls really rub along together? What can be made of the overtones of suspected trickery that the officials worried about? Could the appeals to a sense of family actually be music to the ears of the middle-class overseers, a desperate façade enabling them to get what they wanted? When dealing with responses as individual as these, there are more questions than answers raised by interrogating the text for clues to the reasons behind family strategies.

The Halls' communications in themselves were sometimes treated as acts of criminal deviousness by the overseers. In this context, what were the political aspects of literacy? John Hall was literate, as were his daughters, Elizabeth, Sarah and Mary. However, there is not much evidence that his sons were very experienced at writing. Thomas wrote some of his letters in a very rudimentary hand, but others were dictated. How did access to literacy change people's experience of relief? Paupers who committed themselves to paper may have been seen very differently from those who appeared in person at the vestry. John Thurtle, the south Essex pauper shoemaker (whom I consider elsewhere), was certainly discouraged from writing to his settlement parish.[98] The letters reflect that, as David Vincent has written, elaborating on Roger Schofield's analysis of literacy patterns, in this period literacy and illiteracy were side by side, in families and in communities.[99] As such, literacy could be a resource to be borrowed when the need arose, and also to be used or not used when appropriate.[100]

Literate or not, what the letters do convey is a keen awareness by the poor of their own rights to poor relief. John Hall, for example, argued 'you know Sir Every Poor has A Doctor Allowd them' and, during the negotiations about paying for his wife's funeral, 'As Parrishes do Assist At Such A Time ... I hope I Shall have no Occasion to Trouble you No more for Any thing if the Lord grants me my health as I hope he Will by his Blessing'.[101] The clear idea of a right to poor relief appears in letters from other paupers. John Thurtle wrote in 1831 to the village of his settlement that he was

> great destute of common miserys [necessities] to keep my familey clain and decent and as every parish is giving those things that is nesery [necessary] to keep their one [own] pore clane and decent so i think it my Duty to aply to you for to send me som reliefe to helpe me.[102]

Samuel White, a silk-weaver and Chelmsford parishioner resident in Halstead, must have read the list of outdoor poor as he complained that he had only been sent seven pounds over a period of five years compared with the sixteen pounds that Daniel Rising, a tan-yard worker, had received from Chelmsford in the year of 1821 alone.[103] This man had a clear idea of what he felt his entitlement to relief should be. These rights were open to being contested but it is nevertheless the case that the labouring poor did have a forum for negotiating issues which were crucial to securing their livelihood, even if the boundaries which circumscribed this were tightly drawn and the poverty-stricken had to accept that they fell into a category of 'the poor'. The poor law can be seen as a 'multi-use right' similar to the use of criminal law, and as a result its implementation was open to negotiation.[104]

The language of these letters is interesting. John Hall's letters contain a sense of servility and obligation but this underlying tone is entirely absent in those of his children. A patronage relationship is implied by the fact that the Halls referred to the overseers as 'friends'. John Hall said, 'I have No Other friend but you to go to for Anything', as did his daughter, Sarah: 'I should take you as a Great friend'.[105] In particular, John's phrase, 'Sir I hope you have Not Shut up the Bowels of Compation Intirely Concerning Me' suggests that, since the biblical use of 'bowels' is made in a similar way to references to the heart, affection was almost what the Halls expected from the parish.[106] While John often made religious allusions in his letters ('by the Blessing of God'), this was never done by his children. The Halls did not find it necessary to provide much evidence that they had resorted to self-help in an effort to remedy their situation. There is also very little suggestion of the involvement of employers. John Hall only once mentions that Mr Johns had written to the overseers about his inability to work and that was when Hall was both ill and 60 years old.[107] Hall makes a prior assumption of his entitlement to relief and pursues it despite the distance and the length of time since his family had actually been resident in their settlement parish.

In summary, the poor were well aware of their rights to relief and they could defend them, by appeals to magistrates if necessary. However, in their day-to-day dealings with overseers, they employed strategies to strengthen their case for obtaining a higher level of relief or regular payments. These varied depending on the character of both the pauper and the overseer they were dealing with – some letters are deferential in tone, some obsequious, others demanding. As the case of the Hall family has shown, their family reputation and their appearance were also of issue. Paternalism may have been disappearing in the 1820s but for the poor and their patrons, despite the enormous growth of poverty, an abiding sense of localism – forming networks which connected cities and towns – still shaped the nature of their interactions.

ACKNOWLEDGEMENTS

The original research for this piece was carried out when I was Essex County Council Research Fellow in Local History at the University of Essex, 1990–3. Subsequently, I am grateful to the University of Bristol Faculty of Arts Research Fund for financial help with photocopying. Thanks to Tim Hitchcock and Tom Sokoll for useful comments on the text.

## NOTES

1. G. Himmelfarb, *The Idea of Poverty* (New York, 1984), p.14.
2. They are presently being transcribed into book form by Thomas Sokoll: see his forthcoming *Essex Pauper Letters c.1820–1834* and 'Voices of the Poor: Pauper Letters and Poor Law Provision in Essex 1780–1834' in A. Digby, J. Innes and R.M. Smith (eds), *Poverty and Relief in England from the Sixteenth to the Twentieth Century* (Cambridge University Press, forthcoming). A.P. Hutchings, 'The Relief of the Poor in Chelmsford 1821–1829: Case Histories and Pauper's Correspondence', *Essex Review* 257: LXV (1956), 42–56 puts together some family letters.
3. G. Boyer, *An Economic History of the English Poor Law 1750–1850* (Cambridge, 1990), p.258.
4. Essex Record Office, Chelmsford (hereafter ERO). ERO D/P 94/18/42.
5. J.S. Taylor, *Poverty, Migration and Settlement in the Industrial Revolution: Sojourners' Narratives* (Palo Alto, 1989) analyses the large number of extant letters, bills and petitions for Kirkby Lonsdale. J.S. Taylor, 'A Different Kind of Speenhamland: Non-resident Relief in the Industrial Revolution', *Journal of British Studies*, 30:2 (1991), 183–208: p.199 finds that early nineteenth-century Manchester had as many non-resident as resident poor and calls the system 'industrial speenhamland'. See his contribution to this volume, Chapter 5, 'Voices in the Crowd: The Kirkby Lonsdale Township Letters, 1809–36'. Pauper letters are also used by K.D.M. Snell, *Annals of the Labouring Poor* (Cambridge, 1985).
6. ERO D/P 203/18/1 6/5/1816.
7. J. Booker, *Essex and the Industrial Revolution* (Chelmsford, 1974), p.54. For Essex cloth production in the late eighteenth century, see Chapter 2 of my book *Adapting to Capitalism: Working Women in the English Economy 1700–1850* (Macmillan, 1996).
8. ERO P/Ca9 15/5/1821. This is made clear in this later settlement examination of Susannah Hall, Thomas' widow.
9. The details of John's early married life are not clear. The fact that the earliest children (presumably John and Elizabeth, named for their parents) are born some time after the parents' marriage may be because John was in the militia. His name appears on a list of the St Botolph's militia in 1793 in ERO D/P 203/12/34, when, assuming this is the same John, he is married but childless. At the same time, this may be a different John because he later says that he worked for Johns for 36 years, suggesting no break after gaining his indentures. The first letter appears after the birth of their last child, Henry, in 1811.
10. ERO D/NC22 1/3. Mrs Hall was admitted 4/8/1808; John Junior on 30/7/1817 but shortly afterwards left for London. H.M. Wisbey and R.J. Church, *Our Story 1808–1958: London Road Congregational School, Chelmsford* (Chelmsford, 1958), p.7; H.S.C. 'The olde meeting house, Baddowe Lane, Chelmsford' (1927). Baptisms but no marriage or burial registers are extant for the early nineteenth century.
11. A.V. Sowman, 'The Chelmsford Charity School 1713–1878', *Essex Journal*, 4 (1969), 88–95.

12. ERO D/P 203/12/51 31/12/1811. Although not on regular relief, John had been sent one pound on 29/4/1806 at the same time as another non-resident and again on 27/6/1806.
13. ERO D/P 203/12/51 16/3/1812.
14. ERO D/P 203/18/1 8/12/1814, 19/3/1817, 5/6/1817.
15. ERO P/Ca2 16/1/1816.
16. ERO D/P 203/18/1 29/2/1816. In July 1818 she is on the same level of allowance. In D/P 203/12/50 she is paid three shillings for the child.
17. ERO D/P 203/18/1 6/5/1816.
18. D/P 203/18/1 letter from G. Wiffen, Springfield 7/3/1817 though refers to 'Mary Halls'. It seems likely that she had confused the Hall girls.
19. ERO D/P 203/18/1 4/3/1817.
20. ERO D/P 203/18/1 31/3/1817.
21. ERO D/P 203/18/1 20/5/1817.
22. ERO D/P 203/18/1 24/4/1817
23. ERO D/P 203/18/1 21/6/1819.
24. ERO D/P 203/12/51 c.1820 and other letters in 1820, e.g. 1/11/1820.
25. ERO D/P 203/18/1 2/7/1819.
26. ERO D/P 203/12/51 9/4/1821.
27. For other evidence of fairly generous support to unmarried mothers, see M.E. Fissell, 'Gender, Life-cycle and the Old Poor Law' (unpublished paper, 1992). Evidence from cultural history suggests, to quote Perry, 'the centrality of representations of motherhood to eighteenth-century English culture as a newly elaborated social and sexual identity for women'. See R. Perry, 'Colonizing the Breast: Sexuality and Maternity in Eighteenth-century England' in J.C. Fout (ed.), *Forbidden History* (University of Chicago Press, 1992), pp.107–37 for a stimulating discussion of these issues.
28. ERO D/P 203/18/12 6/8/1818.
29. ERO D/P 203/12/51 5/9/1818. D/P 203/12/50 John Hall was paid one pound in September.
30. ERO D/P 203/18/1 17/5/1818, when a surgeon is called and diagnoses pleurisy.
31. ERO D/P 203/12/51 11/12/1818.
32. ERO D/P 203/18/1 21/12/1818.
33. ERO P/Ca 8.
34. ERO D/P 203/18/1 5/2/1819.
35. ERO D/P 203/18/1 11/2/1819.
36. ERO D/P 203/18/1 4/5/1819, letter from surgeon in Chelmsford.
37. ERO D/P 203/18/1 6/9/1819.
38. ERO D/P 203/18/1 12/11/1819.
39. ERO D/P 203/12/51 1/11/1820 and several other letters about funeral expenses.
40. ERO D/P 203/12/51 5/7/1820.
41. ERO P/Ca8 20/1/1821 and 13/2/1821.
42. ERO D/P 94/8/2 1/1/1821.
43. ERO D/P 203/12/51 22/3/1821.
44. ERO D/P 203/12/5109/6/1821.

45. ERO D/P 203/8/2 11/6/1821.
46. ERO D/P 203/8/203/12/1821.
47. ERO D/P 94/8/4 30/9/1822, Chelmsford vestry minutes record that John Hall is paid four shillings a week by Colchester.
48. ERO D/P 203/8/2 13/5/1823.
49. ERO D/P 203/8/2 26/5/1823.
50. ERO D/P 203/8/2 15/7/1823.
51. ERO D/P 203/18/1 3/9/1826.
52. ERO D/P 203/8/2 5/9/1826.
53. ERO D/P 203/18/1 12/9/1826.
54. ERO D/P 203/8/2 9/1/1827.
55. ERO D/P 203/8/2 23/1/1827.
56. ERO D/P 203/18/1 17/1/1827. For more details on the treatment of the elderly under the Old Poor Law, see M. Barker-Read, 'The Treatment of the Aged Poor in Five Selected West Kent Parishes from Settlement to Speenhamland' (unpublished PhD thesis, Open University, 1988).
57. ERO D/P 94/18/42 23/1/1827. There is no record of a marriage of Mary Hall, but there is no register of marriages conducted in the Independent meeting house on Baddow Lane. However, it could be significant that no evidence of a marriage was produced for the poor law officials.
58. ERO D/P 203/12/45 29/8/1828.
59. ERO D/P 203/18/1 1/12/1829.
60. ERO D/P 203/18/1 8/12/1829.
61. ERO D/P 203/18/1 15/12/1829.
62. ERO D/P 203/12/47 7/9/1832.
63. ERO D/P 203/8/2 22/10/1822.
64. ERO D/P 203/18/2 11/7/1826.
65. D/P 203/8/2 30/5/1826. On 27/2/1827 the rates of pay for work on the streets was drawn up by St Botolph's.
66. ERO D/P 203/18/2 25/7/1826.
67. ERO D/P 203/8/2 29/8/1826.
68. ERO D/P 203/12/45 8/8/1826.
69. *Chelmsford Chronicle* 8/9/1826.
70. C. Vancouver, *General View of the Agriculture in the County of Essex* (London 1795), p.68 commented on the scarcity of hands in the hundreds and the reliance on trampers. Anon., 'Life on an Essex Farm Sixty Years Ago', *Essex Review* 36: IX (1900), 220–7 described how, before the days of fertiliser, south Essex harvests would take place two weeks prior to those on the claylands. The *Chelmsford Chronicle* contains a number of advertisements supporting Milbanks' point, such as, in February 1821, for John Mulley, bricklayer of Ashfield in Suffolk, who 'went to the hundreds of Essex about thirteen years ago, in order to procure work there, and has not since been heard of ...'.
71. ERO D/P 203/18/1 10/9/1826.
72. ERO D/P 203/8/2 15/9/1826.
73. ERO D/P 203/18/1 3/9/1826.
74. ERO D/P 203/18/1 15/9/1826.
75. R. Creighton's 1831 map of London shows these new roads being opened up.

76. ERO D/P 203/18/1 20/12/1826.
77. ERO D/P 203/18/1 14/1/1827.
78. ERO D/P 203/18/1 18/1/1827.
79. ERO D/P 203/18/1 26/1/1827.
80. ERO D/P 203/18/1 8/2/1827.
81. ERO D/P 203/18/1 11/2/1827.
82. ERO D/P 203/8/2 20/3/1827. There are notable differences between John's wife, Elizabeth, and Thomas's wife, Sarah. Sarah is forced to resort to endless attempts to patch the family finances together, which were never mentioned for Elizabeth. On the under-explored subject of female strategies for survival and working-class ideology in this period, see S. D'Cruze, 'Care, Diligence and "Usfull Pride": Gender, Industrialisation and the Domestic Economy c.1770–1840', *Women's History Review* 3:3 (1994), 315–45.
83. ERO D/P 203/8/2 4/9/1827.
84. ERO D/P 203/8/2 18/9/1827, 2/10/1827.
85. ERO D/P 203/8/2 13/10/1827, 27/11/1827.
86. ERO D/P 203/8/2 11/12/1827 sent jacket and trousers; 4/3/1828 sent shoes.
87. ERO D/P 203/8/2 14/12/1827.
88. ERO D/P 203/8/2 29/4/1828.
89. ERO D/P 203/8/2 13/5/1828. An extract from *The Courier* 1/3/1823 described the working of the treadmill in the house of industry in Grimsby. By the weight of four men it ground corn for 100 inmates and was for the purpose of curing all "sham sick", idle and disorderly inmates'. The *Chelmsford Chronicle* 25/2/1825 also contained a report on the use of the treadwheel in several counties.
90. ERO D/P 203/8/2 24/6/1828, 5/8/1828.
91. ERO D/P 203/18/1 25/9/1828, letter from William S. Mason, Limehouse Fields.
92. ERO D/P 203/12/1 26/10/1832, for example.
93. ERO D/P 203/12/1.
94. Comparing what we know of the lives of Thomas Hall and Thomas Carter shows the importance of prevailing economic circumstances. Thomas Carter was a tailor, born in Colchester, who published his autobiography, *Memoirs of a Working Man* (London, 1845). While their characters were obviously very different – Carter tending to pious diligence and Hall to recalcitrance – Carter arrived in the right place, doing the right job of tailoring, at the right time, while Hall was apprenticed in 1816 and came onto the labour market just too late, after the French Wars, when demobilisation combined with poor trade conditions and low wages. Carter married and started his family much later than Hall. Hall applied almost immediately for the poor law allowance scheme whereas Carter never had to resort to parish relief at all. Yet Carter's apprenticeship as an odd-job boy would not have equipped him for high-class tailoring. Carter had many different employers, whereas the Halls maintained a sense of loyalty to the Johns, despite short time working and the fact that the Johns made minimal efforts to alleviate their lack of money or support them in the trials and tribulations of claiming poor relief.
95. Colchester Borough Quarter Sessions Minutes of Session and Bundles, 1792.

96. ERO D/P 203/12/34.
97. L.A. Tilly, 'Individual Lives and Family Strategies in the French Proletariat' in R. Wheaton and T.K. Hareven (eds), *Family and Sexuality in French History* (Philadelphia, 1980), pp.201–23.
98. P. Sharpe, 'Malaria, Machismo and Medical Poor Relief: A Case from Essex 1830–1834' in A. Digby, J. Innes and R.M. Smith (eds), *Poverty and Relief in England from the Sixteenth to the Twentieth Century* (Cambridge University Press, forthcoming).
99. D. Vincent, *Literacy and Popular Culture: England 1750–1914* (Cambridge, 1989); R.S. Schofield, 'Dimensions of Illiteracy in England 1750–1850', *Explorations in Economic History* 10:4 (1973), 437–54. See also M. Sanderson, 'Literacy and Social Mobility in the Industrial Revolution in England', *Past and Present* LVI (1972), 75–104, and debate with T. Laqueur in *Past and Present* LXIV (1974), 96–112.
100. On this point, and for a discussion of 'scriptual power', see T. Sokoll, 'Old Age in Poverty: The Record of Essex Pauper Letters, 1780–1834', Chapter 6 in this volume.
101. ERO D/P 203/12/51 5/7/1820.
102. ERO D/P 238/18/1 2/12/1831.
103. Hutchings, 'The Relief of the Poor' and D/P 94/18/42 letters 1824–9.
104. J. Brewer and J. Styles, *An Ungovernable People* (London, 1980), p.20.
105. ERO D/P 203/18/1 11/1/1827.
106. ERO D/P 203/18/1 5/2/'1719'; D/P 203/18/1 1/8/1826. N. Tadmor, '"Family" and "friend" in *Pamela*: A Case Study in the History of the Family in Eighteenth-century England', *Social History* 14 (1989), 289–306 suggests directly referring to patrons as friends is unusual in the mid-eighteenth century.
107. ERO D/P 203/18/1 1/11/1827.

# 5 Voices in the Crowd: The Kirkby Lonsdale Township Letters, 1809–36
James Stephen Taylor

Mr Stephen Garner I Disier you be so good as to Reed Thoas few lines over be for the gentlemen at the meeting First gentlemen Betty Teabay Disiers you give a Tension To what I going to say I Never was so Ragged Since I A Pension Came I have Not A Clogg to my foot nor A Pettcoat to Put on Nor A Hancorcher to Put on my Neck Nor No Stockins to my legs Nor no Singlets to my Back & for Stase I never had Non this maney years And you Send to me A Bedgoun Which I Never had Send be Fore you Send me a Shiff that was no change What Did you think I must change into while it was washed And I Disier you Send me a gown with those things For I shall be Starved to Deth in this thing Bedgown This Winter And by Doing you much oblidge your obedant Servant Betty Teabay[1]

Innocent of punctuation and idiosyncratic in spelling and capitalisation, this brief letter of 3 September 1809 was written to the poor law authorities of Kirkby Lonsdale by a non-resident pauper. Others like her also wrote home – from Lancaster, Preston, Blackburn, Wigan, Bradford, London, Glasgow and Wales, from 94 identifiable addresses and 22 unidentifiable ones (including Betty Teabay's). It is, by any standard, a valuable record for the social historian exploring the human impact of early industrialism.[2]

From China to Italy to Massachusetts, some historians have traded shovels and picks for spoons and toothbrushes to engage in microhistory.[3] Countervailing preoccupations of social historians are with elites, numbers and borrowings from the social sciences. Whatever one's particular interest, surely no one could argue with the observation that social history has become mightily complex![4] Pullulating avenues of inquiry and theoretical constructs work towards making academic social history an insider's game. On the macrohistorical level there is William McNeill's largely unanswered appeal to professional historians for a history that truly means something – transnational, synthetic and motivated, in McNeill's words, by 'a stubbornly sophomoric urge to understand things'.[5] Yet the macrohistorical may have more in common with the microhistorical than either have with the middle ground, as Lewis Namier suggested long ago.[6] This chapter seeks to explore that assumption by attempting to link the scarcely literate scrawls of deracinated paupers with the beginnings of the most fundamental transformation in modern history – the great technological and social revolution that, whatever the earlier signs and portents, may be said to have begun in northern Britain in the late eighteenth century.[7]

We owe the Kirkby Lonsdale Township letters to Stephen Garnett, who now lies under the best-preserved memorial stone in the churchyard there, sheltered by the boughs of a cedar, and not far from the path to Ruskin's view of the upper Lune valley. Garnett was baptised on Christmas Day, 1763, in the West Riding of Yorkshire church of Marton-in-Craven, and in 1787 married an illiterate woman 14 years his senior at Thornton-in-Lonsdale, but he chose to live the greater part of his life in one of the loveliest valleys in England. At the time of his marriage he was already described as a resident of Kirkby Lonsdale in the county of Westmorland. There he pursued the occupations of grocer, seedsman and auctioneer, occupying a modest house and shop on Main Street. When he died on 17 July 1840 his whole estate was valued at under £800.[8]

It is unclear precisely when he became involved in poor law administration, but Betty Teabay's letter of 1809 is among the earliest he received; the last is dated 22 August 1836. Between those dates Garnett is titled variously but, whatever his precise office, he was the recipient, directly or indirectly, of correspondence from paupers living outside of the township, as well as of letters from other townships' officials and the landlords, friends and family members of individuals, settled for poor law purposes in Kirkby Lonsdale but actually living elsewhere. Perhaps it was Garnett's fine hand that led the open vestry to entrust the correspondence to him. There are only a few letters by him in the some 1250 items now extant but there is enough, together with his marginalia, to state that he wrote well, and that he was intelligent, legalistic and highly organised; so organised that he left what is surely one of the most complete records of local poor law administration for the early nineteenth century.

He was, of course, paid for his services. Ten pounds per annum was specified when he was styled 'Guardian of the Poor' on 3 March 1814, but it was undoubtedly even more indirectly profitable for an outsider, given his various businesses, to employ his considerable talents in bringing order to the township's records, which Frederic Morton Eden had found in 1797 to be 'very confused'.[9]

Eden described Kirkby Lonsdale as a market town where pack-thread, shoes and coarse bags were made for export, and which was well supplied with inns and ale-houses. These last owed something to a location on major roads, north to Kendal and Carlisle, southeast to the West Riding and southwest to Lancaster and beyond to the industrial centres of Lancashire. It was a large town for the region. Indeed, it was second in the county, with 1283 inhabitants in 1801, rising to 1686 in 1831.[10] The Parson and White 1829 *Directory* provides a fuller occupational listing than Eden's, but there are few surprises. There were the expected numbers of attorneys, blacksmiths, confectioners, hairdressers, drapers, painters, spirit merchants, tailors, tanners, tea-dealers and wheelwrights that one might expect in a market town. One significant fact emerges from the listing: there was no single industry of note in a town expanding at the rate of 10 per cent a decade in the early nineteenth century.[11] Little wonder that migration was an attractive option to the unemployed. The routes were easy to the industrial centres to the south and elsewhere. It was certainly not for aesthetic reasons the poor chose to leave. Apart from the urge to find employment, there was an additional incentive – the support migrants could hope to receive from the township should they experience illness or unemployment as sojourners in other townships.

This story is not exceptional. Other townships did the same, and it was one of the ways a labour force emerged in burgeoning centres of industry. What *is* exceptional is that Stephen Garnett saved this particular township's records, including the revelatory correspondence. The letters are tied in bundles, the first covering 1809 to 1817 and the rest by the year, labelled in Garnett's hand. They are part of an extensive collection of poor law records deposited at various times between 1963 and 1981 in the Cumbria Record Office in Kendal by the Parish Council and by the Reverend K.A. Arnold, one-time Vicar of Kirkby Lonsdale.[12]

We owe gratitude to the combination of indifference and enlightenment that has preserved these letters regarding 257 individuals and families. One reason the collection came into being in the first instance, which the letters make clear, was that Garnett was both cautious and dilatory in disbursing the township's relief, even as he was careful in preserving the fruits of those qualities. There are a variety of approaches to the letters – as an element in the study of a particular township's poor law administration, as exemplary of non-resident relief in the industrial north, as the centrepiece of pauper prosopography. The approach attempted here is a reflection on the voices found in the letters. Four are distinctive: the formal, stylised petition, usually commissioned by the applicant; the informational voice, telling of life in a Blackburn or a Manchester, and reminding of needs to be met; the insistent voice, where the need is too compelling for anything other than the expression thereof; and the desperate, even threatening voice, demanding a positive response or the pauper will return to Kirkby Lonsdale or appeal to magistrates. The same correspondent may use different voices at different times, or even in the same letter. However, on the whole, there is a consistency within the letters from a particular claimant (and three-fifths of the correspondents wrote more than once).

In selecting letters for this chapter, geographical diversity and variety of circumstances figured. Only letters presumed to have been written by the paupers themselves are included. The voices are conveyed through the examination of four issues – the truth of the claim; the literacy of the paupers; family relationships; and the common causes (needy children, unemployment, accidents, illness) that united this choir of claimants.

George and Ann Bainbridge were living in Manchester at least as early as 1802 when a printed bill for four of their children's coffins was sent to the overseer of Kirkby Lonsdale (a bill still outstanding in 1811). Ann wrote to her township on 6 March 1814, addressing her letter to the Reverend Joseph Sharp; as other such letters, it ended up in Garnett's collection. She thanked him for 12 shillings received, reported on her own ill-health, and wrote:

> G. Bainbridge is much afflicted with fits several times a Day which has brought him quite unsensible, so that neather knife nor weepen must be in his way had you sent ... somthing weekly as you promisd it might a been a mens of keeping him from being in such a lunicket state.

Things were no better in 1816, when she wrote again of her ill-health and her husband's 'state of derangment'. Shortly after, George returned home to Kirkby Lonsdale, apparently on his own, for Ann wrote on 4 August 1816, asking

> for any information of my husband as i understand he is with you in the work house i wish to know how he is going on and whether it will be nessery to send his clos as they are but a few which i have left as i have been under the nessity of laying sum of them past.

She acknowledged receipt of relief, which was being doled out to her by the Manchester authorities, acting as intermediaries, at 'a trifle pr week', and claimed her continued ill-health

> makes me unable to git my living or travel about i disire that you will consider my state and be so kind as to send me a triffel more Sir please

to send by return of post as i wish to be dericted by you in all things So no more at present from your respectfulley Ann Bainbridge

In subsequent years Ann Bainbridge, widow, wrote for and received relief of various sorts until she was cut off in 1827, thanks to the vigilance of one of Manchester's relieving officers. It appears that Ann had remarried, but not informed her township of her altered state, while another of the township's sojourners resident in Manchester reported to Garnett that Bainbridge was in perfect health.[13]

It was cases like these, so clearly deserving, then ultimately not, that fuelled suspicion, indirectly reflected in Robert Lawson's letter from Lancaster, 17 March 1813.

> Ser mr Bally enformes me that you [Garnett?] have Been over at Lancaster and I should have Been vere glad to have seen you for he teles me that you had ordered him to pay me no more mone wich trabled me vere moch so I arst him if he knod what was the Reason of it so he tauls me that you had heard that I was gon out of town to Work which was a fols Store for upon my oath I have never worked eare sence last november and I was not able so I had a douther of Boultonlemores [Bolton-Le-Moors] and She had Beared her hasbent so she sent to me if I would com over and Stop with hear a fue monthes thes wenter for she heard that I was Porely and she would Pay expences of Comen for I mit com in the Packet Bot to Preston and then com in a fish Cart to Boulton so I went and that is the truth. ... I have allweas don my endevers for to pot the gentelmen to as lettle expence as I posebely could for I have Beared two wifes and I never trabled them for eanething conserning that But I Cant expect that my time can Be long and then they Well Be at no more expence with me for I am in a Clob and now I am 73 years of age. But I cant walkes for or i would have comed over and talked to the gentelmen myself so I tould Mr Bally I would wright to you and he scad it would Be the Best Way so I hop you well Be so Cind as to let the gentelmen se this letter and I hop they ... wel Be so Cind as to order my Penshon as it was Befor Pleas to send me a fue lines as son as you can with Convenence and then I shall know what to do from your hamble servent Rt Lawson.

Lawson had received a township allowance the year before and for a few weeks in 1813 but he seems to have been dropped, at least from regular relief (he had been receiving two shillings a week), most likely because his story revealed a solvent relation.

There is no evidence Garnett himself travelled frequently or far, but he worked through the overseers of other townships, and he relied on carriers and township residents whose business required travel, both to disperse relief and check on the circumstances. They sometimes got it wrong. James Wilson, a coach driver by trade, wrote from Blackburn on 27 June 1827: 'I have received your letter and am sorrey you should charge me with giving a fals Statement of my Situation'. He went on to give a detailed account of his family and their earnings. Then, fearing his own words would be insufficient to convince Garnett, Wilson had his sons' employers, the minister of the local church and a churchwarden sign in confirmation of his story.[14]

There is, in fact, little evidence to suggest that petitioners did more than colour their stories. Only Ann Bainbridge's case and Christopher Grime's under-reporting of family income in 1823 qualify as fraud.[15] The letters contain claims that appear, in fact, to have been true. It is not solely a question of the honesty of the claimants but of unremitting scrutiny, and where Garnett could not scrutinise, he tended to deny.

Wilson's situation was followed up with an inventory of his family's finances on 10 July 1833, at which time he had three children still at home, his older boy employed by a tallow-chandler, the younger boy as an apprentice to a rope-maker, and his girl, aged 11, 'has been under the Doctors hands this twelve months is queit uncapable of doing any thing towards her keep – as she cannot dow any thing we send her to schoal'.

How well-educated were the non-resident paupers? The letters suggest that a significant number had some familiarity with writing. Of course, it was probably the most competent poor who left the township in an attempt to better their fortunes. One should not under-estimate the difficulty of interpreting the writings of claimants, the ultimate challenge being John Thistlethwaite, a frequent recipient of the township's charity, both public and private, throughout the entire period Garnett was in office. Thistlethwaite lived most of those years just a few miles distant, in the West Riding, close enough to return to the vestry meetings of a Sunday evening, and be troublesome. Early in 1824 he wrote an undated letter to 'Garnaff ... groser', 'That other I do or that oure Can I do the rent is on one side my Cradetors on the other side and on the third hand the Touship'. And in March of that year:

> To Mr garnott sir I hop that you will beffrend me at this time or it is up with Me on all sideses for the rent I Canot Pay one fardn towards for it is out of my Pour to get meat at the rate that Potatoes and Meal is at ...

I belev to speak the Truth we have got into all the Det we can this winter for I think that 5 Pound would Not Clear us at this time.

In May of 1824 he wrote: 'sir for the lordes sak have mrce on us as all the Pour restes in your hand Pray be mercful unto us and do Not so vrey hardle with us as to Break us up at this time'.

In 1831, he wrote:

> gentlemen I Diser you will be so Good as to pay Tomas yeats my Rent he is Greatle pot out of Temper at Ben Disapointed of is rent ther is No Dout bot he intends to give me A Notes for he unther stod as will as me that you Would pay my rent.

Flashes of poetic cadence and articulateness may have helped the Thistlethwaites, but still more important was a location but a few miles distant from the township.

The Beck family, as the Thistlethwaites, were in need throughout Garnett's entire time in office, but there the similarity ends. The Becks were usually more obsequious, but also they were more informative of economic conditions, and one reads often of cotton mills lying idle. Writing from Mold, Flintshire, some 75 miles from their township, the Becks (there were two generations of them) could not afford to adopt Thistlethwaite's querulous voice, but they tried many tacks over the 28 years.

A letter of 21 July 1809 began: 'The Humble Petition of Eleanor Beck a Pauper of your Parish To the Churchwardens and Overseers of the Parish of Kirky Lonsdale', and there follows in a beautiful hand an appeal that undoubtedly was taken from a model of how best to petition for relief.[16] Receiving no response to this appeal, the same beautiful hand penned the following lines on 7 September of that year: 'I am surprising that I had no answer from you after I have Send before but I hope that you will consider little towards me for I am in Great distresed and my Eldest Son is very poorly'. On 6 September 1822, again frustrated by unsuccessful appeal, she wrote to 'The Parish Minister of Kirby Lonsdale':

> As the last recourse I apply to you, the character of whose sacred office is charity and benevolence – the application of the Vicar and the Overseer of the Parish of Mold on my behalf have fail'd to obtain any relief from the overseer of Kirby – he is not a Stranger to my case – he knows that I am destitute and aged – Still he singles me out as and ·object worthy of nothing but to be a prey of adversity he deigns not to drop the [least] ingredient of comfort in bitter cup of affliction which I am doom'd to quaff –

This appeal (which netted her ten shillings) was in another hand, and it is clear that at least the first and third of these letters reflect external assistance. Her son Robert may have made a more favourable impression on Garnett. He wrote, for example, on 10 April 1832:

> Mr Garnet Sir I am Sorry To Trouble you as i dew Asure you my wife is verry Poorley and the little Child ever since I wrote to you last as I Mention to you in my last I had nothing but few Potatoes when my wife got her Bed and Dear Sir hear is nithing to due hear is Hundreds out of employment and I have Been fare and near and Cannot get nothing to dow and our factory was on Sale at Manchester on the thurd Instant but it was Not Sold god onley knows what will be Come of us.

The Becks, in fact, received considerable relief over the years. The response to the above was five shillings in casual relief, and over the course of that year Robert Beck received a total of ten pounds and eight shillings in casual relief – a large sum, given the usual levels of relief from this township.

Where did the pauper petitioners learn to write? The Parson and White 1829 *Directory* listed four schools in the township, one of which was a Free Grammar School, which accepted a few poor boys on charity. There was another charity to provide 'good Books' to poor boys, although the funds were only intermittently applied to the purpose.[17] More important, surely, were family tutoring, and the sort of school to which James Wilson sent his daughter, 'as she can not dow anything'. Undoubtedly, circumstances favoured some children, as in the case of Susan King's child. She wrote from Preston on 28 June 1825 concerning a delay in receiving the allowance that permitted her to board her little boy and send him to school while she was in service. In most cases we can only assume the identity of the author of a letter, although a freshness and directness may be some reason to believe in eponymous authorship. Even if it were the pen of a neighbour or family member, writing out of charity or for a pittance, the voice would not be markedly altered, except in an obvious case, such as Eleanor Beck's petitions.

Some of the petitioners wrote clearly and well. Thomas Robinson wrote from Preston on 12 February 1824:

> I was Brought up a Cotton Spinner with my Uncle Robinson at Halton near Lancaster who is dead about 10 Months since and I have been since that time a Preston Their are several new Factories Building at Preston this next summer but at present their are a deal of spinners out of work I get a day or two when t other spinners are off but it is only very little that I can earn by that means.

His literacy led him to a new line of employment, for he wrote again from Preston on 27 June 1829:

> I have for some time been engaged as a canvasser for books and have been able hitherto to support my family in some way by it but Whitsuntide being lately past and now the Races coming on people are very slack at taking in books besides to make it answer it is necessary that I should be from home a good deal and if I had what would keep my famely at home and myself from home a week or two particularly till these Races are over I should then have an equal chance with others and I think there is might be a living got by it but at present I am really reduced to the greatest distress out of which I can see no way of escape.

Robinson had six children, and had once been a candidate for a removal order, subsequently suspended.[18] Literacy for him did not bring health or wealth. 'Sober, quiet, Clane and industrious', their landlord, Charles Albert, had called the family in a letter dated 6 April 1831.

How was money sent? Robinson received his through the post. But postage was not cheap. Between 1816 and 1819 a letter to Preston cost sevenpence, to Manchester eightpence, to Mold tenpence. The township paid anywhere from one to ten pounds a year on postage, printing and stationery. Of course, it was harder on the petitioners, who usually paid their postage, with the added grievance that their letters often would have been unnecessary if Garnett had made timely disbursements. Most payments were made through carriers and peripatetic businessmen from Kirkby Lonsdale. The names of Fawcett, Taylor, Grundy and Davis crop up frequently. The advantage of this method was that delivery could be preceded by scrutiny. We have few of their reports to Garnett (usually of an oral kind), but their role is noted frequently in the letters, as in the case of James Wilson. A third method was to send funds to other townships' overseers for disbursement, relying on them to scrutinise the worth of a claim, as in the case of Ann Bainbridge in Manchester. This system worked well within the northeast, and the post could be as rapid as in our own day (Robert Dales in Manchester received a letter from Garnett on 9 October 1825, only a day after it was posted, a 50-mile delivery). However, distant petitioners were at risk of being denied, although confirmations from local authorities, as in the case of the Becks, could make a difference.[19]

Whatever the method of delivery, petitioners, like many modern recipients of welfare, encountered bewildering delays, leading to additional hardships. William Lowry of Blackburn even offered to pay postage both ways in order not 'to offend you [Garnett] of the Trouble and Expence'.[20]

Lowry is evidence that Scotland did rather well in educating its subjects. Between 1822 and 1832 Garnett received frequent letters from him, chiefly from Blackburn, often filled with information about labour unrest, disease, unemployment, even an account of the 1832 elections.

> There is now four Candidates in the field to Represent this newly made Borough Mr Fielding a Gentlemen of this Nighbourhood and one that has given much Employment to many hundreds of hands is one and a Mr Bowring of London a man they know nothing of But by his political conduct and Mr Hindle a Magistrate ... and Mr William Turner [from] Chesire But careys on Extensive print work in this place the other the Squbs that is going from Day to Day the walle is plasterd with them is astonishing the various Reports about all their Charactor and of all their Tyranny – not one of them is [colleagued?] together every one upon his own Bottom.

Most of Lowry's letters concerned the Marsden children, the issue of his marriage with a person settled in Kirkby Lonsdale. Lowry himself had no claim on the township, but he could appeal to Garnett for maintenance allowances for the children. His letters are those of an intelligent and curious man, living on the edge of desperation. His words and meaning are occasionally obscure, but there is a perceptivity in them rare in the collection.

The letters hide as much as they inform when it comes to family relationships, for the writers had pecuniary reasons for making a strong case. Take the letter from Peter and Elizabeth Barret, writing from Bradford on 25 September 1825:

> Mr Stepen garnet Over seer of now take this oppertunaty of riting to you throw being abblegated to it throw being so destrest With my Children being Out of work witch has put me to much want and destres as all the mills are stopt in Bradford and there is not hearin tell of them starting again so i desire you will Eather send me 3 pounds or take the younger gearl and get her a place for i have tried all ways to get them work for if there be a place there are an hundred for it if you will not send the money you must send an answer how you are for doing or i will sertenly send her by the waggen.

This was a family of long-standing importunities, and Garnett penned to the letter 'Agreed for the girl to come'.[21]

In contrast, John and Margaret Gill of Beverley, Yorkshire, could ill-disguise their love for Margaret's child by a previous marriage. Margaret wrote on 5 June 1827 of 'her poor little thing' which the authorities in Beverley were using to deprive the family of all relief, for the child had a claim on Kirkby Lonsdale by virtue of her deceased father's settlement there. Margaret Gill addressed her letters to Garnett, styling him 'Dear frend', which suggests a personal acquaintanceship, and interlacing her plaints with words of 'cind love' for Garnett and for Margaret's father and her sisters. Her husband, John, was more forceful. He wrote on 28 June 1835:

> Dear Sir i Right this letter to you to Ask you to send my wife Child money ... I ham so mutch oprest and so ill used with our parrish and it would allmoste make a man hang himself and what is it all for becose I have this Child of yours and sir I have a Small famley of my own and small wages and it is more tha i Can Doo and if you will alowe mee something more to assiste mee in getting her Clorth and Shous i will try to keep her in spite of our parresh.

The allowance of one shilling and sixpence per week kept coming, however tardily, but John Gill's particular appeal netted them an additional ten shillings of casual relief under the rubric of 'Cloathing for out Poor', allocated nine days later. It is impossible to know, but it may have been that Garnett was more dilatory with the Gills because he believed they would keep the child, whatever the circumstances. In any case, he kept on paying.

Occasionally, letters addressed to family members then living in the township found their way into the collection. A scarcely penetrable letter, probably by John Dobson, probably from Lancaster, written on 11 January 1824, is addressed to 'Der brother and sester' and concerns a smallpox epidemic. 'Whe ave bur't fire and candle nit and day all this time' and the letter goes on undecipherably, but with a few words emerging into light – blindness, the sharing of beds, nakedness, pain, 'sekness'.

Mary Ann Proctor wrote from Manchester to her husband's family in Kirkby Lonsdale on 28 March 1831:

> Dear Father & Mother I hope these few lines will find you all here in very good helth but sorry to say we are not so here last saturday was the first time John was able to get out of bed for a month and cannot yet without help and my work being so very slack I cannot support him myself and Child without some Relife from his parish and now he will want a deal of meat and a deal of nurishment before he will be able to work again

'Donation money', charitable funds periodically distributed, often figured in such cases. The Churchwardens' Book of Assessments is incomplete, but it is clear that the township received private donations to meet special needs such as those of the Proctors, which are not recorded in the township's records (except for the year 1815). It is, however, also clear that those funds were not large.[22]

Edward Sill, residing in Wigan, wrote to his brother Thomas on 1 August 1826 of his family's plight: 'I beg you will have the goodness to attend the town meeting', he wrote, and went on to say: 'Little Robert is very poorly and has had three teeth drawn lately he has caught cold with gathering dung in the Streets having no other employment'. Sill was well connected, and his pension was paid immediately by order of the vestry, together with a pound note. From 1817 to 1836 the Sills were in frequent need. Family supporters in the home township helped, although when Sill's son fell foul of the law in 1836 and was put in a house of correction, the allowance was stopped by the Wigan authorities pending a definite order from Kirkby Lonsdale to reinstate it.[23] One of the clearest messages in the correspondence is that township relief was closely linked to the perception of the character of the person or family receiving it.

Albert Camus in *The Plague* has the priest, Pencloux, exhort that nothing is 'more important on earth than a child's suffering, the horror it inspires in us, and the reasons we must find to account for it'.[24] Compare that with Mary Kendall, writing from Oldham on 6 May 1835:

> As respects my eldest son Isaac he is 14 years old – he is now Earning me 5/ a week this may be concidered for 10 months in a year – two months may be generally reckoned as lost time from accidents to machinery and holidays.
>
> My Daughter has been a Short while in place – during which time I had to find her all her Clothing – She has not now been in place for a number of weeks and I do not know of another place for her – she is ten years old. Under 13 the law does not allow of a Child to go to a Factory for more than 8 hours a day and Millowners will not have the trouble of Changing their hands each Day – but have One Set of Children of such age as can work a full day – I have her to maintain Thomas is Dead my youngest is too young to be expected to anything.[25]

Widow Kendall was business-like, and had five individuals certify the truth of her statement. Between 1829 and 1831 the township had paid over 15 pounds on a settlement case involving this woman in the hope of saddling another township with her needs, but that effort had failed.[26] The above appeal netted her an allowance of two shillings and sixpence per week. The letters are an imperfect guide to family feeling, but tell us something of how children were regarded, from the compassion of the Gills to the calculation of Kendall.

If it were not the children or other family members in need, then unemployment, accidents and illnesses were the common causes reflected in the letters. The cases were individual, but the causes were common, and they are heartrending in detail and in their frequency. Take Jane Hodgson, writing from Blackburn on 1 March 1826:

> sir it is with paneful feeling that I wright to you at this time it is not my princabel to truble you but at this time I ham compeld for the factory is rely stopt and for some time back we have only alf time but now ther is non a tole dear sir it would pitty the hart of a stone to see blackburn in the distress I ham not by my self and the shop that I get my meats at will trist no more and wot to do I do not know but I trust in god that the will be better times and then I can do again I hope and trust that you will send me a trifel to ceep us from starvan.

Again, the vestry was forthcoming, with five shillings from the rates and a like amount from donation money.

Illness or accident threw the non-resident poor on the mercy of their township. Isabella Pratt wrote from Ulverston on 29 June 1813 that, recovering from illness, she went to a neighbour's house for a little milk, only to have a gate fall upon her. She was granted a shilling a week more to her pension. And William Dodd wrote from Lancaster on 28 February 1835:

> I have only had two Days work since Christmas last & unfortnitely I had a fire which burned nearly all my Whifas Clothes part of mine and some of my Doughters my Wife has nothing but whet she has on her Back if you would get me work I will be glad to come over to you.

He received 30 shillings. Why some were relieved and others denied lies in the long-dead minds of Garnett and his vestry, but the letters suggest a kind of formula: Are these claimants ours? What is their character? Is there anyone in Kirkby Lonsdale to plead their case? Do we have the means to check the accuracy of the claim? Is this a dangerous precedent? What can we afford to give? Only then might compassion enter in.

Children, incapacity, unemployment: this was the trinity upon which most relief requests rested, quite frequently in combination. Weekly pensions, rent, clothing and medical expenses were the quartet of needs usually expressed. Three categories of letters arrived in Garnett's post: letters from petitioners, requests through third parties (clergyman, landlord, employer, friend, relative, hired pen) and correspondence from overseers, magistrates and doctors. Of the three categories, the most trusted was the last. As John Pearson wrote from Whitehaven on 13 December 1818 when most of his family of seven had typhus and all were depending on the ten shillings and sixpence he earned per week: 'I supose as the Doctor and overseers name was not to it you supose it to be fals but I ashewu you we have had 5 out of the 7 lying [ill].'

The overseers' accounts of the township, those still extant, provide relief data from 1813 to 1835 to supplement the letters. We learn from them that the number of weekly non-resident pensions did not change markedly over the years (a high of 39 in 1813, the low at 27 in 1819, but almost every other year in the low 30s), nor did the costs seldom fall below or rise above the £150–200 range annually. Both numbers and costs were slightly higher than relief costs within the township, clearly establishing the importance of relief granted out of the township, but no dramatic trend. Other forms of relief, such as house rents (totalling £1324) and casual relief (£816) are not broken down as in-township or out-township, but specific entries in the books and penned notations on letters indicate a significant portion of both were for non-residents. The overseers' accounts are, in fact, sanitised for presentation, and are not the running accounts that must once have existed. It is not possible to know the full dimensions of out-township relief from these records, any more than we can ever know the extent of donation money. The correspondence itself suggests that not all letters survived; what was kept were the working papers of a busy man. He may have been motivated to save out of prudence in the event of legal complications (removals were rare but, if challenged, could be expensive, the high being £70 in 1819). He may also have been interested in having aids to memory, both to maintain consistency and to avoid dangerous precedents. This is not the place for an analysis of Kirkby Lonsdale's poor law administration, but it is fair to say that non-resident relief was both a steady and significant commitment of expenditure of the township over the period for which there is record. The most noteworthy change over time, at least in humanistic terms, is in fact in the voices of the poor. The letters become less clamorous and there is a trend towards greater servility in tone, although most of the letters to the end of the collection could be described as forthright, reasoned and politely insistent.

Were petitioners truthful? Yes, if only because claims were so closely scrutinised, and Garnett's agents and long experience – with his memory backed by saved correspondence – made him a dangerous man to attempt to deceive. Were petitioners literate? The letters are evidence to show that a form of writing was not rare among the non-resident poor, perhaps upwards of half of them (exactness is impossible because we can never know in every case whether a letter is eponymous or derivative). With regard to family relationships, the gamut is run, but the letters suggest strong attachments and often charity within the family. The causes that led to the correspondence were as exemplified, and it is obvious that most of the correspondence, apart from complaints of delinquent payments, was generated by specific crises in circumstances, usually affecting children, the aged, the ill or the injured.

Were the township authorities caring, competent and conscientious? On the whole, yes, with some significant exceptions where the character of the recipient was suspect.[27] It may be that Garnett and the vestry practised a form of triage. Doubtful claims (or claimants) received nothing; nor did, usually, distant claims where verification and delivery of relief posed difficulties. Another third were non-resident petitioners who exceeded the township's calculations of cost/benefit for allowing them to live elsewhere, or who became annoyingly clamorous; such as these were ordered home, perhaps to be placed in the workhouse. The third group were those given regular or casual relief in circumstances where the township had some means of oversight, and where amounts were less (or at least not more) than relief dispersed to similarly circumstanced paupers within the township.

The letters clearly illustrate how non-resident relief worked in the industrial north, and are full of human interest. If one may be permitted to wax philosophical in support of R.G. Collingwood's simple observation that we study history to attain human self-knowledge, then a study of the range of human need and responses to that need at the outset of Britain's nineteenth century is revelatory and provocative. In the opinion of Samuel Johnson, 'a decent provision for the poor is the true test of civilization'. Yet is the reality much grimmer – that societies gripped by dynamic and creative forces, as was Britain in the Industrial Revolution, lubricate themselves with the wasted, tortured lives of redundant and incapacitated workers? Perhaps the triage provided by Garnett and his like is the best one can hope for until humankind learns to live by a different rule.

Yet, one final observation and illustration follow. Can it not be argued that some credit for the genesis of industrialism goes to workers willing to leave home to seek their fortunes? Credit also may be due to a township, such as Kirkby Lonsdale, which encouraged them – up to a point, as Matthew and Alice Baisbrown discovered. Alice wrote from Covent Garden, London in 1828:

> I am a bilghed to Right to you we have bene virey moch Distressed all this winter and at present whors than ever the Revd William Cares Willson was so cind as to gett me the loan of £12 for a blocking mashean and I have walked the streets this 3 weeks to take logins in town where my work lays and no one will take my famly into logins I have got 5 Children and will have 6 in a virey little time and not one can ern me sixpence the Eldest as been very bad all winter and I have one 8 years lying in Bed and cant be moved she is so bad and the worst of all [Matthew] Baisborn is in such a bad state of elth he is not erning a 1/ a weak we can have a hous with paying 20 pounds going in and if I had that I should be Able to Do and trobel aney one more and pay it Back but as we are we can Do no way and if we take it it will gain us a settlement hear.

The Baisbrowns did receive some relief from their township, but the records end before we can know if it were enough. In another letter from Alice Baisbrown in 1835 she wrote: 'whe have Reaached furder than we can Dow'.[28] 'Ah, but a man's reach should exceed his grasp, Or what's a heaven for?' Robert Browning once wrote. It may not have been heaven, but one hopes the Baisbrowns did achieve their settlement in far-off London.

The township letters contain a choir of voices, some despairing, others hopeful, all reflecting and reinforcing for the reader our common humanity.

## NOTES

1. Cumbria Record Office, Kendal (hereafter CRO/K), Kirkby Lonsdale, WPR/19, Township Letters (hereafter TL) 3/7/1809. I am grateful to The Revd Graham W. Bettridge, Rector of Kirkby Lonsdale, for permission to quote from the township letters; to Sheila MacPherson, former Cumbria County Archivist, for introducing me to this splendid collection; and to Jim Grisenthwaite, Cumbria County Archivist, for his assistance. I am deeply indebted to Brett Harrison, Senior Archivist, Leeds District Archives, for wise counsel, criticism and the checking of the wording of petitions, and the verifying and completing of some of the references. All errors of fact or

## Voices in the Crowd

interpretation are, of course, my own. In quoting from the letters, verbatim extracts are given, the only liberty being a full stop at the end of quoted material to avoid a plethora of ellipses.

2. The township's records, including the letters, have not yet been fully inventoried. As the letters are arranged in rough chronological order, name and date are sufficient to find any particular letter used in this chapter.

3. For an overview, see Edward Muir, 'Introduction: Observing Trifles', in Edward Muir and Guido Ruggiero (eds), *Microhistory and the Lost Peoples of Europe* (Baltimore: Johns Hopkins University Press, 1991), pp.vii–xxviii.

4. See, for example, Adrian Wilson (ed.), *Rethinking Social History: English Society 1570–1920* (Manchester: Manchester University Press, 1993).

5. William H. McNeill, *The Shape of European History* (New York: Oxford University Press, 1974), p.vi.

6. Lewis Namier, 'History', in *Avenues of History* (1952), as quoted in Fritz Stern (ed.), *The Varieties of History* (New York: Vintage, 1972), p.379.

7. For the general relationship between migration, the poor law and industrialism in northern Britain, see J.S. Taylor, 'A Different Kind of Speenhamland: Nonresident Relief in the Industrial Revolution', *Journal of British Studies* 30, April (1991), 183–208.

8. North Yorkshire County Record Office, Marton-in-Craven (then in the West Riding), PR/MRC1/3 25/12/1763; W.H. Chippendall (ed.), *The Parish Registers of Thornton-in-Lonsdale, 1576–1812*, Yorkshire Parish Registers Society, vol. XXXIX (1931), p.261. Lancashire Record Office, Will of Stephen Garnett, proved 2/9/1840.

9. CRO/K, WPR/19, Poor Law Returns, 1801–36. Garnett's salary was raised to fifteen pounds in 1817; Frederic Morton Eden, *The State of the Poor* (London, 1797), III, p.772.

10. Ibid., pp.771–6; Population: *Parliamentary Papers* (1831), vol. XVIII, p.276.

11. William Parson and William White, *History, Directory and Gazetteer of the Counties of Cumberland and Westmorland* (Leeds: W. White, 1829), pp.694–5.

12. The letters were among the earlier deposits, in 1967 or before.

13. CRO/K, WPR/19, TL, George Salkeld to Stephen Garnett, 11/3/1827.

14. Wilson's tactic in seeking confirmation from local witnesses was not unusual, only unusually thorough.

15. CRO/K, WPR/19, TL, Thomas Grundy to Stephen Garnett, 5/6/1823.

16. See, for example, George Brown, *The New and Complete Letter Writer* (London: Alex Hogg, 1800) as a guide to epistolary sophistication. I am grateful to Brett Harrison for this thought and reference.

17. Parson and White, p.39; Reports of the Commissioners, *Charities in England and Wales ... Westmorland, 1818–1837* (London: Henry Gray, n.d.), pp.546–9; CRO/K, WPR/19, Inventory of Funds, Securities and Money Belonging to the Poor, 1838.

18. CRO/K, WPR/19, Removal Orders, 17/8/1827. Formal application of settlement law was the exception, not the rule, for the township. From 1800–34 there were only 24 orders from Kirkby Lonsdale, and for 1800–36, only 31 to the township. Given the volume of migration, this was token.

19. CRO/K, WPR/19, Account Books of Overseers of the Poor, 1813–35. The overseers' accounts and letter marginalia are principal sources for monetary

responses. For the post, see also Howard Robinson, *Britain's Post Office* (London: Oxford University Press, 1953), pp.100–1.
20. CRO/K, WPR/19, TL, William Lowry to Stephen Garnett, 25/6/1827.
21. Betty Barret was a Longhorn. For that family, see J.S. Taylor, *Poverty, Migration and Settlement in the Industrial Revolution* (Palo Alto: SPOSS, 1989), pp.164–7: Chapter 7 of this book treats Kirkby Lonsdale (and the letters) from the standpoint of its poor law administration.
22. CRO/K, WPR/19, Churchwardens' Book for Assessments, 1815–32. The main business of this roughly kept book had to do with the church organ, but charity recipients, 35 in all, and the amounts each received are given for January, May and Christmas, 1815, with distributions ranging from ten shillings to one shilling, the total for that year being a little over ten pounds. There is no way of knowing if this was a typical year. Brett Harrison has found references in estate papers to Garnett being given funds to distribute to the poor. Donation money was distributed at special meetings, but it was also sent throughout the year in response to special needs.
23. CRO/K, WPR/19, TL, Edward Sill to Stephen Garnett, 4/3/1836.
24. Albert Camus, *The Plague*, trans. Stuart Gilbert (New York: Vintage, 1991, f.p. 1947), p.223.
25. Kendall was referring to 3 and 4 William, *cap.* 103 (1833), but she did not take account of the grace periods built into the Factory Act. That may have been true of the mill-owners as well.
26. CRO/K, WPR/19, Township Receipts, 1815–36 29/3/1831.
27. The worst case, possibly indictable, was that of Mary Dixon, who may have starved to death in Preston in 1823, her husband then being in the house of correction for poaching. CRO/K, WPR/19, TL, William Carus-Wilson to Stephen Garnett 19/2, 22/2 and 18/3/1823. For Garnett's overview of the township's poor law administration near the end of his tenure, see Reports from the Assistant Commissioners: Appendix (B.2) Answers to Town Queries: *Parliamentary Papers* (1834), vols XXXV–XXXVI.
28. Like the previous Baisbrown letters, no precise date is given. CRO/K, WPR/19, Township Receipts, 1815–36, has record of five pounds given the family 14/1/1832, and the following year relief was given in kind: washing pot, bed, straw mat and two blankets, valued in all at nine shillings and ninepence.

# 6 Old Age in Poverty: The Record of Essex Pauper Letters, 1780–1834
Thomas Sokoll

Honnerd Genteelmen
I Susannah Halls am very Sorrey to Troubel you with this as I sent before And once troubeled the Church warden to write to you to say I am still living But have had no answer to either I was Afraid they miscaried Genteelmen you Can not Think how bad I have wanted my Weekley alowence I have been very bad in Deed not abel to keep up and am so now Genteelmen had I got my alowen now Hear I Can Truley say not one Farhing is mine I have Got in Det think Gentelmen on my Age is very Grate I think I am 88 years old I think I Shall not Trouble you much longer I am so very feable but Gods will be done I Must ware my apointed time let It be Long or Sort Genteelmen I receved my last alowence very Saft up to Febuary 5th 1824 and I do return you all my sincer Thanks for all your kindness to me a poor helpless Creature I hope Genteelmen you will be So kind as to write as Soon as posebl you Can you now not how Much I wante it Tho its not in my power to reward you Genteelmen I sincerley beg of God to return it to you Ten fould I remaine your poor humble parishner Susannah Halls.

This letter was written on 21 June 1824. Susannah Halls lived in St Nicholas parish, Ipswich, but the letter was addressed and sent to the overseers of the poor at Chelmsford, because that was the place where she had her settlement and from which she received her allowance.[1]

The references to old age in this letter are striking. She does not know precisely how old she is, though certainly old enough to make her feel she won't trouble her parish much longer; she faces her death in the firm belief that when it comes it will be a fulfilment of God's will. Concise statements, which immediately reveal the unique quality of pauper letters: they provide a rare direct personal record of what the poorest people of society felt and thought, including such intimate matters as the suffering from illness and the experience of old age.

In using the evidence of pauper letters with respect to old age, this chapter pursues two aims. First, to show how historical research into ageing may profit from the personal record of the elderly themselves, and second, to demonstrate the richness of that source itself, and its value for the study of poverty and welfare provision. Therefore, I hope that the example presented here will encourage not only students of ageing to make use of these and other types of personal records, but also students of the poor law to explore the rich archive of pauper letters for other themes and purposes.

The following discussion draws on all pauper letters surviving among overseers' papers of Essex parishes, a corpus of evidence comprising some 1000 pieces.[2] It goes without saying that the sheer volume of the material must preclude any attempt at comprehensive coverage of even the subsample of letters directly concerned with old age. Rather, I shall restrict myself to an exemplary illustration of a few selected cases under three themes: the role of the family, the question of removal and the experience of old age.

I should also make it clear at the outset that I present no more than some first fruits of a larger research project, which also involves the critical edition of some 300 pauper letters from the entire collection.[3] In other words, what follows are preliminary findings. My aim is not so much to offer conclusive answers as to pose questions and open a new perspective towards the social experience of poverty and old age as recorded in the written word of ordinary people. Caution is required also, because in drawing on pauper letters we are entering an almost entirely new field of historical research. There is a variety of sources recording (or coming pretty close to recording) the words of ordinary people, a number of which, like autobiographies of working people, threatening letters or certain types of court and other legal records, have been dealt with competently in previous research (that this has still been far less than they deserve is another matter).[4] More specifically, Keith Snell, in his pathbreaking work on settlement examinations, has made us fully aware of the rich record of personal testimonies of the labouring poor that was produced under the Old Poor Law – a unique collective archive of ordinary people which is probably unrivalled among all historic civilisations.[5] But the most compelling type of record within that collective archive, that of pauper letters, has only just begun to be explored, with J.S. Taylor's reconstruction of individual case histories from such letters in the form of carefully annotated narratives.[6]

Since social historical research on pauper letters is still in its initial stage, where even such elementary exercises as their proper literary critique have not been approached, I have found it necessary to cover a number of methodological questions before turning to the substance of pauper letters.[7] Thus, I shall first explain the institutional background from which the records arise (I) and consider some basic elements of source criticism (II); then look into the sources themselves, with respect to the three themes already mentioned: the role of the family (III), the question of removal (IV) and the experience of old age (V); and finally round off the exercise with a brief conclusion (VI).

## I INSTITUTIONAL BACKGROUND: NON-RESIDENT RELIEF UNDER THE OLD POOR LAW

Why did people – sometimes people who were hardly literate – take the trouble to write to the overseers of the poor? Would it not have been easier to call on them? Indeed, if you could, it *was* easier to go and talk to your overseer, and this we must assume is what most people did when they applied for relief. A letter was only written when the overseer was too far away to go to, that is to say, when someone lived outside the parish in which he had his settlement. People who resided 'at home' had no reason to write to their overseer.

This also explains the way in which pauper letters have come down to us: as part of the overseers' correspondence of the parish to which they were sent – and apart from a few exceptions these were always sent from outside. Thus, strictly speaking, they do not form a historical source in themselves but only as part of another, larger corpus of evidence, a point which may seem a bit pedantic at first sight, but which is essential in considering the question of their authorship, as we shall see later on.

Pauper letters of that type derive from a specific institutional setting: the practice of non-resident or out-parish relief. This means that paupers who resided in a parish other than that of their settlement were relieved at that place, on the basis of informal arrangements between the two parishes concerned, to the effect that the overseers of the 'host' parish advanced the necessary payments which were then reimbursed by the 'home' parish. In order to appreciate the significance of such arrangements it is important to understand that they practically circumvented the legal requirements under the settlement laws, according to which a pauper who had become chargeable in another parish was supposed, at the expense of that parish, to be sent (if necessary removed) to his or her place of settlement and then to be relieved there.[8]

The practice of non-resident (or out-parish) relief has only recently become a subject of serious research. And that research has mainly been concerned with the situation in industrial parishes in the northern counties, where the support to unemployed labourers from rural parishes during periods of trade depression has been described as a 'system of parochially funded labour migration that promoted a work force for the expanding industries', while at the same time it also benefited the rural parishes, who preferred such limited relief payments to the constant burden which returning out-migrants would have incurred 'at home'.[9] The extent of the system in the rural areas of the south is still entirely unclear. But the point developed by J.S. Taylor that non-resident relief was a common practice whenever it suited each of the three parties involved (the pauper, his host parish and his home parish), is not restricted to the conditions of 'Industrial Speenhamland'. It is equally applicable to other situations, as his case histories from Devon illustrate.

The wider implication, which will become even more apparent in the light of the cases reported below, is that the whole issue of the practical consequences of the settlement laws, including the recent debate over the question of whether they formed a means of 'monitoring' migration of the labouring poor in rural areas and of enhancing their 'surveillance',[10] will have to be reconsidered as more evidence from pauper letters and other kinds of overseers' correspondence is being gathered. For our present purposes, though, it is sufficient to repeat that it is essentially to the institution of non-resident relief, that is, inter-parochial arrangements *below* the level of the costly procedures stipulated in the settlement laws, that we owe pauper letters.

## II STRATEGIC WRITING: CONSIDERATIONS TOWARDS A SOURCE CRITICISM OF PAUPER LETTERS

For a closer assessment of the peculiar properties of pauper letters as a historical source, it is convenient to return to the letter from Susannah Halls quoted at the beginning of this chapter. The language of the document is telling. There is no epistolary phraseology, but plain words which address the issues in a straightforward manner. The style, the lack of punctuation, and most particularly the characteristic phonetic spelling suggest the close connection of the written text to the spoken word: 'I have Got in Det ... my Age is very Grate ... you now not how Much I wante it'. It is not only that the modern reader may find that reading aloud facilitates his or her understanding. It is rather that, from a strictly historical point of view, such documents *ought* to be read aloud, since in many cases someone must actually have been speaking in the act of writing.

Nevertheless, the letter from Susannah Halls is definitely and decidedly a genuine piece of literary communication. It bears references to other letters, including those of other people. In fact, apart from her own letter, some of these records have also survived and we shall consult them in due course. Thus, her letter forms part of a larger correspondence. The negotiations between the parties concerned with the welfare of this elderly lady were conducted on the basis of written records.

Pauper letters, even the ones which are so intimate in their tone and in their detailed description of personal affairs that they might almost be mistaken for private correspondence,[11] are always 'official' pieces of writing. They are addressed to people responsible for the administration of the poor laws. They are written for a specific purpose. And most – though by no means all – of them convey a clear message. In the present case, the message is that Susannah Halls has not received her regular pension, needs it desperately and urges the overseers to send it: 'You Can not Think how bad I have wanted my Weekley alowance ... I Can Truley say not one Far [t]hing is mine I have Got in Det ... you [k]now not how Much I wante it'.

Due to their official addressee and the specific interest which they pursue, pauper letters are highly strategic pieces of writing. Most of them – although again with interesting exceptions – display a characteristic rhetoric of deferential gratitude. Susannah Halls' letter is replete with acknowledgements of the relief she received on previous occasions. The biblical image of man being but a 'poor helpless Creature' is alluded to, and at the end of the letter the idea of balancing retributive justice is conjured up: 'Tho its not in my power to reward you Genteelmen I sincerley beg of God to return it to you Ten fould'. Often, the acknowledgements are phrased in very similar terms. Thus, in an undated letter written early in 1824, it says in virtually the same words as in the letter quoted at the beginning: 'I Susannah Halls receved my Last alowence verry Safe and do return you all Gentelmen my Sincer Thanks to all For your kindeness to me apoor helpless Feable creature. I Can but just Creep about I have bean very bad indeed.'[12]

It is obvious, then, that in interpreting a pauper letter we have to watch out for stereotypes, exaggerations or even literary make-ups which must not be taken literally. And yet, despite this, we may normally still regard it as a true record of the specific circumstances of an individual case, providing that the account is not grossly inconsistent or unlikely. There would appear to be no reason, for example, why we should not believe that Susannah Halls was confined to her bed ('I have been very bad in Deed not abel to keep up and am so now'), and that she had run into debt because she had not received her weekly pension. Indebtedness caused by ill-health in old age is an almost universal face of poverty, witnessed in countless records.

More important, however, is the fact that for a pauper writing a letter, plain lying would not have made much sense, given that the addressed overseer of his or her home parish could always ask the overseer in the host parish to comment on the statements made in the letter and to check on the circumstances of the sender. Thus, even though paupers might physically be well beyond the reach of the parish in which they were settled, they were still enmeshed into the relief system of the parish in which they resided – and this, it would seem, often to an even greater extent than the paupers belonging to that parish – since they found themselves under the responsibility of two parties, with each of whom they communicated in a different way: the overseer of the host parish, to whom they would talk, and the overseer of the home parish, to whom they would write. Naturally, whatever has come down to us is only a record of the latter type of communication. But it is clear that the former type was no less – if not in fact more – frequent and important. Again, it is right at the beginning of the letter from Susannah Halls itself that this point is referred to, where it is mentioned that she had asked the churchwarden of Ipswich St Nicholas, her host parish, to let the overseer of Chelmsford know that she was still living. This is because at an earlier occasion she had indeed been asked by the latter to 'send ... a Certificate ... that you ar[e] living'.[13]

Apart from the correspondence concerning her case, we have the record of the payments she received from the overseers of Chelmford (where she had her settlement) from Lady Day 1822 until 15 November 1825, the day on which she died. Throughout that period, she received a regular pension of two shillings and sixpence per week – a common rate for an elderly widow at that time. The overseers of Chelmsford sent the money – by bank order – to the overseers at Ipswich in the form of quarterly payments, quite sensibly in advance at the beginning of each quarter. Occasionally, however, the payments were delayed, and since the overseers at Ipswich were apparently not prepared to advance her pension from their own parochial purse, it is no wonder that the poor old woman got into difficulties.[14] Three of her letters, including the one quoted in full at the beginning of this chapter, were written for that reason.[15] Apart from such difficulties, however, the pension as such can be regarded as providing her with a moderate but relatively fair subsistence, given that an agricultural labourer in that region would hardly have earned more than ten shillings a week – that is, four times as much.[16]

The record of her case as given in the surviving letters is absolutely consistent with the external evidence in the overseers' accounts and vestry minutes of Chelmsford, except for the fact that the latter put her age somewhat lower, at 81 or 82, for the time of her death.[17]

However, one problem remains. Although all her letters were written in her name, she did not put pen to paper herself. The letters are all written in the same hand, and so is the following:

> Honnerd Genteelmen
> This is to inform you that Susan Halls died this Morning. I would be So much ablidght to you if you Will be so kind as to Send what the parish alowes For bering. She is had a very heavey affliction We wear ablidght to have Two to do for her. Her Paines was So Grate one Could not do for her alone that maid it so very heavey for me and bissnes so very dull or I would not asked you but you may depend that is the Truth. Genteelmen I return my sincer Thanks to you all for all your kindness to My poor old Mother I remaine your Humbel S alexander.[18]

This is 'her' last letter, written on 15 November 1825 and signed by her daughter. It was received at Chelmsford two days later – the postage of sevenpence is duly entered in the minute book of the select vestry, along with an allowance of one pound towards her burial which was sent to her son-in-law James Alexander, who had also received all previous payments on her behalf.[19]

Given that Susannah Halls had apparently not written a single letter herself, it may seem a little daring if I present her of all paupers as my crown witness for the case of source criticism. However, for the question of the evidential validity of pauper letters to be tackled it needs to be carried to the extreme. And the extreme case I want to make is that a letter may justifiably count as a pauper letter as long as it was written and signed in the name of a pauper, even if it was not put down in his or her own hand.

A brief consideration of the wider context may help to clarify the point. Recent research in the history and cross-cultural study of literacy has made it abundantly clear that for societies before the enforcement of universal literacy the notion of the individual writer, acting in the remote sphere of private seclusion, is misleading – no less misleading than that of the individual reader.[20] Just as reading remained essentially a social activity well into the nineteenth century, so did the composition and production of written documents often involve the co-operation of a number of individuals. In the context of the social history of language, terms like 'author', 'writer' or 'scribe' are insufficient and inappropriate if understood in their conventional sense. Charlemagne could not write. But he dictated assiduously and has thus 'written' hundreds of records. In the history of written records, hand and mouth need to be distinguished, and this not only analytically but, for most cases, physically and personally as well. And if this is true of Charlemagne around 800, why should it not hold for Susannah Halls some thousand years later?

Peter Burke has recently declared that 'one of the most immediate tasks for social historians of language is to work out who, in a given place at a given time, used the medium of writing to communicate with whom about what'.[21] I want to suggest that his proposition does not yet reach far enough, since the fact that someone used the medium of writing does not necessarily mean that he or she used their own hand. It could also mean – and has indeed meant over long periods of history for which we possess written evidence – that, on whatever grounds and for whatever purposes, the hands of others were at their disposal. The power of writing is not confined to those who were themselves able to write. It also applies to any one who *had* a piece being written in a given place at a given time.[22]

It is in this sense that I insist that what I would like to call the *scriptual power* of the labouring poor of late eighteenth- and early nineteenth-century England, as it is witnessed in pauper letters, but also in similar pieces of writing like threatening letters, resolutions and proclamations, needs to be seen as a complex cultural practice, or as a spectrum of practices which can only be appreciated within the social context in which the documents were produced.

This spectrum of practices may conveniently be broken down into typical situations of writing. Thus, most of the pauper letters we are concerned with here were presumably written by the applicants themselves and in their own hands. After all, even among labourers, about a third of all grown-up males were literate in England by the end of the eighteenth century, a fairly high proportion by international standards.[23] However, even if most pauper letters were written by the paupers themselves, it does not necessarily follow that they were also composed by them alone. Many a pauper must have had someone else to assist him in the writing – in some cases he must even have written no more than what that person dictated to him. Conversely, lots of pauper letters were written by other people, and here again it is important to envisage a broad spectrum of possibilities. Some paupers must have dictated their letters. Others had them written, like 70-year-old Jane Hills, who sent a letter from London to Chelmsford in the summer of 1824, asking for her allowance and ending with the telling remark: 'I can neither Read nor write and ham Abbot [am about] to Trouble Some body every time to write'.[24] In other cases, letters must have been written for paupers, even in their names, who did not know about it themselves. Naturally, Susannah Halls did not know about

## Old Age in Poverty

'her' last letter of 15 November 1825 – but it may well be that she did not know anything about her other letters either, even though they were all written as if she were speaking herself.

Finally, there are those letters in which other people wrote on behalf of a pauper, but on their own initiative and in their own name. The close relative, the intimate companion, the faithful friend, the concerned neighbour, the benevolent master, the dutiful clergyman, the zealous surgeon, even the overseer of the host parish – they all are in evidence as epistolary advocates of the poor. Naturally, such letters cannot – even under the most generous definition – be counted as pauper letters. But as a complementary source, they are nevertheless useful for the interpretation of pauper letters proper, in that they show to what extent certain attitudes, images and beliefs were shared across social groups, thus providing important insights into the social range of contemporary notions such as the nature of poverty, the duty to work and the right to public assistance.

### III  THE ROLE OF THE FAMILY

Pauper letters reveal a unique insight into the domestic arrangements of the elderly poor, especially with respect to the role for their support of the family and the kin group. In the case of Susannah Halls, we have already seen the moving account of how she was looked after, right up to her death, by the family of her son-in-law, although it is not altogether clear whether she actually lived in his household. Her daughter's statement that they were obliged to have two people 'to do for her' during her last days might suggest that she lived on her own, though it is equally possible that when it says 'Her Paines was So Grate one Could not do for her alone', it is simply meant that she was attended day and night.

But there are many other cases which quite clearly indicate the existence of extended family households among the poor, with elderly paupers actually living with their kin who looked after them. Jane Hills, the elderly lady whom we have already heard to have had her letters written because she could neither read nor write, resided with her widowed daughter-in-law and her children.[25] Rachel Brown, who also wrote from London, asking for an allowance of one pound 'as i want A gown and other nercurys which i know not how to do without', lived with her elderly father.[26] Elizabeth Reilly in London wrote that her 80 year old mother had lived with them for ten years but had now become so infirm that they could no longer keep her, unless they were assisted by the parish.[27] It is on similar lines that the possible formation of extended households is discussed, where people say they would be prepared to take in an elderly relative, but needed financial assistance. Thus, the daughter of Elizabeth Philbrick, a 68-year-old widow, wrote from Wivenhoe that she would take in her mother when she was given a small weekly allowance towards her keep.[28]

Unfortunately, it is impossible to say to what extent the parish officers gave financial support to such arrangements, since there is no way – despite their enormous number – to quantify the evidence of pauper letters for that purpose. Many cases, again like that of Susannah Halls, are vague (was she cared for in the household of her daughter or not?), whereas quantification demands counting, and counting is impossible with ambiguous cases which cannot be determined one way or the other. Yet, even if we were to count only the unequivocal instances of domestic care, that number would be meaningless, since there is no numerical frame of reference. It is simply impossible to establish the number of 'all' elderly poor, against which the tiny subgroup of those could be set who lived in other people's households, wrote letters (or had them written) and even talked about the household in these letters.[29]

Nevertheless, in discussing the question of the role of household and family for the care of elderly people, the evidence of pauper letters is not to be underrated since these documents reveal a lot more about the motives, interests and options of the parties involved – the poor, their relatives and the parish officers – than most other records. So far, the instances we have quoted would suggest that publicly funded domestic care of the elderly poor by their relatives was probably far more widespread than it has hitherto been assumed. Many parish officers would seem to have agreed if suggestions of that kind were put to them, since they knew only too well that communal support of private care at home incurred far lower costs than the institutional care of old people.

This contention is further supported by cases in which the parish authorities arranged for the care of an elderly bedridden pauper by paying someone – be he or she a relative or not – to live with the old person in his or her household and look after him or her. Mary Elvin, for example, until she died at the age of 87, had been provided for in this way by a young woman. In a letter to Mary's home parish, the vicar of Ingrave (the parish in which she had resided) reported: 'I think I have before appraized to you that she was gradually wearing out, but no one could suppose that she would have lasted so long! ... the poor old Dame had to struggle hard to exist'. He asked for the grant of 'a trifle towards the expense of entereing her decently, as she has always been respected her[e]'.[30] Ann Thudgett, living in the London parish of St Giles, was looked after by her niece. She had received a weekly allowance of three shillings and sixpence from her home parish, Steeple Bumpstead, for some time, which was handed over to her (or to her niece?) by a contact man, a certain Mr Earl. But apparently the allowance had then been reduced, because when she wrote to her parish she asked for Mr Earl to be instructed to hand her the full amount of three shillings and sixpence as before. This, she said, was what she needed,

> for I cannot live hear and Starve a[s] I am a Poor Oflic[t]ed woman and Cannot work for my Living and likewise that my Nece has to dress and un dress me and has had for years gentelmen Mary Ann Page I am Ann Thudgett['s] Nece I have don for my poor oflic[t]ed old a[u]nt for years with your assistance I have Boarded lodg wash and Every other thing that Laid in my Pour for 6d per day.[31]

The letter is also interesting in that it highlights once more the problem of scriptual power. The whole letter was written by Mary Ann Page, Ann Thudgett's niece, but the first lines are written in her aunt's name – as if she were writing. Or should we imagine that in the first lines Mary Ann Page only wrote what her aunt dictated her – up to the point where the report turns to the niece and where the same, all of a sudden, reveals herself as the writer? We cannot tell. Neither do we know how the two women fared later on. Apparently, there were further attempts at reducing or even cancelling Ann Thudgett's allowance. Six years later the overseers of Steeple Bumpstead were told by the London police that she was too old to be removed and that she should be given relief further on.[32]

Even if, as in the last case, the public assistance of private care of elderly people might be debated between their relatives and the parish officers, it is nevertheless clear that even such cases cast heavy doubts on the idea of social isolation as a typical concomitant of poverty in old age – an idea that has become prominent in recent research on the history of poverty. Paul Slack, for instance, in his masterly survey of poverty in Tudor and Stuart England, has written to this effect: 'A lonely old age was the lot of most of the labouring poor.'[33] To support that view, he refers to the evidence of early modern English pauper censuses in which a high proportion of elderly people, especially women (and here again widows in particular), seem to be recorded as solitaries.[34]

However, as I have shown elsewhere, it is almost certain that these pauper censuses do not record households, but recipients of poor relief, which means that it is misleading to assume that they provide any proof of the existence of isolated pauper households. In such documents, a widow for example is recorded as a 'family' on her own if she 'counts' as a relief recipient in her own right, even if she lived in (say) the household of her son-in-law – and even if her relief payments were actually made to the son-in-law (as in the case of Susannah Halls).[35] Moreover, for the two Essex communities of Ardleigh and Braintree (unfortunately, there are as yet no further comparable studies), it has been possible to show, by combining local census material with poor law records, that elderly poor relief recipients, especially women, did in fact live in the households of their children or shared their households with other women. The solitary pauper household was simply not in evidence at all. In clear contrast to the rule formulated by Peter Laslett that, in the world we have lost, household size was a simple function of social class (the lower the status the smaller and simpler the household), the households of the poor were not particularly small in these two communities, and the proportion of complex households was in fact higher among the poor than in the rest of the population.[36]

The evidence of pauper letters lends further support to those findings in that they too reveal cases in which elderly women in receipt of poor relief actually lived with their children or, conversely, that the children, as household heads, received assistance towards their living-in relatives. The question as to how often the payments were handed over to either side, and on what grounds, cannot be carried further at this point. But it is obvious that these cases support the suggestion long ago made by Hans Medick (against Laslett's rule) that the formation of complex households could be understood as a means for the labouring classes of redistributing poverty through the system of family and kinship – and, I would here add, with the assistance of the local welfare system.[37]

Middle-class observers who showed themselves shocked that the poor had their care of parents and other elderly relatives publicly funded in this way and who denounced the 'deficiencies of parental and filial affection' among the labouring classes,[38] should have known better that most elderly people in poverty could hardly expect their children to support them, given the latter's responsibilities for their own offspring. This dilemma was neatly expressed in 1810 in a letter from Rachel Shoregh from Bethnal Green: 'my children are all married and got familys which these dear times they have as much as they can do to support and therefore are not able to assist me'.[39]

The question of how the poor organised their households is closely related to that of lodging arrangements. As we have learned from numerous studies, the practice of taking in lodgers was widespread in working-class communities well into the nineteenth and even into the twentieth centuries. Various types of lodgers, inmates, *Schlafgänger* (people who claimed no more than a bed) and others were welcomed for various reasons, with financial and social considerations probably being the most important ones. Lodgers made an additional contribution to the family income, and their inclusion in the household was a means to create and maintain wider kinship and community networks.[40] Because of the prominence of lodgers, the notion of a 'half-open family structure' has been suggested for the industrial working class.[41] Similar practices are in evidence for the rural labouring classes. By the late eighteenth century, contemporaries were aware of this. For example, in the path-breaking sociographic analysis of agricultural labourers published by David Davies in 1795, the report from Surrey records several families who 'take in lodgers which lessens their rents, and for whom the wives wash and mend'.[42]

Pauper letters provide further examples. Thus, we hear of an elderly couple at Upminster who would have had to make do with the insufficient wages of the man had it not been for 'the benefits they derived from a lodger or two'.[43] Or take Mary Parnell in Hertford, a widow with six children, of whom only three were 'able to get their own bread', with one of the other three suffering from a serious injury of the spine. 'By taking in lodgers & other means [she] is able to do a little for herself', wrote her brother-in-law, adding that thereby she earned 'more perhaps than in a place in which she was not known – it would not be worthwhile nor indeed expedient to insist on her removal'.[44]

## IV THE ARGUMENT ABOUT REMOVAL

The last words in the last quotation point to an issue which is often brought up in letters which carry information on the householding patterns of the poor: the issue of the removal – or threatening removal – of paupers to their parish of settlement. In most cases, the removal does *not* in fact seem to have been undertaken, presumably because the parish officers were willing to learn better, as in the case of Mary Parnell, who stayed in Hertford and received her allowance there.[45]

It is indeed in no few pauper letters that strong arguments are put forward against the removal of elderly people, a measure by which, it is held, they would not just be ejected from their own households but uprooted from their entire social environment. And it is interesting to see that it is particularly such letters which reveal a self-confidence of their writers that is in clear contrast to the deferential gratitude we have witnessed so far. This is what 72-year-old Samuel Hearsum, who lived in London in the parish of St Marylebone, wrote in his letter to the overseers of Chelmsford, the place of his settlement, on 4 February 1824:

> According to promise I Expected a line from you before now to lit me Know Wether the Gent[n]. of the Committe p[l]ease to allow me a small Trifle weekly, I think it very hard as I have pay[d]. so much into the poor

fund to be Forsed in to the Workhouse for the Triflon sum of 1$^s$: 6$^d$ per week, which I will endevour to make shift with, Gentalmen If not I hope you will be so good as to let me know wether you would pay M$^r$. French to bring me Down or to Appley to Marylebone Parish to Pass me home which will be very Expenseiv as I Am not Able to Walk.[46]

This man does not even feel obliged to ask for relief. He simply claims it. What is more, he takes the overseer to task. He complains that the latter has not kept his promise, and that he is supposed to be subjected to what was later to come to be known as the 'workhouse test' for the trifling sum of one shilling and sixpence (the regular weekly allowance he received) even though he used to pay poor rates himself. And with a cunning stylistic swing ('Gentalmen If not I hope you will be so good as to let me know') he gets to his major point: that, as he is not willing to come 'home' voluntarily, it would be quite expensive for the parish if he were to be brought home. An assessment of comparative advantages is suggested here. The implicit message of Samuel Hearsum's letter is that the overseers ought to consider whether it would not be cheaper to give him a regular pension and leave him where he was rather than to engage in the complicated procedure of a formal removal, given further that he would also have to be relieved once he had come 'home'.

Other paupers were more explicit on this point. For example, in June 1833, Susan Spooner wrote from Norwich, where she lived with her bedridden sister Elizabeth:

> I hope Gentleman you will allow me as us[u]al for I have no way of getting a living for I ham so very lame for I cannot wo[r]k if not I must Come home then my sister must have some body to do for her therefore it will be more expence to you she cannot be alone nor cannot be moved I have expected her death for several weeks.[47]

The two Spooner sisters had their settlement in Braintree. A thriving centre of the north Essex cloth industry during the seventeenth century, the town had since suffered from the decline of cloth production. By the early nineteenth century, it supported a large group of paupers living elsewhere – people who had moved to other places in search of employment, but had not gained new settlements. No less than a fifth of the paupers chargeable to Braintree lived elsewhere, not only in the closer vicinity, but also in places like London, Norwich, Leeds and York.[48] Norwich, itself an old centre of cloth production, had one of the largest communities of Braintree paupers, a group whose members were visited several times by representatives of the select vestry of Braintree, who inquired into their condition

## Old Age in Poverty

and checked on whether their allowances were still appropriate. In the report of the visit of July 1831, it was said about Susan and Elizabeth Spooner that one of them had a lame knee and that 'both weave Silk but can get very little to do – a complaint general throughout the trade'.[49] At that time, each of them received a weekly allowance of two shillings, which was sent by bank order to the overseers of Norwich who then handed it out to them.[50]

The other Braintree poor at Norwich received their allowances in the same way. Judged by the levels of these payments and the repeated assessments and revisions of the allowances through the select vestry, it appears that the relief policy of Braintree was not particularly generous, but fairly reasonable. The earnings of the recipients were – negatively – taken into account but, on the other hand, there were positive social criteria like the number of dependent children.[51] It may be noted in passing that more or less the same rules were also applied to the paupers residing in Braintree itself, who altogether made up about a quarter of the population.[52]

In 1833, a stern 'reform' faction emerged within Braintree's select vestry, who opposed current relief practices and intended to have all 'outstanding' paupers brought 'home' and delivered into the workhouse. In the previous year, the Royal Commission on the Poor Laws had been appointed and (even if there is no direct proof of this) it would not seem unreasonable to assume that the attempts at reorganising poor relief at Braintree were also influenced by the public debate on the reform of the poor law generated by the work of the Commission. At any rate, in July 1833 – three weeks after the receipt of the letter from Susan Spooner quoted above – the select vestry of Braintree decided 'to cut off all distant Paupers belonging to us'. In a letter which was sent out to all parishes concerned with such paupers, it was said that if someone still needed relief, 'he must come home, into our Workhouse'[53] – a procedure which anticipated precisely the 'workhouse test' that was to be recommended in the *Poor Law Report* of 1834 and then made compulsory for all newly established Poor Law Unions in the Poor Law Amendment Act of the same year.[54]

However, just as, in the event, the New Poor Law was not implemented in the brutal fashion which had been planned,[55] so did many a resolution that had been passed in the select vestry at Braintree prove a dead letter. There is no evidence that elderly paupers residing elsewhere were actually removed to Braintree and put into the workhouse. Susan and Elizabeth Spooner definitely stayed in Norwich and still received their weekly allowance. By September 1833 it was reduced from two shillings to one shilling and sixpence for each of them, but they still received it regularly, at least until midsummer 1835 – maybe even longer, though this is impossible to tell as the relief books do not survive beyond that point in time.[56]

The account of high prospective removal costs against regular relief payments was not only brought up by the poor themselves. It was also referred to by people who wrote on their behalf. A good example is that of 74-year-old widow Parminter at Bromsgrove (near Birmingham) whose settlement was also in Braintree. She too was supposed either to do without her pension or to go 'home' – where in fact she had never been – and enter the workhouse. This is what her former master, for whom she and her husband had worked for 20 years, wrote in June 1833:

> She is a native of this neighbourhood – & never was 23 miles distant – here she has kind neighbours & old social relations ... Such is the state of the poor woman's mind that I verily believe her removal would prove the breaking down of her mind & the shortening of her days – & so reluctant is the poor creature to come to a workhouse – that I am sure nothing will move her whilst she has a penny or a chair or Table to sell to produce a loaf of bread – & the difference between the expenses of her long removal & the expenses at Braintree when there & her allowance here would be pretty nearly balanced in the end – considering her great age & infirmities & probability of short existance – Unless indeed a Saving be calculated upon in shortening of life by distress of mind – I hope ... that you will allow 2/6 weekly – & allow the old creature to die peaceably in her native county.[57]

Like the Spooner sisters, this woman was not removed to Braintree but stayed in Bromsgrove, the place where she was really – though not legally – 'at home', and still received her weekly pension of two shillings and sixpence.[58]

Even if she had never been to Braintree herself, widow Parminter was still well known to the overseers of that place. As early as the summer of 1826, the overseers of Bromsgrove had thanked their colleagues at Braintree for the receipt of her allowance payments, and told them that she had 'for many years laboried under rheumatic gout in the wrists and knees', and that 'she would be unable to support herself with the allowance of 3/ weekly did she not occasionally receive a small sum by taken a lodger'.[59] In the following year, she planned to move to Wordesley where 'sume Friend will take her in to make her Comfortable'. The overseer of Wordesley gave his consent, on the condition of being reimbursed, to which in turn the overseers of Braintree agreed. They would, it was said, cover the advance costs 'as is our useal way'.[60]

We do not know whether widow Parminter ever moved to Wordesley. Presumably she did not but stayed in Bromsgrove, since all later references to her – like the letter of her former master quoted above – mention only that place. Nevertheless, her plan is interesting in itself in that it suggests that even paupers who resided in a parish in which they were not settled were not necessarily restricted to remain at that place once and for all, but might well be able to move about without having to worry about their relief as long as the parishes concerned made the necessary arrangements. No less telling are the references to the household arrangements involved in her plan: at Wordesley, she would have lived as a lodger, just as she had previously taken in lodgers herself. Sharing your premises with other people in a similar condition seems to have been a common experience of the poor.

## V  EXPERIENCES OF OLD AGE

The experience of old age has already been touched upon, though in no more than the most fragmentary fashion, in the letters written in the name of Susannah Halls. Still, these fragments alone are telling enough: the image of the 'poor helpless creature' who could 'just creep about', or the fact that she was not able (and neither was her daughter) to tell her age in precise years – a numerical uncertainty with respect to ageing which, if Keith Thomas is right, was widespread well into the nineteenth century.[61]

Isolated references to the experience of ageing are to be found in many pauper letters. In some cases, however, the images become so 'dense' that a more or less coherent picture emerges. Perhaps the most compelling example is that of William James. It is an extreme case, not in terms of the experiences as such, but with respect to the sheer extent and extraordinary literary power of his testimony. This poor man has left no less than 53 letters behind, apparently all written by himself, from Chelmsford to Colchester St Peter, covering a period of ten years from July 1818 to August 1828. It is the richest record of any one pauper I have seen.

At the time of his first letter he is 65, his wife 70 (she dies in early 1823). Their daughter is chronically ill (unfortunately he does not specify the nature of her disease) and confined to her bed. There are certain recurrent themes in his letters. First, the insufficiency of his earnings. He seems to be (or to have become) an unskilled day labourer doing all sorts of 'jobs', if he gets work at all. Second, there is the issue of his growing debility. He complains of being unable to do hard work, of his illnesses, of his weakness and fatigue. Third, he frequently refers to the illness of his wife and daughter, especially the latter's constant confinement to bed, but also the former's unableness to work. Fourth, he dwells on the trouble with his landlady, who keeps threatening to have his few goods distrained whenever he has been unable to pay his rent. Fifth, he reflects on the difficulties of making ends meet, stressing the necessity of drawing on the help from friends and neighbours.

For our purposes, the most compelling theme is complaint about the infirmities of old age, the torment of illness, the exhaustion of body and soul. 'My strength, and all my faculties', he writes in the summer of 1823, 'fail me very fast'.[62] Or in the spring of 1824: 'it cannot be long, [and for] E[v]er my head must be laid in the dust'.[63] In another letter, there is a particularly interesting passage which draws a clear association between ill-health, infirmity and deficient diet. It is also the most explicit record I have come across of the experience of work in which that experience is not only expressed in the words of a poor man, but also put down in his own hand:

> for many weeks past, sometimes work, & sometimes none, my Earnings have been but small, not more on Average, than six Shillings or six, and sixpence, a week, as near as I can tell – (I may say for some Months this have been my case) with which we cannot procure Necessaries, to support health, nor nature, for the want of which, I find health and strengh decaying fast, so that when I have a little work to do, I find myself, through Age, and fatige, incapable to perform it, Walking into the Country five or six Miles in a morning, working the day, and returning home at Night, is a task that I cannot, but without great dif[f]iculty perform serveral times I have thought, I could not gett home, and it have been the Occasion, of my being Ill, for two or three days, this I attribute in a great degree, to the want, of constant nourishment, to keep up my strength, and of Age ad[d]ed theretoo, being now within one Year of Seventy – at this time I am Unwell, and have been several days[64]

As already said, this is an extreme case. The wide scope of his writing, the minute detail of his descriptions, and above all his stunning literary power are quite extraordinary. So is the comprehensive picture of old age as it emerges from his letters. And yet, the individual components of that picture are by no means exceptional, but turn up in many other pauper letters. Take the example of work. Nearly all pauper letters touch on it, even if no other one gets anywhere near the extraordinary testimony just quoted. But many letters deal with the connection of work and subsistence in that it is pointed out, for example, that an elderly person is still working but not able to subsist, without drawing poor relief, because of insufficient earnings; or it is said that an elderly person cannot work any longer, for the simple reason that he or she is too ill or too weak. Or we hear that someone who wants to work cannot find employment because of his age, a trap which is succinctly described in a letter in the summer of 1818: 'they will not Employ a Old Hand while they can get Plenty of Young ones'.[65]

To some extent, of course, the permanent references to work have to be regarded as mere rhetoric. In a society which conceived itself as being built upon labour, and where the notion of poverty – as distinguished from indigence – was the negative image of labour, it would have been foolish not to cover the question of work in a letter concerned with matters of poor relief.[66] And yet, it would seem to me that the sense of pride in the strength of your body – as it is so vividly brought out in William James' account of how he feels his power waning – is a clear testimony of a deeply rooted positive attitude to work and a firm belief in its social function that was typical of the labouring poor, and should not simply be regarded as a rhetorical concession to middle-class values.

It is also from this attitude to labour that the notion of retirement emerges, the idea that you had a right to relief when your labour power had gone; and, that in recognition of the work you had performed as long as you could, you were entitled to spend the autumn of your life without having to worry about it. This view was neatly put by John Hides, an elderly pauper whom the overseer of Cheshunt, Hertfordshire, where he lived, described as 'worn out by hard labour'. In 1805, he wrote to the overseers of Upminster where he was settled: 'I need not enumerate my distresses to you I am sure you can judge and feel for me; as I grow older I get more Infirm, my Wife quite helpless  I leave all to you, hopeing you will get something done to make me tollerable comfortable'.[67] A similar view was expressed by Isaac Harriage in London, who wrote to the overseers of Chelmsford, in an absolutely remarkable self-conscious mood: 'I hope You will Consider me worthey of your Consideration to allow me my Salery As I had which is three Shillings Pers Weeke ... my Wife is Seventy there [three] Years of Age w[h]ich You Cannot Expect but wee must be Troubleson to the Parrish'.[68]

In interpreting such statements we must not, of course, mistake them for expressions of generally acknowledged standards of welfare provision. While support for the elderly *could* be fairly generous under the Old Poor Law, this was by no means the norm. Rather, with the evidence on the value and availability of old age 'pensions' before the twentieth century still being so limited, and at the same time so conflicting, there is every reason to be sceptical about the achievements in the field of public assistance for the elderly poor during the period of the pre-history of the modern welfare state.[69]

Nevertheless, within the field of the images of the elderly poor, as witnessed in their own testimonies with which we have been concerned in this chapter, the contrast of Isaac Harriage's notion of old age to that expressed in Susannah Hall's letter quoted at the beginning could hardly be greater. Where for her old age is a matter of shame for which you apologise: 'I think I Shall not Trouble you much longer', to him it is a source of self-confidence to take a position from which poor relief is regarded as of right: 'my Wife is Seventy there Years of Age w[h]ich You Cannot Expect but wee must be Troubleson to the Parrish'.

## VI  CONCLUSION

In trying to sum up, I want to begin with a methodological point. Every pauper letter is a narrative account written for a specific purpose, and as such it is bound up with strategic interests. However, no pauper letter can be reduced to those interests. This is because in the course of writing, a narrative potential is released through which the writer loses the firm track of his rhetoric strategy and is 'misled' onto the wide territory of unintended asides and bypasses. It is this territory of narrative imagination which provides us with the rich subject matter for the historical interpretation of pauper letters.

Turning to substantive issues, I shall take up the three themes under which the material has been presented and posit some wider implications. I should like to stress that these are tentative suggestions which go beyond the scope of the evidence found in pauper letters, and which therefore can probably never be fully substantiated on the basis of that material alone. But they are meant to point out certain directions in which that material may be interpreted, in the context of our general knowledge of the Old Poor Law and of the conditions of the labouring poor in late eighteenth- and early nineteenth-century England.

First, then, the household arrangements of the elderly: here the evidence of pauper letters seems to support the findings of recent research into the demographic profiles of pauper populations, according to which the households of the poor were not smaller in size and simpler in structure than those in the rest of the population, but displayed a variety of household forms and family patterns, including those which involved the presence of relatives and lodgers. The formation of such non-nuclear households seems to have rested on the initiative of the poor themselves. There is as

## Old Age in Poverty

yet no indication, for example, that the local authorities would ever have ordered an elderly widow to be placed in the household of a relative of hers. This suggests that under the Old Poor Law there was no interference of the welfare agencies with your household arrangements. Rather, you could expect to be supported in whatever household you had chosen to live. Naturally, this rule does not hold for those who were not in the position to make that choice, like orphaned children, sick people or, in fact, elderly paupers who were boarded out by parish officers. We know that the boarding out of individual paupers was a common form of welfare provision under the Old Poor Law. Unfortunately though, there is as yet no systematic research on the extent of this practice which would enable us to make it a critical variable against which to judge how far the principle of individual independence in household formation extended.

Second, the question of removal: in opening a balance of high prospective expenses which would arise from their removal against a moderate level of regular non-resident relief, it is striking how the poor took up financial considerations in order to turn them *against* the overseers. This means that the Old Poor Law provided a platform for negotiation on which both sides could pursue their interests.

Third, the experience of old age in relation to the question of physical capacity and labour power: pauper letters reveal a strong determination to make your own living, to support yourself and your family and succeed in the precarious 'economy of makeshifts'.[70] Connected to this, we find a deeply rooted pride in the ability to work, and in exerting your physical powers as long as you possibly could. The wider implication here is the complex way in which the Old Poor Law acted as a vital institutional channel through which that peculiar type of economy was supported, not just in the form of regular relief during critical phases of the lifecycle, but also by providing working materials, tools and credit on special occasions.

Finally, the experience of old age as it impinges on the formation of the idea of retirement and old age pension. Naturally, in this context the notion of entitlement relates to elderly people: people, that is, who had a particular claim to communal support. But again, there is a wider implication. It is not only that Isaac Harriage referred to his relief as his 'salary' – the striking point here is that this notion is echoed in numerous other letters where people, and not just elderly ones, demand it as their 'pay', their 'money', even their 'wage'. This suggests that by the late eighteenth century the Old Poor Law was understood by the labouring poor as providing them with a right to relief, over the extent of which there might be (or perhaps even had to be) arguments with the parish officers, but which was (in their view at any rate) no longer questionable in principle.

## NOTES

1. Essex Record Office, Chelmsford (hereafter ERO), D/P 94/18/1, Chelmsford overseers' correspondence.
2. Among the 400 or so historic parishes of Essex, there are 56 which possess records classed as 'overseers' correspondence', a corpus of letters which consists of some 5000 pieces dating from the 1680s to the 1840s. About 1000 of these are letters received from paupers, which survive mainly from the 1820s and early 1830s.
3. The first volume, under the provisional title *Voices of the Labouring Poor: Essex Pauper Letters, 1820-1834* (Oxford: British Academy), is in preparation for the 'Records of Social and Economic History. New Series'. I should like to take this opportunity to record my thanks to the British Academy's RSEH Committee for inviting me to prepare that volume. Thanks are also due to Richard Smith and Ludolf Kuchenbuch for their unfailing interest and encouragement; to Stefan Hanemann, who has been a model research assistant; and to the Cambridge Group for the History of Population and Social Structure, the Wellcome Unit for the History of Medicine at the University of Oxford and the FernUniversität Hagen for their financial support.
4. For working-class autobiographies, we have the anthologies edited by J. Burnett, *Useful Toil. Autobiographies of Working People from the 1820s to the 1920s* (Harmondsworth: Penguin, 1977); *Destiny Obscure. Autobiographies of Childhood, Education and Family from the 1820s to the 1920s* (Harmondsworth: Penguin, 1982), and the masterly analysis by D. Vincent, *Bread, Knowledge and Freedom. A Study of Nineteenth-Century Working Class Autobiography* (London: Europa Publications, 1981). Similar standard works could be named for other countries, like Wolfgang Emmerich, *Proletarische Lebensläufe. Autobiographische Dokumente zur Enstehung der Zweiten Kultur in Deutschland*, 2 vols (Reinbek: Rowohlt, 1974–5), for Germany. For threatening letters, see the seminal contribution by E.P. Thompson, 'The Crime of Anonymity', in D. Hay et al., *Albion's Fatal Tree. Crime and Society in Eighteenth-Century England* (Harmondsworth: Penguin, 1977), pp.255–344 (with selected pieces, pp.309–44). Famous analyses of personal testimonies in legal records include A. Farge and M. Foucault, *Le Désordre des familles. Lettres de cachet des Archives de la Bastille* (Paris: Gallimard, 1982) and N.Z. Davis, *Fiction in the Archives. Pardon Tales and Their Tellers in Sixteenth-Century France* (Palo Alto: Stanford University Press, 1987).
5. K.D.M. Snell, *Annals of the Labouring Poor. Social Change and Agrarian England 1660–1900* (Cambridge: Cambridge University Press, 1985).
6. J.S. Taylor, *Poverty, Migration, and Settlement in the Industrial Revolution. Sojourners' Narratives* (Palo Alto, California: Society for the Promotion of Science and Scholarship, 1989).
7. For a first attempt at a literary critique of pauper letters, see T. Sokoll, 'Sprechende Briefe: Englische Armenbriefe, 1750–1850', in W. Schulze (ed.), *Ego-Dokumente. Annäherungen an den Menschen in der Geschichte* (Berlin: Akademie-Verlag, 1995). An extended English version of that paper will be found in A. Digby, J. Innes and R.M. Smith (eds), *Poverty and*

*Relief in England from the Sixteenth to the Twentieth Century* (Cambridge: Cambridge University Press, forthcoming).

8. A settlement certificate made no difference in this respect. For if paupers had moved with a settlement certificate from their home parish, this only meant that the overseers of the 'host' parish had not been able to send (or remove) them on their arrival (which, until 1795, they could do if the paupers had no certificate), but could (or rather should) only do so when they became chargeable. Likewise, the extension (in 1795) of the latter provision to all paupers, including those travelling without a settlement certificate, made no difference, since the universal application of the principle 'removable only if chargeable' implied the removal of 'alien' paupers in need of relief to their place of settlement. In other words, the settlement laws never provided for the relief of a pauper *in* a parish other than that of his or her settlement. The best account of complicated provisions and the practical effects of the settlement laws is J.S. Taylor, 'The Impact of Pauper Settlement 1691–1834', *Past and Present* 73 (1976), 42–74; for the pre-1795 situation, see also the lucid sketch by Paul Slack, *The English Poor Law 1531–1782* (London: Macmillan, 1990), pp.35–9.

9. J.S. Taylor, 'A Different Kind of Speenhamland: Nonresident Relief in the Industrial Revolution', *Journal of British Studies* 30 (1991), 183–208 (the quotation: 184); Taylor, *Poverty, Migration, and Settlement in the Industrial Revolution*. There is also a brief discussion in G.R. Boyer, *An Economic History of the English Poor Law, 1750–1850* (Cambridge: Cambridge University Press, 1990), pp.257–9. The notable exception to the neglect of the issue in the older literature is E.M. Hampson, 'Settlement and Removal in Cambridgeshire, 1662–1834', *Cambridge Historical Journal* 2 (1926–8), 287–9; E.M. Hampson, *The Treatment of Poverty in Cambridgeshire 1597–1834* (Cambridge: Cambridge University Press, 1934), pp.148–51.

10. N. Landau, 'The Laws of Settlement and the Surveillance of Immigration in Eighteenth-century Kent', *Continuity and Change* 3 (1988), 391–420; K.D.M. Snell, 'Pauper Settlement and the Right to Poor Relief in England and Wales', *Continuity and Change* 6 (1991), 375–415; N. Landau, 'The Eighteenth-century Context of the Laws of Settlement', *Continuity and Change* 6 (1991), 417–39; K.D.M. Snell, 'Settlement, Poor Law and the Rural Historian: New Approaches and Opportunities', *Rural History* 3 (1992), 145–72.

11. The rather informal tone of English pauper letters is in sharp contrast to records of that kind from other countries. German pauper letters, for example, are extremely formal, abounding with deferential phraseology and all sorts of epistolary conventions. See J. Karweick, '"Tiefgebeugt von Nahrungssorgen und Gram". Schreiben an Behörden', in S. Grosse *et al.*, *'Denn das Schreiben gehört nicht zu meiner täglichen Beschäftigung'. Der Alltag Kleiner Leute in Bittschriften, Briefen und Berichten aus dem 19. Jahrhundert. Ein Lesebuch* (Bonn: Dietz 1989), pp.17–87, 188–89, especially the applications for poor relief to the magistrate of the town of Essen for 1804–5 (pp.32–40).

12. ERO, D/P 94/18/1, Chelmsford overseers' correspondence. Another example is the letter of (?)/11/1825: 'I Susannah Halls Do return my Sincear

Thanks to you all Genteelmen For all your kindness to me a poor feable Creature'.

13. ERO, D/P 94/18/42, Chelmsford overseers' correspondence, 1800–34, letter of 13/5/1825 (copy).
14. ERO, D/P 94/12/36, Chelmsford overseers' accounts.
15. ERO, D/P 94/18/42, Chelmsford overseers' correspondence, 1800–34, letters of 1/2/1824, 21/6/1824 and 4/11/1824.
16. Lord Ernle, *English Farming Past and Present*, 6th edn, introd. G.E. Fussel and O.R. McGregor (London: Longman, 1961), p.314; T.L. Richardson, 'Agricultural Labourers' Wages and the Cost of Living in Essex, 1790–1834: a Contribution to the Standard of Living Debate', in B.A. Holderness and M. Turner (eds), *Land, Labour and Agriculture, 1790–1920. Essays for Gordon Mingay* (London: Hambledon, 1991), pp.69–90.
17. ERO, D/P 94/12/36, Chelmsford overseers' accounts; D/P 94/8/6, Chelmsford select vestry minutes, 1824–6.
18. D/P 94/18/42, Chelmsford overseers' correspondence, 1800–34, letter of 15/11/1825.
19. ERO, D/P 94/8/6, Chelmsford select vestry minutes, entry of 17/11/1825; D/P 94/12/36, Chelmsford overseers' accounts.
20. R. Chartier, 'The Practical Impact of Writing', in P. Ariès and G. Duby (eds), *The History of Private Life*, vol. 3: R. Chartier (ed.), *Renaissance to Enlightenment* (London: Harvard University Press, 1989), pp.111–59, 615–17 (the title is misleading, as Chartier deals almost exclusively with the practices of reading); R. Chartier, 'Leisure and Sociability. Reading Aloud in Early Modern Europe', in S. Zimmermann and R. Weissmann (eds), *Urban Life in the Renaissance* (London and Toronto: Associate University Press, 1989), pp.103–20 [R. Chartier, 'Muße und Geselligkeit. Lautes Lesen im Europa der Neuzeit', in R. Chartier, *Lesewelten. Buch und Lektüre in der frühen Neuzeit* (Frankfurt and New York: Campus, 1990), pp.146–68].
21. P. Burke, 'Introduction', in P. Burke and R. Porter (eds), *The Social History of Language* (Cambridge: Cambridge University Press, 1987), p.10.
22. For a brilliant survey of the historical analysis of the dialectics of orality and literacy, see W.J. Ong, *Orality and Literacy. The Technologizing of the Word* (London and New York: Methuen, 1982). A wide range of material is provided in L. Kuchenbuch, T. Sokoll *et al.*, *Einführungskurs Alteuropäische Schriftlichkeit* (Hagen: FernUniversität Hagen, 1988).
23. R.S. Schofield, 'Dimensions of Illiteracy, 1750–1850', *Explorations in Economic History* 10 (1972/3), 450. In counties like Essex, Suffolk and Norfolk, the level of literacy was of course lower. See W.B. Stephens, *Education, Literacy and Society, 1830–1870. The Geography of Diversity in Provincial England* (Manchester: Manchester University Press, 1987), pp.79–81. For the European comparison, see C.M. Cipolla, *Literacy and Development in the West* (Harmondsworth: Penguin, 1969), Chap. 3 and statistical appendix; H.J. Graff, *The Legacies of Literacy. Continuities and Contradictions in Western Culture and Society* (Bloomington and Indianapolis: Indiana University Press, 1987), Chap. 6.
24. ERO, D/P 94/18/42, Chelmsford overseers' correspondence, 1800–34, letter of 8/7/1824.

25. Ibid., letter of 28/6/1825. For her letter on letter writing, see previous note.
26. Ibid., letter of 27/12/1825.
27. ERO, D/P 322/18/1, Rayleigh overseers' correspondence, 1799–1837, letter of 25/3/1828.
28. ERO, D/P 94/18/42, Chelmsford overseers' correspondence, 1800–34, letter of 21/11/1827 from Wivenhoe.
29. This is not to say that I would altogether exclude the possibility, within the small compass of an individual community over a shorter period of time, to determine the place of the group of letter-writing paupers within the circle of all recipients of poor relief and to assess the evidence of their letters in the context of the adopted relief policies. But this would be an extremely lucky singular case, and the historical reconstruction itself would be an extremely time-consuming business.
30. ERO, D/P 264/18/24, Braintree overseers' correspondence, 1685–1835, letter of 22/4/1833.
31. ERO, D/P 21/18/3, Steeple Bumpstead overseers' correspondence, 1817–57, undated letter (notice of receipt 27/9/1825).
32. ERO, D/P 21/16/4, Steeple Bumpstead overseers' settlement correspondence, letter of 12/12/1831.
33. P. Slack, *Poverty and Policy in Tudor and Stuart England* (London: Longman, 1988), p.85.
34. Ibid., pp.73–80.
35. T. Sokoll, 'The Pauper Household Small and Simple? The Evidence from Listings of Inhabitants and Pauper Lists of Early Modern England Reassessed', *Ethnologia Europaea* 17 (1987), 30–2; T. Sokoll, *Household and Family Among the Poor: the Case of Two Essex Communities in the Late Eighteenth and Early Nineteenth Centuries* (Bochum: Brockmeyer, 1993), pp.59–74.
36. Sokoll, *Household and Family Among the Poor*, Chaps 6, 9 and 10; T. Sokoll, 'The Household Position of Elderly Widows in Poverty: Evidence from Two English Communities in the Late Eighteenth and Early Nineteenth Centuries', in J. Henderson and R. Wall (eds), *Poor Women and Children in the Past* (London: Routledge, 1994), pp.207–24. For Laslett's 'rule', see P. Laslett, *The World We Have Lost – Further Explored* (London: Methuen, 1983), p.46 (the point was already made in the first edition of 1965).
37. H. Medick, 'The Proto-industrial Family Economy: the Structural Function of Household and Family during the Transition from Peasant Society to Industrial Capitalism', *Social History* 1 (1976), 308–9. It should be noted, however, that for the evidence on householding patterns of elderly paupers to be properly understood it needs to be judged against the evidence on the living arrangements of elderly people in general. The latter is still rather limited itself, but some material may be found in R. Wall, 'Residential Isolation of the Elderly: a Comparison over Time', *Ageing and Society* 4 (1984), 483–503; P. Laslett, *A Fresh Map of Life. The Emergence of the Third Age* (London: Weidenfeld & Nicolson, 1989), pp.111–15; R. Wall, 'Elderly Persons and Members of their Households in England and Wales from Preindustrial Times to the Present', in D.I. Kertzer and P. Laslett (eds), *Aging in the Past: Demography, Society, and Old Age* (Berkeley and Los

Angeles: University of California Press, 1995), pp.81–106; and J. Ehmer, *Sozialgeschichte des Alters* (Frankfurt am Main: Suhrkamp, 1990), pp.177–87.

38. S.G. and E.O.A. Checkland (eds), *The Poor Law Report of 1834* (Harmondsworth: Penguin 1974), p.115.
39. ERO D/P 138/18/1+11, Colchester St James overseers' correspondence, 1810–33, letter of 15/10/1810. On later debates concerning the supposedly 'natural' duty of inter-generational assistance, especially of children towards their parents, see M. Anderson, 'The Impact on the Family Relationships of the Elderly of Changes since Victorian Times in Governmental Income Maintenance Provision', in E. Shanas and M.B. Sussman (eds), *Family, Bureaucracy and the Elderly* (Durham, NC: Duke University Press, 1977), pp.36–59; M.A. Crowther, 'Family Responsibility and State Responsibility in Britain Before the Welfare State', *Historical Journal* 25 (1982), 131–45; D. Thomson, '"I Am Not My Father's Keeper": Families and the Elderly in Nineteenth-century England', *Law and History Review* 2 (1984), 265–86.
40. M. Anderson, *Family Structure in Nineteenth-Century Lancashire* (Cambridge: Cambridge University Press, 1971), pp.45–53; M. Anderson, 'Household Structure and the Industrial Revolution; Mid-nineteenth-century Preston in Comparative Perspective', in P. Laslett and R. Wall (eds), *Household and Family in Past Time* (Cambridge: Cambridge University Press, 1972), pp.224–6; J. Foster, *Class Struggle and the Industrial Revolution. Early Industrial Capitalism in Three English Towns* (London: Methuen, 1974), pp.95–7; J. Ehmer, *Familienstruktur und Arbeitsorganisation im frühindustriellen Wien* (Munich: Oldenbourg, 1980), pp.150–61; R. Sieder, *Sozialgeschichte der Familie* (Frankfurt am Main: Suhrkamp, 1978), pp.183–6.
41. L. Niethammer and F.-J. Brüggemeier, 'Wie wohnten die Arbeiter im Kaiserreich?', *Archiv für Sozialgeschichte* 16 (1976), 150–4; F.-J. Brüggemeier, *Leben vor Ort. Ruhrbergleute und Ruhrbergbau 1889–1819* (Munich: Beck, 1983), pp.62–8.
42. D. Davies, *The Case of Labourers in Husbandry* (London: Robinson, 1795), p.181. For further material on lodgers in pauper households, see Sokoll, *Household and Family Among the Poor*, pp.82–9.
43. ERO, D/P 157/18/12, Aveley overseers' correspondence, 1751–1838, letter of 1/8/1822.
44. ERO, D/P 21/18/13, Steeple Bumpstead overseers' correspondence, 1817–37, letter of 3/5/1832.
45. ERO, D/P 21/18/13, Steeple Bumpstead overseers' correspondence, 1817–37, letters of 10/5/1832, 7/6/1832, 12/7/1832, 22/12/1833, 29/12/1834, 18/3/1836 and 7/9/1836. At the time of the letter quoted in the previous note, her weekly allowance amounted to seven shillings. It was later reduced to five shillings.
46. ERO, D/P 94/18/42, Chelmsford overseers' correspondence, 1800–34, letter of 4/2/1824.
47. ERO, D/P 264/18/24, Braintree overseers' correspondence, 1685–1835, letter of 21/6/1833.
48. This is evident from ERO, D/DO 09, Braintree Poor Book 1821, and D/Ub 29, Braintree Poor Books 1822–4. For details, see Sokoll, *Household and Family Among the Poor*, Chap. 8.

## Old Age in Poverty

49. ERO, D/P 264/8/10, Braintree, select vestry, Book of memoranda, 1817–36, report on the condition of the Braintree poor at Norwich of 22/7/1831.
50. ERO, D/P 264/12/31–2, Braintree overseers' accounts. According to the recordings of regular relief payments between Easter 1824 and midsummer 1835 given in that source, Susan Spooner received a regular weekly allowance of two shillings since Michaelmas 1829 (possibly even before that date: there are no surviving records from Michaelmas 1827 until Lady Day 1829), and her sister the same amount since Christmas 1830.
51. ERO, D/P 264/8/10, Braintree, select vestry, Book of memoranda, 1817–36, reports on the paupers residing in Norwich of 23/6/1825, 18/8/1827 and 22/7/1831.
52. For details, see Sokoll, *Household and Family Among the Poor*, Chap. 8.
53. ERO, D/P 264/8/10, Braintree, select vestry, Book of memoranda, 1817–36, entry of 10/7/1833.
54. The work of the Royal Commission, their Report and the final Act are well summarised in U.R.Q. Henriques, *Before the Welfare State. Social Administration in Early Industrial Britain* (London: Longman, 1979), pp.26–34, 39–52.
55. See ibid., pp.52–9, and M.E. Rose, *The Relief of Poverty 1834–1914*, 2nd edn (London: Macmillan, 1986), pp.11–14, for convenient sketches of the opposition against the New Poor Law.
56. ERO, D/P 264/12/32, Braintree overseers' accounts.
57. ERO, D/P 264/18/24, Braintree overseers' correspondence 1685–1835, letter of John Adams of 19/6/1833.
58. Incidentally, it is not at all exceptional that she should have been chargeable to a parish she had never been to herself. Upon her marriage, a woman gained the settlement of her husband. Thus, widow Parminter's deceased husband might have moved from Braintree, where he was settled (be it by birth or later acquisition through apprenticeship, service or otherwise), to Bromsgrove without gaining a new settlement. But it might as well be that his father had moved from Braintree to Bromsgrove in the first place, thereby 'carrying' his settlement along with him, and had then bequeathed it to his son. In that case, widow Parminter's deceased husband would have been settled in Braintree even if he had never been there himself, whereas her own settlement, passed on to her through her father-in-law and her husband, would also have been in Braintree. Cases like these, which could span over several generations and involve a whole range of different places, were dealt with under the notion of 'derivative settlement' by eighteenth-century lawyers, and contemporary commentators reported the most ludicrous examples of such settlement 'chains'. See S. and B. Webb, *English Poor Law History, Part I: The Old Poor Law* (London: Longman, 1927), pp.333–4.
59. ERO, D/P 264/8/10, Braintree, select vestry, Book of memoranda, 1817–36, copy of a letter by John Pearce, assistant overseer at Bromsgrove, of 3/11/1826. In August 1832 her weekly allowance was reduced from three shillings to two shillings and sixpence, the amount she still received after her master's letter quoted above.
60. ERO, D/P 264/18/24, Braintree overseers' correspondence 1685–1835, letter of the vestry clerk to the overseers of Bromsgrove, 18/9/1827. See also the letter to widow Parminter of 18/9/1827, saying that there was no

objection to her moving to her friend at Wordesley and that the overseer of that place had been informed about her plan.
61. K. Thomas, 'Age and Authority in Early Modern England', *Proceedings of the British Academy* 62 (1976), 205.
62. ERO, D/P 178/18/23, Colchester St Peter overseers' correspondence, 1815–38, letter of 25/6/1823.
63. Ibid., letter of (?)/4/1824.
64. Ibid., letter of 29/7/1822.
65. Ibid., letter of J. Berry from London of 19/7/1818.
66. The distinction between 'indigence' and 'poverty' in the 1834 Poor Law Report is a telling example. Indigent, and therefore worthy of public assistance, it was said, was any one 'unable to labour, or unable to obtain, in return for his labour, the means of subsistence'. Poverty, by contrast, was held to be 'the state of one who, in order to obtain a mere subsistence, is forced to have recourse to labour': *Poor Law Report*, p.334. See also P. Colquhoun, *A Treatise on Indigence* (London: Hatchard, 1806), p.8. The best survey of the ideological background is still J.R. Poynter, *Society and Pauperism. English Ideas on Poor Relief, 1795–1834* (London: Routledge & Kegan Paul, 1969). Other useful works include P. Mathias, 'Adam's Burden: Historical Diagnoses of Poverty', in P. Mathias, *The Transformation of England. Essay on the Economic and Social History of England in the Eighteenth Century* (London: Methuen, 1979), pp.131–47; G. Himmelfarb, *The Idea of Poverty: England in the Early Industrial Age* (London: Faber & Faber, 1984). For a European perspective, see the brilliant discussion by V. Hunecke, 'Überlegungen zur Geschichte der Armut im vorindustriellen Europa', *Geschichte und Gesellschaft* 9 (1983), 488–512, esp. 383–4 and 509–12.
67. ERO, D/P 117/18/2A, Upminster overseers' correspondence, letter of 2/1/1805; letter of 6/3/1805 for the quotation of the overseer.
68. ERO, D/P 94/18/42, Chelmsford overseers' correspondence, 1800–34, letter of 19/3/1827.
69. D. Thomson, 'The Decline of Social Welfare: Falling State Support for the Elderly since Early Victorian Times', *Ageing and Society* 4 (1984), 451–82; E.H. Hunt, 'Paupers and Pensioners: Past and Present', *Ageing and Society* 9 (1990), 407–30; P. Thane, 'Old Age in English History', in C. Conrad and H.-J. von Kondratowitz (eds), *Zur Kulturgeschichte des Alterns/Toward a Cultural History of Aging* (Berlin: Deutsches Zentrum für Altersfragen, 1993), pp.24–6.
70. O. Hufton, 'Women without Men: Widows and Spinsters in Britain and France in the Eighteenth Century', *Journal of Family History* 9 (1984), p.363.

# 7 Pauper Inventories and the Material Lives of the Poor in the Eighteenth and Early Nineteenth Centuries
Peter King

A substantial history of the physical environments in which the eighteenth-century poor lived has yet to be written. The material world of the eighteenth and early nineteenth centuries has recently become an increasing focus for the work of historians.[1] The growing demand for products and services, and changing patterns of consumer behaviour, have each received fairly comprehensive treatment. The extent to which these new patterns of consumption and demand extended from the middling sort to the labouring poor has, however, been largely ignored.[2] While Malcolmson argues in *Life and Labour in England 1700–1780* that the 'expanding culture of consumerism ... was almost entirely inaccessible to the great majority of the nation's population',[3] the relevant parts of his book focus on the ways the poor put together a living rather than on an analysis of their material possessions. The vibrant plebeian culture of the eighteenth century – its recreations, customary practices and popular protests – has been subjected to detailed scrutiny by social historians,[4] while the wide-ranging standard-of-living debate has resulted in the detailed exploitation of the limited data available on wages, prices and other indicators of changing real wage levels and overall consumption patterns.[5] However, neither of these approaches has focused on the household items and everyday material world of the poor.

This lacuna may partly reflect the preoccupations of these two very different schools of historical study (the first with social relations and social conflict, the second with macroeconomic indicators and complex formulae applied to often woefully inadequate data series), but it could be argued that it is mainly the result of a lack of source materials. Contemporary observers rarely wrote in any detail about such matters. The surveys of Davies and Eden, for example, included a detailed series of family budgets, listing both expenditure and earnings, but they contained very few descriptions of the immediate material circumstances of the poor or of their household possessions.[6] Contemporary observations about the consumption habits of the poor are also so contradictory that they are of little use in this context. Complaints about the extravagance of the poor, in aping the consumption habits of their betters, were often coupled with a continued belief in what was later called the theory of leisure-preference, which assumed that if the poor were given an increase in wages they would simply work fewer hours, taking out their increased remuneration in the form of greater leisure.[7] Unfortunately, the main body of sources that might have filled this gap – probate inventories – contain very few documents relating to labouring families, because the vast majority of such families remained outside the scope of the probate system. Only 28 of the sample of 2902 inventories Lorna Weatherill used to study the period 1675–1725 involved those labelled as 'labourers', and these were almost certainly an untypical sample.[8] Labourers' probate inventories can still be useful where they are available, but it is difficult to gauge the extent to which the few labouring families that left inventories were from the higher end of the wealth spectrum within their social group. Moreover, since probate inventories do not survive in significant numbers in most counties beyond the mid-eighteenth century, at the very latest, they also impose severe chronological limitations.

Despite these problems, this chapter will suggest that it is too early to conclude with Weatherill that 'there is a lack of reliable evidence about the possessions of those who did not leave inventories or accounts; we simply do not know what they owned or how they spent their incomes'. Pauper inventories, complex though they are, can, when properly contextualised, begin to open up the material worlds of the poor. Moreover, when used in conjunction with probate inventories (where these survive in sufficient numbers for relatively lowly groups such as labourers and husbandmen), they may enable us to evaluate more fully Weatherill's conclusions that the 'lower limit to the market for household goods' came higher in the social hierarchy than these two groups. Is she correct to assume that 'there was a limit to consumption in the eighteenth century, just as there was in the seventeenth century, for there is no evidence in the inventories that wage-earners were able and willing to spend their incomes on many domestic goods' and that 'wage-earners and the less well-off farmers were not acquiring the goods [she] examined'?[9] Pauper inventories offer a new way of approaching these questions, and since many were written in the later eighteenth century, they may also provide vital evidence on the period in which probate inventories became extremely sparse. These questions will be returned to briefly at the end of this chapter, but the main aim here is to establish the nature and potential of this virtually unexploited source. This will be done by looking at the main contexts in which pauper inventories were created, by analysing three inventories in greater detail and then by tracing about 50 individual inventories into the relevant parish records. This sample of contextualised pauper inventories will then be analysed and compared to a sample of probate inventories in order to raise further questions about the material lives of the poor and about the extent to which they were, or were not, involved in the burgeoning consumer society of the eighteenth century.

I

Pauper inventories are not as easy to find as probate inventories. They are sometimes stored in separate series within the poor law records of an individual parish but they are frequently interspersed within other records such as routine overseers' accounts, and lengthy searches may therefore be required unless the relevant county has a detailed and accessible catalogue of its poor law records. The sample used here has been selected from nearly 350 Essex inventories found and transcribed by Thomas Sokoll as part of his broader research on the Essex poor, the first fruits of which have recently appeared in his book *Household and Family among the Poor*.[10] All these inventories will, it is hoped, eventually be published in full with a detailed introduction indicating the varied contexts from which they arose. In this chapter therefore, those contexts will be analysed only briefly in order to explain why certain types of inventory have been selected as useful for our purposes here.

The term 'pauper inventory' is itself a highly problematic one. Broadly speaking, pauper inventories are defined here as all inventories of household goods and chattels found in parish records, apart from those relating to institutions owned and run by the parish such as workhouses and pesthouses. However, a number of the inventories that fall within this definition clearly do not relate to paupers. In 1758 an inventory of the household goods of George Wright, farmer, appears in the Great Canfield records, for example, not because he was poor (which the inventory clearly indicates he was not), but because he had run away and left his wife and four children potentially chargeable to the parish. As Burn's 1764 *History of the Poor Laws* recorded, 'where a man's actions left wives and children upon the charge of the parish: the church wardens and overseers, by order of the justices, may seize their effects'. This is precisely what the parish officers proceeded to do. The deserted wife thus lost not only her husband but also her material possessions.[11] Inventories, or more frequently lists of goods distrained which may or may not have constituted a full appraisal of the person's possessions, were also made in other contexts where it is clear that the individual whose goods are being recorded was not a pauper. The Saint Osyth parish records, for example, contain a list of Daniel Keeble's goods 'lodged in the workhouse to indemnify the parish from a bastard child'. More common were inventories taken 'as a distraint for arrears for rent' or 'seized for rent due to his landlord'. These were sometimes accompanied by a legal statement from the landlord that 'if you do not pay the ... arrears or replevy the said goods and chattels within five days ... I shall cause the said goods and chattels to be appraised and sold'.[12] Sometimes these documents related to arrears of rent incurred by those who had just become dependent on parish relief, but on other occasions it is by no means certain that the individuals involved were either paupers or labourers. Since the aim here is to identify and analyse a group of inventories that both relate to individuals known to be paupers, and contain a reasonably full list of the household possessions of those individuals, the inventories or partial lists of goods created in the above situations must be set aside. They may be useful in illustrating the effects of other aspects of parochial administration on the lives of the poor, but they are relatively few in number and they do not suit our purposes here. The same must be said for the more numerous inventories of 'goods delivered into the workhouse', which appear in a number of parish collections.[13] These documents suggest that for many ageing or infirm paupers their final journey into the parish workhouse was not only the moment when they lost their independence but also effectively the moment at which they lost control of their possessions.

Given the lack of parochial storage space and the publicly acknowledged tendency for potential inmates to hide or redistribute their possessions before their removal to the workhouse, it is not surprising to find that inventories headed 'goods delivered into the workhouse' often contain only a few basic items. Nor do they describe the rooms in which the goods stood before their removal. These inventories (and the few documents that recorded goods taken out of the workhouse when a pauper, not in terminal decline, found an alternative place in the community, and was allowed to leave the parish's residential institution) have therefore also been laid aside.[14]

The majority of pauper inventories do not fall into any of these more problematic categories. They are headed simply 'an inventory of the household goods of X taken by Y' (who is usually an overseer), and give no indication as to why they were compiled. Many appear very similar to probate inventories, listing the rooms in the house and the contents of each room – the only difference being that few include valuations of the goods being described. A few of these inventories may have arisen from the special types of case already analysed – family abandonment, bastard paternity, rent arrears, and so on – but the vast majority arose from a widespread set of practices whereby those who became chargeable to a parish effectively relinquished the long-term ownership of their movable possessions in return for the right to reasonable out-relief until their deaths. The transaction was basically a simple one. The paupers would get relief and would usually be allowed to keep their remaining household possessions throughout their lifetime. In exchange, the parish would inherit their goods on their demise and could either sell them, redistribute them to other paupers, or use them to furnish their workhouse, poorhouse or pesthouse.

The legal basis for these practices was somewhat ill-defined. Under the heading 'defects in the justices law' in his 1764 *History*, Burn suggested that:

> In case of removing poor persons to the workhouse, a power (as it seemeth) should be given to the overseers, to take with them their clothes, bedding, tools of their trade, or other effects: These they often make away to their relations. So when they die, it seemeth reasonable, that the overseers should have power to dispose of their clothes, and other effects, in aid of the parish for their funeral and other expenses.[15]

In reality, many vestries did not worry about such legal niceties in their dealings with the goods of paupers, whether they had died in the workhouse or after a period as regular receivers of out-relief. In some places, the position of the parish was reinforced by insisting that any old people who became dependent on the parish made 'a will and act of surrender' leaving all their goods to the overseers.[16] Elsewhere, vestries simply assumed the right to act as if the poor had made such a surrender. In 1779, for example, a Northamptonshire parish recorded that 'Any person that dies that received relief and leaves household goods, they are to be for the use of the parish and no other use.' To prevent the poor from quietly selling off goods which were future assets for the parish, an inventory was often made and the goods branded with a parish mark. The Northamptonshire labourer, John Clare, had to watch his father go through this process. 'As soon as he went to the parish for relief', Clare wrote, 'they came to clap the town brand on his goods and set them down in their parish books because he should not sell or get out of them.'[17] Clare clearly hated the practice and in his poem 'The Parish' he openly criticised the vestry for 'clapping on [the pauper's] goods the Parish Brand, lest he should sell them for the want of bread, on parish bounty rather pind than fed'.[18] Since disputes could arise with the relatives of dead paupers, overseers in east Kent made sure that they had 'a list of the goods that none of them is made away with'.[19] Essex vestries followed similar practices. In 1756, for example, the Wethersfield vestry 'resolved that the overseer go to Willoughby Strait and give her proper relief and likewise take account of her effects'.[20]

The two points at which a pauper's goods were most likely to be listed by the overseers were therefore at the time he or she first became regularly chargeable to the parish, and at the time of his or her death. Where a husband died leaving a wife unable to support herself, the two points coincided. An inventory was taken at his death because that death was also the point at which she became reliant on the parish. A few parishes made periodic checks on the goods of regular receivers who had been on relief for some time and had not recently died. The parish officers of Little Baddow, for example, took 'an account of the goods of the poor which receive weekly collection' in 1766. In 1735 the parish officers of Theydon Garnon appraised the goods of John North, Widow Wilson and Thomas Lincoln, all of whom had already been regular receivers for years and continued to be so for many years to come.[21] These practices do not, however, seem to have been followed in the majority of parishes. Most of the pauper inventories taken by overseers in the expectation that the goods listed would eventually pass to the parish, were taken at the point when the pauper lost either his or her financial independence or his or her life.

The only way that we can be sure that a particular inventory found in the parish records related to a pauper receiving relief rather than to a tenant in arrears, a runaway farmer or a bastard's father is to trace the individual concerned into the overseers' account books or into other relevant parish records. Since these often do not survive for the relevant years, the contexts from which many pauper inventories arose are irrecoverable. However, it has so far been possible to trace 51 of the Essex pauper inventories (45 of which were made between 1730 and 1799) into other records and to establish that the person concerned already was, or was about to become, reliant upon the parish.[22] Forty-one of these 51 inventories list rooms as well as goods and must therefore have been taken in the pauper's home. These form the core sample analysed and compared to data from Essex probate inventories in Tables 7.1 and 7.2. The remaining ten do not list rooms but give no indication that they were partial inventories or simply lists of goods taken into the workhouse. Since many ageing paupers lived in single rooms, often as lodgers, it is likely that almost all of these are also fairly full lists of the relevant pauper's goods. They have therefore been added to the core sample in order to form the broader sample analysed in Tables 7.1 and 7.2.

## II

The problems encountered in analysing pauper inventories are often very similar to those found in the extensive literature about probate inventories. They did not usually record real-estate or immovable items attached permanently to the fabric of the house. They listed only the goods owned by the subject of the inventory although, if the individual involved was part of a larger household, he or she would have enjoyed access to a much broader range of goods. They rarely recorded debts owed by the subject and, in the case of pauper inventories, debts owed to him or her are rarely mentioned. They were unable to record any goods given away or hidden prior to the making of the inventory. They do not usually record the age of the individual involved or the size and structure of the household he or she lived in. Moreover, overseers (like probate inventory appraisers) varied in their assiduousness. Fewer pauper inventories contain the tell-tale words 'and other items' used by some probate inventory makers, but it cannot be assumed that the parish officers who wrote them either saw everything that was there, or recorded absolutely everything they saw. Because they were legally obliged to do so, those who wrote probate inventories always valued the goods they recorded, but overseers were under no such obligation and valuations are therefore relatively rare.[23] Although probate valuations are themselves by no means a perfect guide to wealth levels, this makes it particularly difficult to develop any sense of the relative poverty of those whose goods are recorded in pauper inventories. Like probate inventories, pauper ones rarely recorded the colour or texture of the goods they listed. Nor did they give any direct indication of the ways the objects were arranged within each room, or of their purpose, whether practical, decorative or representational.

The absence of any clear indication of the age of the individual concerned may be less important for pauper inventories than for probate ones, since parish records often enable the lifecycle stage at which the inventory was taken to be fairly accurately estimated. However, the impact of the lifecycle dimension on each inventory should not be under-estimated. Paupers entered the list of regular receivers, and thus became vulnerable to the pauper inventory process, by a number of very different routes. Some of the men involved were unskilled landless labourers who had always

Table 7.1 Essex probate and pauper inventories, later seventeenth to early nineteenth centuries: percentages containing selected goods

|  | Essex 1710–1819 (pauper) || Mid-Essex 1658–1731 (probate) ||| N.E. Essex 1700–1750 (probate) |||
|---|---|---|---|---|---|---|---|---|
|  | Core sample | Broader sample | Total sample (incl. widows) | Tradesmen & artisans | Yeomen & farmers | Husbandmen & labourers | Total sample (incl. widows, etc.) | Tradesmen & artisans | Yeomen & farmers |
| Chairs (any type) | 95 | 94 | 96 | 89 | 100 | 94 | 94 | 91 | 97 |
| Cane chairs | 0 | 0 | 1 | 0 | 3 | 0 | 8 | 0 | 8 |
| Oval table | 7 | 8 | 9 | 11 | 8 | 0 | 17 | 14 | 11 |
| Chest of drawers | 32 | 31 | 18 | 22 | 17 | 0 | 67 | 71 | 68 |
| Mahog. furniture | 5 | 4 | 0 | 0 | 0 | 0 | 1 | 0 | 0 |
| Walnut furniture | 2 | 2 | 0 | 0 | 0 | 0 | 0 | 0 | 0 |
| Looking-glass | 27 | 27 | 19 | 14 | 24 | 0 | 51 | 62 | 53 |
| Clocks/watches | 20 | 16 | 16 | 11 | 22 | 0 | 71 | 71 | 68 |
| Pictures/prints | 10 | 12 | 2 | 0 | 3 | 0 | 13 | 19 | 8 |
| Books | 0 | 2 | 24 | 11 | 32 | 0 | 18 | 24 | 13 |
| Candlesticks | 49 | 43 | 28 | 19 | 38 | 6 | 53 | 48 | 55 |
| Lanterns | 7 | 8 | 8 | 11 | 8 | 0 | 22 | 5 | 32 |
| Weapons | 2 | 2 | 22 | 22 | 29 | 6 | 26 | 19 | 37 |
| Silver items | 0 | 0 | 21 | 17 | 26 | 6 | 25 | 19 | 26 |
| Fire jack | 2 | 2 | 40 | 42 | 43 | 0 | 57 | 67 | 58 |
| Poker | 12 | 10 | 1 | 0 | 0 | 0 | 8 | 10 | 3 |
| Fender | 10 | 10 | 4 | 0 | 3 | 0 | 13 | 14 | 11 |
| Earthenware | 61 | 56 | 23 | 25 | 22 | 25 | 36 | 29 | 37 |
| Knives & forks | 0 | 0 | 1 | 0 | 0 | 0 | 4 | 0 | 0 |

Table 7.1 Continued

|  | Essex 1710–1819 (pauper) | | Mid-Essex 1658–1731 (probate) | | | | N.E. Essex 1700–1750 (probate) | |
|---|---|---|---|---|---|---|---|---|
|  | Core sample | Broader sample | Total sample (incl. widows) | Tradesmen & artisans | Yeomen & farmers | Husband-men & labourers | Total sample (incl. widows, etc.) | Tradesmen & artisans | Yeomen & farmers |
| Salt box | 12 | 12 | 12 | 19 | 10 | 6 | 24 | 19 | 29 |
| Pepper box | 10 | 10 | 1 | 3 | 0 | 0 | 6 | 5 | 3 |
| Tea-related items | 46 | 41 | 1 | 0 | 0 | 0 | 15 | 19 | 13 |
| Coffee items | 10 | 8 | 1 | 0 | 0 | 0 | 7 | 5 | 8 |
| Tobacco items | 0 | 0 | 1 | 0 | 1 | 0 | 4 | 9 | 0 |
| Coal items | 7 | 6 | 9 | 8 | 10 | 0 | 24 | 38 | 13 |
| Sample size | 41 | 51 | 139 | 36 | 72 | 16 | 72 | 38 | 21 |
| Average value of listed assets | (10) | (9) | 162 | 87 | 249 | 38 | 150 | 91 | 216 |
| Average number of rooms | 3.6 | 3.6 | 9.6 | 8.1 | 12.0 | 6.3 | 8.1 | 7.2 | 9.7 |
| Average number of beds | 2.1 | 2.0 | 4.4 | 3.4 | 5.4 | 3.1 | 3.6 | 3.8 | 4.2 |

*Note* Apart from the final 4 lines (sample size, etc.) numbers represent the percentage of inventories that mentioned a particular item.

Table 7.2  Essex probate and pauper inventories, later seventeenth to early nineteenth centuries: bedding, linen, bedroom-heating and fire equipment

|  | Essex 1710–1819 (pauper) |  | Mid-Essex area 1658–1731 (probate) |  |  |  |
|---|---|---|---|---|---|---|
|  | Core sample | Broader sample | Total sample (incl. widows) | Tradesmen & artisans | Yeomen & farmers | Husbandmen & labourers |
| **Bedding**, quality of where bed described |  |  |  |  |  |  |
| % straw | 14 | 16 | 4 | 4 | 4 | 3 |
| % flock | 33 | 37 | 30 | 29 | 29 | 46 |
| % feather | 53 | 46 | 66 | 68 | 67 | 51 |
| **Linen** |  |  |  |  |  |  |
| % of inventories making some mention of linen | 68 | 65 | 89 | 86 | 93 | 75 |
| % mentioning sheets | 68 | 65 | 71 | 78 | 65 | 63 |
| % mentioning pillows | 7 | 8 | 53 | 53 | 60 | 19 |
| % mentioning napkins | 7 | 8 | 55 | 58 | 56 | 31 |
| % mentioning tablecloths | 5 | 4 | 55 | 61 | 56 | 31 |
| % mentioning towels | 5 | 4 | 24 | 22 | 29 | 13 |
| Amongst those whose linen is listed in detail |  |  |  |  |  |  |
| Average number of sheets | 3.9 | 3.8 | 8.8 | 6.6 | 11.6 | 4.3 |
| Average number of pillows | 2.0 | 2.0 | 6.9 | 5.6 | 8.1 | 2.3 |
| Average number of napkins | 4.3 | 3.8 | 23.9 | 18.4 | 32.3 | 13.5 |
| Average number of tablecloths | 1.5 | 1.5 | 4.3 | 3.4 | 5.1 | 2.8 |
| Average number of towels | 2.5 | 2.5 | 5.4 | 5.3 | 5.9 | 4.0 |

Table 7.2  Continued

|  | Essex 1710–1819 (pauper) |  | Mid-Essex area 1658–1731 (probate) |  |  |  |
|---|---|---|---|---|---|---|
|  | Core sample | Broader sample | Total sample (incl. widows) | Tradesmen & artisans | Yeomen & farmers | Husbandmen & labourers |
| *Bedroom-heating equipment* |  |  |  |  |  |  |
| % of inventories with fire equipment in a bedroom | 5 | 4 | 30 | 19 | 43 | 6 |
| *Fire equipment* |  |  |  |  |  |  |
| % of inventories making mention of |  |  |  |  |  |  |
| tongs | 73 | 75 | 74 | 86 | 79 | 50 |
| fire shovel | 49 | 49 | 69 | 80 | 76 | 38 |
| bellows | 68 | 63 | 40 | 44 | 35 | 19 |

*Note* Apart from the final 4 lines (sample size, etc.), numbers represent the percentage of inventories that mentioned a particular item.

lived close to the margins of subsistence. As they grew older they often suffered increasingly long periods of under-employment and/or partial disability, which eroded their meagre assets and left them with few possessions. Other men who spent their final days on poor relief had been relatively prosperous artisans, tradesmen or husbandmen (and possibly minor ratepayers) until they were fairly rapidly pushed into poverty by the onset of illness or old age.[24] Amongst the women, some would enter the pauper lists whilst still in the prime of life, usually because the death of their husband had left them unable to support a family of young children.[25] Others were single women who had never been able to make more than a meagre living but who found even this impossible to sustain once they reached old age. Two of these four scenarios would probably have resulted in the material world of the prospective pauper still being relatively rich when the overseer first made an inventory of his or her effects – a situation which might have continued until the pauper's death, given that the goods listed were not supposed to be sold. The other two scenarios would have had the opposite effect.

It is not surprising, therefore, that the amount and range of goods listed in the 51 inventories spotlighted here varied enormously. Some give the impression that a busy family was still, or had been until fairly recently, occupying the household space described. These inventories include a wide range of food-producing and heating equipment as well as of furniture, bedding, linen, eating utensils and so on. Other inventories, by contrast, clearly described the sparse environment of an impoverished person living out the final stage of the lifecycle.[26] A range of examples could be used to illustrate these contrasts but three cases that can be more deeply contextualised than most will suffice here. (See Appendices 1–3.)

The first concerns Joseph Smith of Ashdon – a rural parish in northwest Essex, where the farmer-dominated vestry held a relatively tight grip on the local poor.[27] The excellent Ashdon parish records allow us to reconstruct much more deeply than is usually possible the context within which this document was created. Smith's inventory (which is part of the broader sample used in Tables 7.1 and 7.2 rather than the core sample, because it contains no reference to the room or rooms the goods were in) suggests a fairly sparse material world. The basics for eating, sleeping, cooking and sitting are there, as are certain productive artifacts – a kneading trough, a spinning wheel (see Appendix 1). The bedding is of poor quality – a flock bed and a straw bed rather than a feather one – and there are no luxurious curtains, valances or bed-linen. Although there are some items that might be regarded as semi-luxuries and which occur in only a minority of pauper inventories – notably a looking-glass and candlesticks – this inventory conforms fairly well to the relatively austere view many historians have taken of the material life of the poor in the late eighteenth and early nineteenth centuries. It is probably describing a household living in one room, although it is possible that Joseph Smith occupied a two- or three-roomed cottage.[28]

Joseph Smith's age, occupation, family earnings and household size all suggest that this was probably a relatively impoverished household within the labouring community of Ashdon at this time. The inventory was taken immediately after Joseph's death at the ripe old age of 81. He does not seem to have become a regular receiver of weekly out-relief until he was 79, although he was sometimes given temporary assistance at times of particular difficulty before that point.[29] The 1801 census describes Joseph's household as containing himself and two women, neither of whom were said to be following either agricultural or trade occupations. Joseph was listed as employed in agriculture and, since he was not among the occupiers or landowners listed in the Ashdon Land Tax of 1801 or in the rate assessments of the 1790s, these records suggest he was an agricultural labourer.[30] This is confirmed by a document listing all the Ashdon families who were given temporary relief and subsidised flour during the harvest crisis of 1800–1.[31] There Joseph is described as a labourer with no dependent children under 12, earning eleven shillings a week. Since the 1801 documents give the earnings of almost every labouring family in Ashdon as well as information on household size, Joseph Smith's relative position around his seventieth year can be analysed (Figures 7.1, 7.2 and 7.3). Not surprisingly, since his children were now grown up, the size of his household was well below the mean for his community (Figure 7.3). His family's earnings were about average for the labouring households of Ashdon, which was a considerable achievement given his age and the probability that neither of the women in the household were bringing in much income.[32] He earned less than the average artisan family but more than double the highest earnings achieved by a widow or single woman (see Figures 7.1 and 7.2).[33] Joseph kept his relative independence well on into his life. I have found no reference to him as a regular receiver of relief between 1801 and 1810. In July 1810 he began to appear fairly frequently as a recipient of out-relief and at the end of October he was finally added to the list of regular receivers. Once there he received a regular dole of three shillings a week until May 1812, when nine shillings extra was paid out to 'Joseph Smith, ill' as the overseers' account book described him. By June 1812 he was dead.[34]

Joseph's income was never large and in striving to stay off relief throughout his seventies he would almost certainly have drained his few

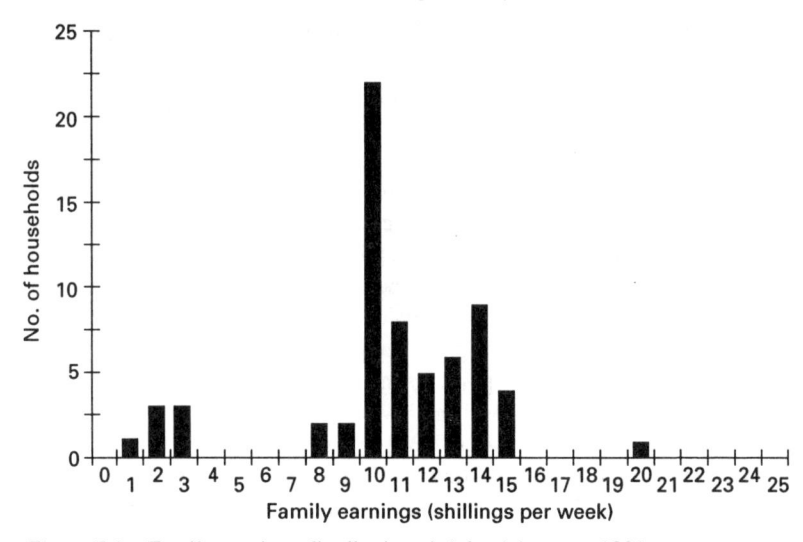

*Figure* 7.1   Family earnings distribution, Ashdon labourers, 1801

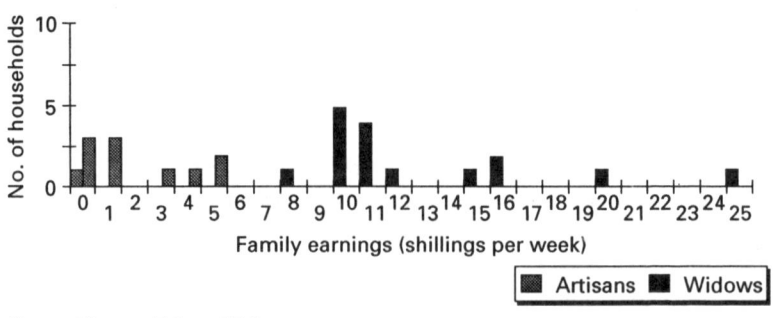

*Key to Figures 7.1 and 7.2*
Family earnings grouped within each shilling unit
e.g.   0  =  0–11d
       1  =  1s–1s11d
       2  =  2s–2s11d

*Source*   E/R/O, D/P 18/1/6 & 14. Ashdon Pauper Census.
*Note*   The vertical axis represents the number of households.

*Figure* 7.2   Family earnings distribution, Ashdon artisans and widows, 1801

assets even further. Given that he then had nearly two years on regular poor relief at a level equivalent to around a third of what he had been earning as a 70-year-old labourer, and that only 6 per cent of Ashdon residents survived further into old age than he did (Figure 7.4),[35] the inventory

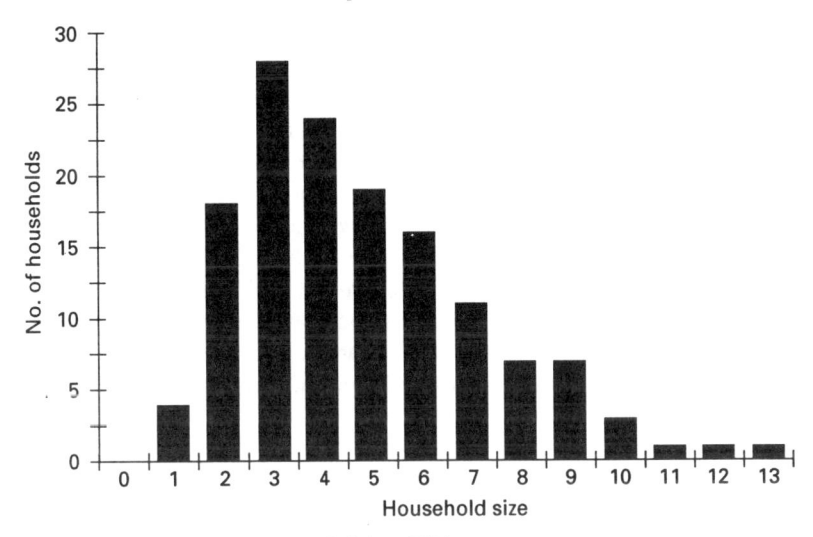

*Figure* 7.3  Household size in Ashdon, 1801 census

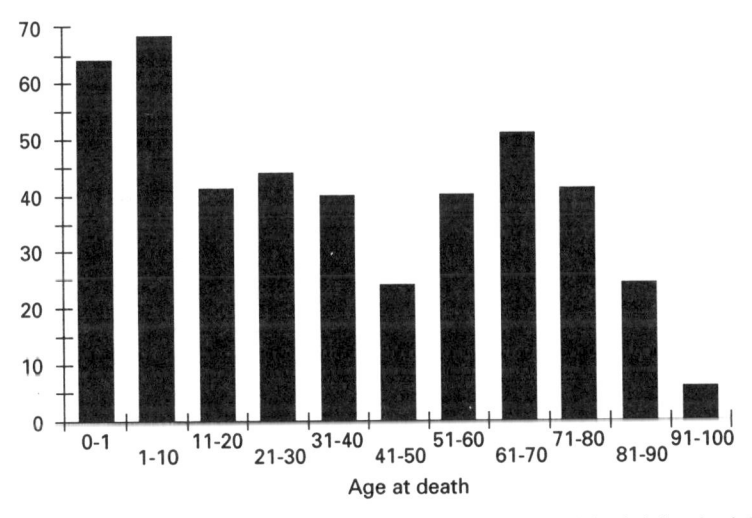

*Source*  E/R/O/, D/P 18/1/6 & 14. Age at death as recorded in Ashdon burial register.

*Figure* 7.4  Ages at death, Ashdon, 1795–1820

written at his death takes on a rather different light. It is certainly less persuasive evidence of the sparse lifestyles of the labouring poor than it would have been if it had proved to be a description of the material world of a labouring household earlier in the lifecycle of the main breadwinner.

The second example used here (Appendix 2), the inventory of John Tadgell, labourer,[36] taken two years earlier in 1810, challenges our preconceptions about the material life of the poor far more fundamentally. We know much less about the background to this inventory but it was also, it seems, taken at the death of the labourer whose household goods it lists. 'Widow Tadgell' appears for the first time on the list of regular receivers of relief in the rural parish of Hatfield Broad Oak immediately after the inventory was made and continues for some years to receive two shillings per week.[37] John Tadgell's age at his death is not known but, from the amount she received after her husband's death, it is highly unlikely that widow Tadgell still had young children to support. The couple had almost certainly reached a fairly advanced middle-age at the very least before John died and the inventory was taken.

Their house was not a large one. The inventory does not describe the precise arrangement of either the rooms or the furniture, but the house probably consisted of two chambers above a larger downstairs room with a buttery attached. The 'dwelling room' was either fairly large or very crowded with household goods. There were three tables, including a long oak one, plenty of chairs and a settle. The fire equipment was fairly sophisticated, including a fender, poker and bellows as well as the standard cooking equipment. There was plenty of storage space – two dressers, two cupboards, and at least two sets of shelves – and it was needed to house and/or display a considerable array of items. This included 67 pieces of teacups, glasses and crockery ware, 16 Delph plates, seven green-edged plates and various wooden, tin and pewter pieces. Unlike the homes of an increasing proportion of the middling sort, there was no division here between 'frontstage' and 'backstage', between a parlour for entertaining and a kitchen for working and everyday living. The Tadgells' dwelling room is a living room, a cooking room and a show room all in one. The bedroom furnishings are of relatively high quality – four-poster beds, linen and quilts or coverlets, feather-bedding on the main beds. There is a looking-glass in one of the bedrooms as well as in the dwelling room. The house is full of colour and variety. Colourful plates, a different colour for each set of bedroom furniture, a variety of woods including mahogany and a japanned tea board. The Tadgells' inventory can also be read as conveying a sense of conviviality – the long oak table with many chairs that could be gathered round it, the settle and the fire, the facilities for making and enjoying both coffee and tea. However, there are many problems in reading such documents. Did the parish officers who made this inventory simply have a greater awareness of colour than others who created such documents? Had the Tadgells experienced a sudden bereavement which had not given them an opportunity to share out, hide or sell some of these possessions? This is one of the few pauper inventories that gives the occupation of the household head, but had John Tadgell always been a labourer? The overseers' account books do not include rate assessments for this period[38] but if the Land Tax Assessments of 1790, 1800 and 1809 are any guide, the Tadgells had no taxable landholdings during the 20 years before John's death.[39] They may have had a tiny holding too small to be included in the land tax schedules and/or a cottage to which certain customary rights were attached, but there is no evidence that they were not what the inventory described them as – a labouring family. Thus, although widow Tadgell may not have taken all these goods with her as she journeyed on through the lifecycle after her husband's death, this document remains a fascinating insight into the relative richness of the material world of one labouring family in the early nineteenth century.

To balance these two contrasting early nineteenth-century examples – the meagre living-space of the 81-year-old Joseph Smith and the much fuller material diversity with which Mrs Tadgell faced her widowhood – a variety of inventories would need to be contextualised and then scrutinised in detail. While a majority of the 51 Essex inventories whose subjects have been verified as receivers of poor relief reveal a material world more diverse than the Smiths' and less abundant than the Tadgells', there are considerable numbers of inventories that are very similar to those of these two families. The sample contains, for example, several widows' inventories from the mid-eighteenth century that are not dissimilar to Joseph Smith's.[40] Equally, it was not just in the early nineteenth century or in the rather exceptional parish of Hatfield Broad Oak that pauper inventories can be found which include a range of household goods similar to that of the Tadgells.

The 1775 inventory of the goods of Thomas Burgh of Theydon Garnon (Appendix 3), for example, described a five-roomed house with a separate kitchen and parlour, two well-equipped bedrooms and a washhouse. It had two separate fireplaces, a fair range of furniture and a selection of goods – looking-glass, candlesticks, tea-related items, chest of drawers, eight-day clock, and so on – not always found in the probate inventories of the better-off tradesmen and farmers of Essex 75 years earlier (Table 7.1). It has not been possible to find any evidence about Thomas' occupation but it is clear that this is the inventory of an old man's household. Thomas started receiving relief just before the document was drawn up. He was referred to by the overseers as 'Old Burgh' and from then on he was a regular receiver.[41]

Thus, pauper inventories describing households with a reasonably sizeable dwelling and a fairly diverse range of household goods were not confined to subjects who died suddenly and relatively early in their life-cycle. Nor were they confined to the early nineteenth century. Examples of this kind can be found in the majority of the parishes from which inventories were traced into the poor law records, and across most of the period (1710–1812) from which the sample was drawn. Thus, even a fairly cursory reading of the three examples reproduced in Appendices 1–3, and of the broader sample of 51 inventories from which they were drawn, indicates not only the wide range of material circumstances of those who became regular receivers of relief, but also the possibility that a significant proportion of them were not completely excluded from the market for household goods by the later eighteenth century.

III

Before any firmer conclusions can be drawn it will be necessary both to contextualise a much larger sample of pauper inventories, and to address in more detail the complex methodological problems posed by this particular source. The most that this preliminary survey can do is to raise some of the most obvious of those problems and make some preliminary soundings suggesting ways that the material can be used. The problems posed by the recording practices of those who wrote both pauper and probate inventories have already been explored at the beginning of Section II, but another equally important set of questions is raised by the need to assess more precisely which subgroups of the local community are actually represented in the pauper inventories that have survived. Men and women in extreme poverty may rarely have featured in these records. Those who were almost completely destitute by the time they applied for relief would not have had sufficient goods to merit the taking of an inventory. They would also be much more likely to be deemed in need of indoor relief, in which case the only record that would have been made of their material goods would often have been a very selective list of the goods they were allowed to 'remove into the workhouse'. It is also important, but very difficult without detailed life histories, to explore the opposite question – how high up the social spectrum is it necessary to go before we reach the point at which a family's accumulated wealth and ability to mobilise the resources available from grown-up children, kin, friendly societies, benevolent ex-employers, local charities, and continued access to customary rights, gardens and so on would have been sufficient to prevent it from needing to claim relief throughout the lifecycle. What proportion of artisans, tradesmen, tenant farmers and husbandmen were vulnerable, as the landless labouring poor clearly were, to becoming subjects of a pauper inventory in old age or in cases when the husband met an early death?

The very wide variations in poor relief practices between parishes raise further problems. Pauper inventories survive for less than a quarter of Essex parishes. This could mean that the practice was followed by only a minority of parishes or (as seems more likely) that it was very widespread, but that few parishes saw any point in keeping these documents once they were no longer useful.[42] How typical are the parishes where pauper inventories (and the overseers' account books in which their subjects can be traced as receivers) have survived? To what extent did policies about the point in the lifecycle at which an inventory was taken (at death, at the point of first dependence, and so on) vary between parishes and over time? As the Old Poor Law underwent a major crisis in the late eighteenth and early nineteenth centuries, and as the able-bodied poor began to play an increasingly important role as receivers, were the attitudes and practices that underpinned the making of pauper inventories undermined or radically changed? These are complex problems and their impact should not be under-estimated, but by exploring two quantitative research strategies and by a brief qualitative analysis of the inventories of a specific parish, the remainder of this chapter will explore the potential as well as the pitfalls of pauper inventories as historical sources.

IV

Given that pauper inventories appear to offer a window into the material life of precisely those social groups that probate inventories largely ignore, an obvious strategy is to compare the data from these two sources for the same geographical area. Tables 7.1 and 7.2 are a preliminary attempt to quantify, across various broad occupational groups, the proportion of Essex inventories mentioning particular types of household goods.[43] They also compare data on other relevant indices of wealth, such as the average number of rooms, beds and so on per household and the type of bedding used. Unfortunately, relatively few probate inventories survive for Essex. Only two small areas of the county, both of them 'peculiar' jurisdictions, provide more than a handful for the later seventeenth and eighteenth centuries.[44] Both of these were predominantly rural areas – Writtle and Good Easter in central Essex, and Kirby, Thorpe and Walton in the northeast.

Although the periods covered by each series overlap, there are significant differences. Discounting pre-1658 inventories, the central Essex sample includes 139 individuals from the period 1658–1731 but more than two-thirds of these, including all the husbandmen and labourers, are dated before 1700.[45] The northeast Essex sample is biased towards a slightly later period, the 72 inventories available being fairly evenly divided across the years 1701 to 1758. Unfortunately, it also includes even fewer inventories from less wealthy households. Only one inventory is ascribed to a husbandman or labourer.[46] A comparison of the mainly late seventeenth-century mid-Essex inventories with those of northeast Essex in the first half of the eighteenth century confirms the picture of change that Weatherill's broader work has uncovered. The proportion of inventories in which new 'luxury' items, such as clocks, looking-glasses, tea- and coffee-related items and pictures or maps are mentioned, increased very significantly.[47] So did the ownership of other items Weatherill did not include in her work, such as chests of drawers, candlesticks, pokers, fenders and so on (Table 7.1). Although these two wheat and pastoral farming areas of Essex are fairly similar in some respects, using comparisons across different regions to look at change over time is, of course, highly problematic.

More important for our analysis here is the clear pattern of differentiation in wealth levels by social class seen in both areas. Since neither of these areas contained many rich merchants or dealers, the hierarchy of wealth within the three broad categories used here is fairly clear-cut. Average wealth levels, as measured by the total value of the commodities listed, the number of rooms and outbuildings and the number of beds, all follow the same pattern. The yeomen/farmers are much wealthier on average than the tradesmen and artisans, and that group in turn are very considerably better-off than the husbandmen or labourers. Differences in the proportion of each group owning household items that might be considered relative luxuries indicate a two- rather than a three-level hierarchy. As Weatherill's work also indicates, differences in ownership levels were much less clear-cut between the yeoman group and the artisans and tradesmen. However, despite the relatively small sample,[48] it is clear that while most of the middling sort of mid-Essex owned a range of household goods such as looking-glasses, clocks, pictures, books, candlesticks, lanterns, pokers, fenders, silver items, fire jacks, or tea- and coffee-related items, husbandmen and labourers very rarely possessed such things in the late seventeenth century (Table 7.1). The latter were also less likely to sleep on feather rather than flock beds, to have a fireplace in any of their bedrooms, or to own the more luxurious items of linen such as pillows, napkins, tablecloths and so on (Table 7.2). Where they did own these things they possessed fewer of them, just as fewer of their households contained fireside items such as bellows, tongs and fire shovels. The Essex probate inventory evidence therefore broadly confirms Weatherill's conclusion that in the early eighteenth century 'the lower boundary for those tending to own a variety of household goods was between the craftsmen and the husbandmen, since husbandmen's inventories were unlikely to record new and decorative items; even staple goods were less frequent here, and the few labourers' inventories are similar'.[49] To what extent can this conclusion be extended to the later eighteenth century? To wrestle with this question it is necessary to return to the pauper inventories.

Given that the process of contextualising each inventory is so time-consuming, a small subsample had to be selected from the many inventories found in the Essex parish records that make no reference to rent arrears, bastardy and so on, and are therefore potentially useful for the purposes of this chapter. In order to concentrate on inventories which were indisputably taken in the subject's dwelling, and which therefore provide information about that dwelling as well as a relatively complete listing of their goods, this subsample was not chosen on a random basis. Rather, those inventories which listed the rooms in which the goods were standing were given priority. Forty-one of these were eventually traced into other parish records which linked them to regular receivers of relief.[50] These 41 form the core sample in Tables 7.1 and 7.2. This selection strategy inevitably skews the sample away from some of the more destitute subgroups. In particular, it excludes all those living in one room either as lodgers or as residents of hovels with no separate sleeping, living and cooking spaces. However, the distorting effect of concentrating on inventories mentioning rooms may not have been very strong. Many old people, such as Thomas Burgh (Appendix 3), were still inhabiting multi-room dwellings when they became receivers of relief. Moreover, many of the inventories which do not include rooms contain long lists of household goods[51] and suggest that, although they were taken in multi-room dwellings, the overseers simply did not bother to record the rooms the goods were in.

Thus, the core sample probably contains a higher than average proportion of relatively well-off paupers, of widows (such as John Tadgell's) whose husbands had just died, and of inventories taken at the moment the pauper came onto relief rather than at the time of the pauper's death. Joseph Smith's inventory (Appendix 1), for example, which was made at his death, contains no references to rooms. Following the analysis of the

41 core inventories, another 10 inventories (including Joseph Smith's) which do not contain room information but which can also be linked to regular receivers of relief, were analysed and included in the broader sample of 51 seen in Tables 7.1 and 7.2. Further research on this type of inventory is clearly needed before the impact of focusing mainly on inventories listing rooms is understood. However, given the diverse nature of the pauper host, and the presence within it of groups (such as orphans and ex-servant girls with illegitimate children) who became receivers before ever having an opportunity to establish a household of their own, it is clear that no combination of the different types of pauper inventories available would produce a 'typical' sample of all poor relief recipients. It may therefore be more helpful to regard the core and broader samples not as a selection of paupers but rather as representing a certain fairly broad stratum of the labouring poor. More specifically, the pauper inventories in Tables 7.1 and 7.2 were drawn from those sub-groups of the local working population who were sufficiently vulnerable to long-term poverty in widowhood, infirmity or old age to become regular receivers, but who also had enough goods to be worth subjecting to the inventory process, and (in the case of the core sample) who had enough wealth or good fortune to still be in a multi-roomed dwelling when their inventory was taken.

V

In using Tables 7.1 and 7.2 to compare the material world of the substrata of the labouring poor represented in pauper inventories with the few husbandmen and labourers whose probate inventories have survived, the small size of the samples involved is not the only problem. The time-periods are very different. All the probate inventories were written before 1700. All the pauper inventories were dated after 1710, and 95 per cent of them came from the period 1730–1812. Nor is this, of course, a comparison of like with like. The few labourers leaving probate inventories were almost certainly from the richer end of the labouring class, while some of those labelled as husbandmen may have had considerable landholdings. The occupational structure of those included in the pauper inventories would almost certainly have included some individuals from both these groups as well as some artisans, but direct occupational information is rarely available and it is quite probable that unskilled and virtually landless labourers, or their widows, formed the main bulk of the pauper inventory sample.

The three overall wealth indicators available – the average value of listed assets, the number of rooms and outhouses, and the number of beds – all suggest that the husbandmen and labourers who became subjects of probate inventories were generally better-off than those who later appeared in pauper inventories. The former had nearly 50 per cent more beds and 75 per cent more rooms/outhouses. Their total assets were also valued 3.8 times higher (Table 7.1). The latter measure is highly problematic. Few pauper inventories contain price information and the impact of price changes is difficult to measure. More important, different recording practices in relation to debts and other assets make comparisons very difficult.[52] However, a number of other fairly basic indices show a similar decline or lack of positive change between the earlier probate and the later pauper inventory sample. The proportion of inventories recording fireplaces in bedrooms was negligible in both samples. The proportion of inventories mentioning linen declined slightly and the proportion with a range of different kinds of linen fell considerably. The information on bedding types indicates no substantial increase in feather-bedding but suggests that pauper inventory subjects were more likely to use the poorest bedding material – straw – than did the husbandmen and labourers of the previous century.

These indicators therefore suggest that, on average, the eighteenth-century pauper inventories may well cover a subgroup of working people that was positioned lower in the social scale than the subgroups whose goods were listed in the probate inventories of husbandmen and labourers that survive for late seventeenth-century Essex. This makes it all the more interesting that, by the mid- to late eighteenth century, even that relatively low subgroup of the labouring poor owned a much greater variety of household goods and of decorative or semi-luxury items than that seen in the slightly more affluent subgroup of husbandmen and labourers about whom late seventeenth-century probate data is available (Table 7.1). None of the earlier sample owned looking-glasses, clocks or watches. A fifth to a quarter of pauper inventories include these items. The ownership of earthenware had increased threefold. Candlesticks were now owned by half of the households inventoried, instead of 6 per cent. Ownership of many fire-related items such as pokers, fenders, tongs, fire shovels and bellows increased considerably. So had mentions of chests of drawers, pictures, maps, lanterns, salt and pepper boxes, oval tables, and coffee-related items. The rise of tea-related items from nil to 46 per cent indicates a major change in the drinking habits of the labouring poor (Table 7.1).

The precise significance of each of these changes needs, of course, to be explored in more detail than is possible here. The arrival of prints and maps in the homes of the labouring poor, for example, may have been mainly a function of the growth of cheap reproduction techniques in this period. The decline in the number of households openly displaying weapons needs to be placed in the context of the aftermath of the Civil War and of changes in the game laws.[53] However, despite the slight decline in the percentage of inventories containing articles such as books and silver items, the overall pattern is fairly clear. The range of household goods that working people might expect to own expanded fairly rapidly in the century after 1700. A comparison of the late eighteenth- and early nineteenth-century pauper inventories with those of the yeomen and tradesmen of the later seventeenth and early eighteenth centuries suggests that, by the later period, the poor had reached beyond the middling sorts' former ownership levels in relation to a small number of household items such as earthenware, tea-related goods, bellows and pokers.

Too much should not be made of this, of course. The items involved are minor and changes in fashion and in cooking practices could alter the significance of the ownership of certain goods in ways that make such comparisons almost meaningless. More important, the few probate inventories that survive for late eighteenth- and early nineteenth-century Essex suggest that there had been a vast increase in the array of household goods owned by families of the middling sort since the period covered by the mid-Essex and northeast Essex probate inventory series shown in Tables 7.1 and 7.2. The 'polite and commercial people' of Essex moved rapidly into much greater decorative, representational and conspicuous forms of consumption during the eighteenth century,[54] in ways which the labouring poor could never begin to match. However, this should not be allowed to obscure the fact that the material world of the labouring poor was changing too. Although the subjects of pauper inventories were probably not as high in the social hierarchy as the range of labourers and husbandmen whose goods were listed in the probate inventories made 50 to 100 years earlier, they were increasingly engaged in the market for household goods (albeit perhaps the second-hand one).

Table 7.3, which divides the core sample of 41 into half, comparing the period 1711–69 with 1770–1812, suggests that much, although by no means all, of that engagement took place after 1770. This was par-

*Table* 7.3  Essex pauper inventories: analysis of subsamples

|  | Hatfield Broad Oak only | All other parishes | Up to 1769 | 1770 upwards |
|---|---|---|---|---|
| Chairs (any type) | 100 | 92 | 95 | 95 |
| Cane chairs | 0 | 0 | 0 | 0 |
| Oval table | 7 | 8 | 5 | 9 |
| Chest of drawers | 13 | 42 | 25 | 38 |
| Mahogany furniture | 7 | 4 | 0 | 10 |
| Walnut furniture | 7 | 0 | 0 | 5 |
| Looking-glass | 40 | 19 | 10 | 43 |
| Clocks/watches | 13 | 38 | 20 | 38 |
| Pictures/prints | 20 | 4 | 0 | 19 |
| Books | 0 | 0 | 0 | 0 |
| Candlesticks | 60 | 42 | 40 | 57 |
| Lanterns | 20 | 0 | 0 | 14 |
| Weapons | 0 | 4 | 0 | 5 |
| Silver items | 0 | 0 | 0 | 0 |
| Fire jack | 7 | 0 | 0 | 5 |
| Poker | 13 | 12 | 0 | 24 |
| Fender | 20 | 4 | 0 | 19 |
| Earthenware | 80 | 50 | 60 | 62 |
| Knives & forks | 0 | 0 | 0 | 0 |
| Salt box | 13 | 4 | 15 | 14 |
| Pepper box | 13 | 0 | 20 | 0 |
| Tea-related items | 67 | 35 | 20 | 71 |
| Coffee items | 13 | 8 | 5 | 14 |
| Tobacco items | 0 | 0 | 0 | 0 |
| Coal items | 7 | 8 | 5 | 10 |
| Sample size | 15 | 26 | 20 | 21 |
| Average number of rooms | 4.1 | 3.2 | 3.2 | 3.9 |
| Average number of beds | 2.3 | 2.0 | 1.9 | 2.3 |

*Note* Apart from the final 4 lines (sample size, etc.) numbers represent the percentage of inventories that mentioned a particular item.

ticularly the case with decorative and semi-luxury items such as looking-glasses, clocks, pictures, mahogany and walnut furniture, and tea- or coffee-related items. The average number of rooms/outhouses and beds had also risen. Despite the small sample sizes involved, it is therefore tempting to conclude that the major advance came not during the so-called golden age of the agricultural labourer in the early and mid eighteenth century but in the years after 1770. However, many historians, including those who have studied Essex, have portrayed this period as one of declining or static living standards among the poor,[55] and a closer inspection of the post-1770 pauper inventory evidence is therefore necessary. This is best done by concentrating on one parish, Hatfield Broad Oak.

## VI

The pauper inventory sample used in Tables 7.1–7.3 was drawn from nine predominantly rural parishes scattered throughout central and northern Essex. However, three parishes with particularly rich collections supplied three-quarters of these documents. One of these was John Tadgell's parish of Hatfield Broad Oak, which contributed 13 post-1770 and two pre-1770 inventories (that is, 10 per cent of the early sample and nearly two-thirds of the post-1770 sample). This might not have been a problem if Hatfield Broad Oak had been a reasonably typical rural parish, but it was not. It was one of the largest parishes in Essex and, more importantly, it contained an 1100-acre forest, a substantial heath, and a variety of other commonable areas, including a common marsh. The forest was not enclosed until the mid-nineteenth century. The common marsh is still referred to in the 1809 Land Tax, and as late as the 1840s the parish still contained no less than 19 named commons.[56] Since most of Essex contained little woodland by this period and since the great majority of parishes did not have commons or heathlands on this scale, the labouring poor of Hatfield Broad Oak were exceptionally fortunate in their access to pasture and other customary rights. To a limited extent, the information about animal ownership in their pauper inventories reflected this. Only five of the 41 inventories in the core sample mentioned animals. In 1767, a Weathersfield pauper had three old geese, a gander and seventeen goslings 'on the green'. In 1711, a Feering pauper inventory mentioned 'a pig in the yard'. The other three mentions of animal ownership were all in Hatfield Broad Oak inventories. Twenty per cent of inventory subjects in that parish owned an animal with much greater earning potential – a cow.[57]

Although some of the Hatfield Broad Oak inventories are brief and suggest a lifestyle closer to that of Joseph Smith than to that of their neighbour John Tadgell (Appendices 1 and 2), others are very similar to Tadgell's. The inventory of 'the widow of the late Joshua Adams', taken in 1796, for example, describes a house similar in size and furnishings. Widow Adams became a regular receiver soon afterwards. The inventory of 'Edward Bird and Dorothy his wife', taken six years later, included three 'chambers' and a large dwelling-space as well as various outhouses. Moreover, it contained a slightly greater diversity of household goods than that of the Tadgells. Edward Bird was a regular receiver of poor relief in the year it was taken.[58]

It should not, of course, be assumed that all these households were reliant solely on income from unskilled labour. As Paul Slack has recently pointed out, the poor were 'a jumble of social groups and individuals with little in common besides their poverty'. Edward Bird, like Tadgell, cannot be traced in the Land Tax but he may well have had considerable resources to call upon since there is a reference at the end of his inventory to 'a cottage at Garson Green'. Joshua Adams was a smallholder who, if the Land Tax is any guide, rented about 1.5 per cent of the land of the parish. His inventory, which includes a 'four year old milch cow' and some 'barley and peas' in the straw, not only confirms that he was farming on a similar scale to many who were labelled husbandmen, but also suggests that he was a wheelwright with an outhouse and a workshop containing the relevant tools and raw materials.[59] Although the subjects of most of the Hatfield Broad Oak pauper inventories in this sample had no landholdings recorded in the Land Tax, Joshua Adams was not unique in this respect. Thomas Warner, for example, had a tiny holding with the lowest possible Land Tax rating (equivalent to 0.2 per cent of the parish land) and his inventory, taken in 1799, included a cow, three sheep and a lamb 'in the yard'.[60] Clearly many of the labourers, smallholders and artisans of Hatfield Broad Oak had much better access to pasture and other customary rights than those of similar status elsewhere in Essex, and the fact that their dwellings were slightly larger and that they were rather more likely to own some relative luxuries such as looking-glasses, candlesticks and pictures (Table 7.3) was almost certainly linked to this. The differences were not immense and may have been partly caused by the fact that 11 of the 15 Hatfield inventories were taken very late, between 1793 and 1810. But Hatfield Broad Oak's dominance among the 1770–1812 subsample makes it impossible to draw firm conclusions about changes over time within the pauper inventory data. There is much further work to be done on the unique pauper inventory collection of Hatfield Broad Oak but the sample of inventories contextualised here serves as a timely reminder of the problems of using sources so unevenly spread across space and time. Clearly, the quantitative exercises attempted in Tables 7.1–7.3 have many drawbacks and it is important to regard the figures they contain as preliminary and problematic.

## VII

Although the work presented here has already pinpointed a series of questions about this particular source, it has by no means exhausted the range of issues that pauper inventories raise about the lives and strategies of the poor. What was the nature of the bargain, whether implicit or explicit, that was made when a pauper's goods were inventoried at the point that he or she became a regular receiver? Did those whose goods were inventoried receive more or less out-relief than other paupers? Did ex-ratepayers get better treatment and have a better chance of keeping their household goods whilst on relief? Do cases like those of Joshua Adams and Thomas Warner, who almost certainly moved from being ratepayers to being regular receivers as they went through the final stages of the lifecycle, offer insights into why the Old Poor Law had such widespread support outside the ranks of the very poor? A welfare system that offers the prospect of later benefits to the taxpaying middling sort, or at least to the lower or more vulnerable groups within it, will be regarded much more positively than one that does not. So will a system that offers some support to the widows of fairly substantial householders.[61]

The making of pauper inventories needs to be located within these life-cycle-related issues and expectations if we are to understand them as a strategy not only of the parish officers but also of the poor, by unravelling the transactions, reciprocities and tactics that lay beneath them. These inventories can be seen as instruments of oppression and appropriation by the parish authorities, and as another stigma for the poor to suffer. John Clare certainly regarded them as such by the early nineteenth century. However, they can equally be seen in some contexts as a humane means by which ratepayers could be persuaded to leave regular receivers not only in their own family homes but also in complete control of their possessions – at least for their own lifetimes. When a man or woman first entered the list of regular receivers, their material goods might become a vital plank in their bargaining strategies. Only detailed studies of vestry minutes in parishes where inventories have survived in abundance will reveal how much, or how little, room for manoeuvre the poor had in such situations, or how the strategies of the poor law authorities and the poor changed over time.

This chapter has focused primarily on the questions this source raises about the material life of the poor, but even here many questions have remained unanswered. The inventories tells us very little, for example, about the proportion of their earnings that the poor spent on household goods rather than on basic necessities, on the purchase and feeding of productive animals, or on forms of non-subsistence-based expenditure – recreations, drinking, gambling, travelling, pets, friendly societies, mutual support and so on; nor can the Essex inventories offer any insights into regional variations. Equally, the inventories do not reveal where the poor obtained their widening range of household goods. Did they buy them new or secondhand, barter them, make them for themselves or for each other, appropriate them, hand them down to family and kin, or receive them as cast-offs from richer groups?[62]

The main aim here has been to raise questions rather than to answer them, but one conclusion can be tentatively advanced. By the later eighteenth century, Weatherill's suggestion that wage-earners were not acquiring a wide range of household items almost certainly no longer applies. The extent to which the poor had bought into 'the culture of consumerism' either mentally or literally remains unclear. In Essex, at least, the division between backstage and frontstage, for example, had yet to embed itself in plebeian culture. Moreover, the main findings that emerge from the comparison attempted here between the wealth and household goods of the labourers and husbandmen of the later seventeenth-century sample, and those found in the pauper inventories 1711–1812, are paradoxical. Although the latter sample owned a much wider range of household goods, their general wealth-levels as measured by house size and so on, remained lower. Thus, while the pauper inventories of the eighteenth and early nineteenth centuries challenge, to some extent, our assumptions about the austere lives of the poor and about their lack of material reserves in times of need,[63] the picture that emerges is by no means an optimistic one. Indeed, given the rapid increases in material wealth experienced by many farming and other middling households during this period, it seems likely that in relative terms the labouring families of Essex were getting poorer rather than richer. Larger and better-balanced samples that allow for such factors as differences in the availability of customary rights are necessary before firmer conclusions can be drawn, but the potential as well as the pitfalls of these sources remains immense. Pauper inventories, such as those reproduced in Appendices 1–3, when properly located within their life-cycle, administrative and broader economic contexts, offer unique insights into the material world of working people. They have been neglected by social historians for far too long.

## APPENDIX 1: ASHDON, ESSEX

**An Inventory of Joseph Smith's House-Hold goods taken 2 June 1812**

2 Bedsteds   1 Flock Bed   1 Bolster   2 Pillars   1 straw Bed   1 Quilt   1 Blanket & 4 Sheets   1 trunk & 2 boxes   1 Ale Stall   1 Corner Cupboard   2 Tables   1 Copper Boiler   1 Kneading trough   1 stool   1 Foarm   4 Chairs   4 Shelves   1 Clothes Basket   a pair of Bellows Tongs and Fire-shovel   1 trammel   1 Tea-kettle   1 Lock-Iron & 2 heaters   7 trenchers – 4 plates   1 looking glass   2 Candle sticks   2 pitchers   1 Wheel & 1 Reel.

*Reference* E/R/O/, D/P 18/12/7

## APPENDIX 2: HATFIELD BROAD OAK, ESSEX, 12 JULY 1810

**An Inventory of the goods and chattels belonging to John Tadgell Labourer taken by: Mr J° Spellar Acting Overseer and Tho[s] Richard – Vestry Clerk**

*In the Dwelling Room*
a square Deal Table & Dresser   a small D°   an Elm Cubboard D°   shelf   a Kneading Trough w[t] 4 Leggs   a Round Tea Table   a Long Oak Table wt frame & drawer,   7 Chairs & a Childs Do   a Small Cubboard & Shelf   a Settle wt Seat,   a small nest of Shelves,   a Bracket wt two Shelves;   a warming pan   a Brass Frying pan Do   a Cettle   two Fire Shovels   a poker & tongs,   a Tramel & two hooks   a Gridiron fender and iron Bar,   a Flat iron   a Box iron and rest   a Chopping knife   a Saw & three hammers,   a Cup Cobiron   a Mahogany Tea Chest   a gepand Tea board – a pair of Bellows,   two Bills,   a Table Brush,   a Coffee pot   a canister,   7 green edg'd Plates   a small Do Dish.   16 Large Delph Plates   3 Course Dishes;   67 Pieces of Teacups Glasses and Crockery Ware;   9 Pieces of Tin ware,   4 wooden bottles   11 Pieces of wooden ware,   a Looking-Glass,   a Stool and a Pitcher,   2 pewter plates & a Dish.

*First Chamber*
A Four Post Sacking bottomd Bed Stead with red Furniture,   a Feather Bed Bolster & 2 Pillows   a pair sheets & 2 Blankets & a Quilt,   5 Candlesticks   two Straw Beds,   two Sythes   six Sickles   a Landithing Hoe   a Stable Lanthorn,   one Elm Hutch   3 Chairs & round Table,   3 deal Boxes,   a Stool   a Close Basket and a Deal Cradle.

*Second Chamber*
a Four Post Sacking bottomd Bed Stead and Crimson plod Furniture, a Feather Bed Bolster & 2 Pillows  a pair Sheets,  3 Blankets and Civerlid,  a Deal Chest  a Tea Chest and two oak Hutches  3 deal Boxes  2 small Boxes and 2 Stools,  a looking glass –  2 Chairs  2 hand basons  one Chamber pot,  one Stone jar  a tin Candlestick and Extinguisher,  a Tinder Box, & Steel,  a Dustpan & hearth Brush,  a Close Basket & Quilting Frame  13 Bottles Glass and Lanthorn.

*Buttery*
a Copper Boiler  2 Do Tea Cettles  a Warming pan,  a sinder sifter and 3 Earthen pots,  a ladle  a Water Pail,  two Mattocks  two landtichen Spades and Do hoe,  a Large Brass Kettle,  two Iron Shovels,  a fork & 2 hoes,  a Bean hook  a wooden Peal & Garden Rake,  a wash Tub & Lye Letch  a Kneading trough and Spening Wheel  a pair wooden Scales & 4 Weights

*Yard*
Two Herdles  a Stool  a Tub & Small Jar.

*Reference* E/R/O/, D/P 4/18/8


APPENDIX 3: THEYDON GARNON, ESSEX

**18 August 1775 The account of Mr. Thos Burgh's Goods**

*In the Kitchen*
A grate and hanging Oyrn and pork Oyrn and fire shovell poker & sifter Bellows and Tramell and Trevett and Fender Tongs  Chafing Dish and 6 Dishes and 6 plates pewter and warming pan  Deal table 5  Chares and a table with 2 Drawers and a Old Chess Tea Chest and 2 Tea Boards  a Corner Cubbard  3 Candlesticks Brass and a Morter and Sniffers,  a Tea Table and a gun  2 oyrn Candle Sticks and 1 Tinon  a Box Oyrn and Rack  a Cloath Brush and Whip

*Parlour*
A pair of Cob Oyrns Brass Nobs & Bellows,  fire Shovell and Tongs and Fender  a Great Arm Chear and Cushen and 1 other and 5 pichters

*Stair Case*
an 8 Day Clock

*First Chamber*
a hangar   a Bed Stead and Furniture   a Bed Bolster and 2 pillows   3 blanketts and quilt and Trunde and a pair of Chester Draws and Dressing Box and Looking glass and 2 Cheers and [illeg.] Stool Bason and Valleno belongin to the Bed

*Second Chamber*
A Bed Stead and Yellow Furniture   a Feather bed and Bolster and 2 pillows   4 Blanketts and 1 quilt   4 Cheers   2 Cob Oyrns and Table Box and Table   2 Window Curtains

*Wash House*
A Table and Tea Kittle and 2 Saucepans   a Pair of Stillards and Beef fork and Brass Ladle and a Brass porridge pott and 1 oyrn Do and Brass Lidd and 2 Brass Kittles   1 Cheer

*Reference* E/R/O/, D/P 152/18/9

NOTES

I would like to record my deep debt to Thomas Sokoll who made available transcripts of the 350 Essex pauper inventories from which the 51 that are more deeply contextualised here were selected. I am also thankful for his comments on the original version of this chapter which was given as a paper to the 'Words of the Poor, Lives of the Poor 1700–1850' Conference at the University of North London in January 1995. The many questions raised by the audience at that Conference were also immensely useful. I am particularly grateful to Roger Wells for his critical written comments and to Cris Gostlow for her work on Figures 7.1–7.4. I would like to thank the staff of the ERO for producing much of the relevant material at very short notice.

Place of publication is London, unless otherwise indicated.

1. J. Brewer and R. Porter (eds), *Consumption and the World of Goods* (1993); L. Weatherill, *Consumer Behaviour and Material Culture in Britain 1660–1760* (1988); P. Langford, *A Polite and Commercial People, England 1727–1783* (Oxford 1989).
2. N. McKendrick, J. Brewer and J. Plumb, *The Birth of a Consumer Society. The Commercialisation of Eighteenth-Century England* (1982), esp. Chap. 1.
3. R. Malcolmson, *Life and Labour in England 1700–1780* (1981).

4. Much of this work was inspired by E.P. Thompson's influence, some of which reached its final printed form in E.P. Thompson, *Customs in Common* (1991). For a discussion see P. King, 'Edward Thompson's Contribution to Eighteenth-Century Studies. The Patrician–Plebeian Model Re-examined', *Social History* 21 (1996), 215–28.
5. For brief recent observations on the vast historiography of the standard-of-living debate see P. Hudson, *The Industrial Revolution* (1992), pp.29–32. R. Floud, 'Standards of Living and Industrialisation' in A. Digby and C. Feinstein (eds), *New Directions in Economic and Social History* (1989), pp.117–29. For another useful overview see P. O'Brien and S. Engerman, 'Changes in Income and its Distribution during the Industrial Revolution' in R. Floud and D. McCloskey (eds), *The Economic History of Britain since 1700*. I. *1700–1860* (Cambridge, 1981), pp.164–81.
6. F. Eden, *The State of the Poor* (3 vols, 1797); D. Davies, *The Case of Labourers in Husbandry* (1795). See also T. Sokoll, 'Early Attempts at Accounting the Unaccountable: Davies' and Eden's Budgets of Agricultural Labouring Families in Late Eighteenth-Century England' in T. Pierenkemper (ed.), *Zur Okonomik des Private-Haushalts* (Frankfurt, 1991).
7. P. Mathias, *The Transformation of England. Essays in the Economic and Social History of England in the Eighteenth Century* (1979), pp.148–67.
8. Weatherill, *Consumer Behaviour*, pp.168–76. Similar problems have been experienced by others working on inventories – see Mathias, *Transformation*, pp.148–67.
9. Weatherill, *Consumer Behaviour*, pp.192–9.
10. T. Sokoll, *Household and Family among the Poor. The Case of Two Essex Communities in the Late Eighteenth and Early Nineteenth Centuries* (Bochum, 1993).
11. R. Burn, *The History of the Poor Laws: with Observations* (1764), p.101; Essex Record Office (hereafter E/R/O/) Q/SBb 215/2. According to T. Williams, *The Whole Law Relative to the Duty and Office of a Justice of the Peace* (4 vols, 1794) 3, pp.665 and 727, the rents and profits of her husband's lands and tenements could also be taken (following a JP's order) by the parish.
12. E/R/O/ D/P 322/18/31 for Daniel Keeble's inventory. The legal background to this can be found in Williams, *The Whole Law Relative*, 3, pp.663–4. For rent arrears see, for example, E/R/O/ D/P 36/18/1 inventory of George Rogers; D/P 4/18/8 inventory of Robert Bird, D/P 11/18/3 William Foulder.
13. For examples see E/R/O/ D/P 264/18/14 inventories of Sarah Slaughter and of William Watson; D/P 219/12/29 of Mrs Worley; D/P 193/12/2 of Widow Draper and of Ann Bacon.
14. Inventories made at paupers' departures from institutional care were rare: see the list of 'Banisters goods when he went out of the poor house', E/R/O/ D/P 55/12/1. Other lists of goods taken from one pauper and then redistributed amongst others do occasionally occur, E/R/O/ D/P 4/18/8. For a dispute in which a pauper used the potential restoration of his furniture and bedding as a bargaining tool, Q/SBb 336/71.
15. Burn, *History*, p.281.

16. This was the practice in the Hertfordshire village of Little Gaddesden where 'old people who had no one to care for them were given shelter in the town houses; and when they had thus become the bedes folk of the parish they made a "will and act of surrender", leaving all their goods to the overseers. At their death their belongings were sold for the relief of the poor rate.' V. Bell, *To Meet Mr Ellis, Little Gaddesden in the Eighteenth Century* (1956).
17. R. Robinson, *John Clare's Autobiographical Writings* (Oxford, 1986), p.115; S. Nesbitt, 'Implications and Outcomes of the Poor Law Amendment Act' (BA dissertation, Nene College, 1993) p.10, quoting poor rate assessment book, Northants Record Office, 325 P/179.
18. J. Clare, *The Parish. A Satire* (1985), pp.62–3 – a work written in the early 1820s.
19. A. Newman, 'The Old Poor Law in East Kent 1606–1834. A Social and Demographic Analysis' (PhD, University of Kent, 1979), p.154, who also observes that a pauper's goods went to the parish after his or her death.
20. E/R/O/ D/P 119/8/2.
21. E/R/O/ D/P 35/8/1; D/P 152/12/2. On 11 June 1792 the Canewdon vestry ordered inventories to be taken of the household goods of six paupers and recorded one shilling and sixpence as the cost of this activity, E/R/O/ M/F 471 (D/P 219/12/29).
22. These 51 came from: Weathersfield (D/P 119/12/1) 14; Theydon Garnon (D/P 152/18/9 and 12/2) 10; Purleigh (D/P 197/18/4 and 12/6) 2; Willingale Spain (D/P 337/12/1) 1; Canewdon (D/P 219/12/29) 4; Ashdon (D/P 18/12/1 and 18/12/7) 2; Hatfield Broad Oak (D/P 4/18/8) 15; Feering (D/P 231/12/1) 2; Great Coggeshall (D/P 36/11/6A) 1. Apart from the final parish, which was a small town with a cloth industrial base, these were all predominantly rural parishes spread around various rural hundreds from northwest Essex to central and southeastern Essex. The sample selected here does not represent all the inventories which it may be possible to contextualise from these or other Essex parishes. Given that this is a very time-consuming process, it was confined to these 51 inventories.
23. For critical reviews of probate inventories and their problems see, for example, Weatherill, *Consumer Behaviour*; D. Vaisey, *Probate Inventories of Lichfield and District 1568–1680* (Staffordshire Record Society, 1969); R. Garrard, 'English Probate Inventories and their Use in Studying the Significance of the Domestic Interior, 1570–1700', *A.A.G. Bijdragen* 23 (1980), 55–85; N. and J. Cox, 'Probate Inventories: the Legal Background', *The Local Historian* 16 (nos 3 and 4, 1984), 'Part 1', 133–45, 'Part 2', 217–27. M. Spufford, 'The Limitations of the Probate Inventory' in J. Chartres and D. Hey (eds), *English Rural Society 1500–1800* (Cambridge, 1990), pp.139–74 is an excellent recent critique. For a brief discussion of pauper inventories see B. Cornford, 'Inventories of the Poor', *Norfolk Archaeology* 25, 118–25 and Anon., 'Inventories of Poor People's Furniture at Clyffe Pypard 1767', *The Wiltshire Magazine* 48 (1938), 193–6.
24. Four of the 15 paupers whose inventories are discussed by Cornford, 'Inventories', had been ratepayers earlier in their lives.
25. A number of the Hatfield Broad Oak inventories in particular appear to arise from this context: E/R/O/, D/P 4/18/8 and 4/12/13–14.

## Pauper Inventories

26. The same variation is seen in the 15 Norfolk inventories in Cornford, 'Inventories'.
27. J. North, 'State of the Poor in the Parish of Ashdon', *Annals of Agriculture* 35 (1800), 459–73; E/R/O/ D/P 18/8/3.
28. E/R/O/ D/P 18/12/7.
29. E/R/O/ D/P 18/12/6–7.
30. E/R/O/ D/P 18/18/4, Q/RPL 389; D/P 18/5/1 rate assessments.
31. E/R/O/ D/P 18/18/2.
32. E/R/O/, D/P 18/18/2 and D/P/ 18/18/4 compared suggest he and his wife shared their household with one other non-family member. By 1810 his household size was down to two, D/P 18/18/5.
33. This rare document (E/R/O/, D/P 18/18/2) gives us considerable insight into the range of earnings of labouring families in this period – information which is rarely considered by those attempting to use one-wage series as 'typical' of any given community or occupation in order to create time series that can be used to measure changes in real earnings. It lists 97 family units and their earnings, 94 of which have occupations assigned or are widows or single women. The census taken two months later contains 143 households. While there are problems in comparing across documents, almost all the labouring families of Ashdon appear to be listed.
34. E/R/O/, D/P 18/12/7–8; D/P 18/1/6.
35. E/R/O/ D/P 18/1/6 and 18/1/14 contain the ages at death of all those buried in Ashdon as recorded in the Anglican registers.
36. E/R/O/, D/P 4/18/8.
37. E/R/O/, D/P 4/12/14.
38. E/R/O/, D/P 4/12/13–15. The Hatfield Broad Oak collection is virtually the only set of parish documents not yet fully catalogued by the Essex Record Office. In the 67 boxes of material – many of them containing loose overseers' bills, accounts, etc. – this information may eventually be recoverable.
39. E/R/O/, Q/RPL 431, 441, 450
40. E/R/O/, D/P 119/12/1 inventories of Widow Birds, Widow Doe, and D/P 119/8/2 for context as regular receivers
41. E/R/O/, D/P 152/18/9 and 152/12/5.
42. Thomas Sokoll has found 75 parishes with probate inventories. Unlike overseers' account books, which parish officers were legally bound to keep, pauper inventories were informal documents. A considerable number of inventories (such as that of Joseph Smith) survive only because they were recorded in overseers' account books.
43. This use of a 'mentions system' is similar to that used in Weatherill, *Consumer Behaviour*, and was also that used in P. King, 'Changes in Living Standards, Consumption Patterns and Occupations in Kent between the 1680s and the 1740s as seen in Probate Inventories' (undergraduate dissertation, University of Kent, 1972).
44. Scattered later eighteenth-century probate inventories can occasionally be found but the thorough search of the probate records required to find even a small sample has prevented them from being analysed on a quantitative basis here.
45. The 'mid-Essex' sample has been collected by putting together all the inventories in which any detail on household goods is provided from two

sources – the Writtle-with-Roxwell inventories, which are available in print in F. Steer, *Farm and Cottage Inventories of Mid Essex 1634–1749* (Chelmsford, 1950), and the inventories of the Good Easter Peculiar – E/R/O/, D/APgWI. All pre-1658 inventories have been ignored, as have all those where occupation could not be established. The five inventories of 'Gentlemen' have also been left out of the sample.

46. There is a full manuscript transcript in the E/R/O/ of the northeast Essex inventories (E. Wood, 'Soken Probate Inventories 1637–1773'). Only two stray inventories relate to the period either before 1701 and after 1758 and these have been excluded, as have those with no details of the contents of rooms but simply a valuation. The inventories of two gentlemen and two clerics have also been included. This sample includes seven single women, six of whom were widows, five inventories which were clearly not of above farmer or tradesmen status but whose precise occupation is unclear, and one husbandman. Where no occupation was given, but trade goods, tools, or crops/animals enable the inventory subject's occupation to be established, they have been included in the relevant column.
47. Weatherill, *Consumer Behaviour*, pp.25–47.
48. The fact that the husbandmen and labourers in the mid-Essex sample all had inventories dated before 1700, whereas some of the middling sort inventories were made 20 or 30 years later, may partly explain these differences. However, since they fit so well with the work of Weatherill, *Consumer Behaviour*, pp.166–89, which is based on larger samples that do not have these distortions, it seems unlikely that this problem had much impact.
49. Weatherill, *Consumer Behaviour*, p.183.
50. These 41 do not necessarily constitute all the Essex pauper inventories with room information that can be traced into other records. Some of these inventories occur in parishes with very poor records, according to the E/R/O's guide – F. Emmison (ed.), *Catalogue of Essex Parish Records 1240–1894*, (Chelmsford, 2nd edn, 1966).
51. E/R/O/, D/P 119/12/1 inventory of Robert Ward; D/P 20/8/1 Widow Smith; D/P 210/18/4 William Catley.
52. Pauper inventories do not record debts owed to the pauper and only very occasionally record one or more debts owed by them. Probate inventories record debts owed to, but rarely debts owed by the subject of the inventory. For an exploration of the distortions the later practice caused, see Spufford, 'The Limitations'.
53. On the powers given by the 1671 Act allowing guns to be seized, see P. Munsche, *Gentlemen and Poachers. The English Game Laws 1681–1831* (Cambridge, 1981), p.12.
54. For examples see E/R/O/, D/ABW 106, William Benson, Sible Hedingham, Plumber and Glazier (taken 1777) which includes a large, well-provisioned kitchen; a 'Fore Room' well furnished with mahogany and other furniture – tables, chairs, clock, looking-glasses, a wide variety of pictures (including the Rev. Whitfield in a glass and gilt frame), a coal range, tea and coffee things and many other items; a buttery; a parlour even better furnished than the fore room; four bedrooms and a shop. Or see the five-bedroomed house and wide variety of stock of John Page, Prittlewell, Draper, E/R/O/, D/ABWb (1775). Both households had well-established 'frontstage' and

'backstage' rooms. The Essex middling sort were not untypical, see Langford, *A Polite*, pp.69–70.
55. Malcolmson, *Life*, p.146; A. Brown, *Essex at Work 1700–1815* (Chelmsford, 1969) pp.132–4.
56. Three parishes with rich collections are Weathersfield, Theydon Garnon and Hatfield Broad Oak. (See note 22.) For Hatfield Broad Oak see E/R/O, Q/RPL 431, 441, 450; *Victorian History of the Counties of England: Essex* vol. 8, pp.158–86. Hatfield Broad Oak also contained a decaying minor market town. For the importance of customary rights to the poor, see K. Snell, *Annals of the Labouring Poor* (Cambridge, 1985), pp.138–227.
57. E/R/O/, D/P 119/12/1 inventory of George Carder, and D/P 231/12 Walters Northy.
58. E/R/O/, D/P 4/18/8 and 4/12/14.
59. P. Slack, *Poverty and Policy in Tudor and Stuart England* (1988), p.7; E/R/O/, D/P 4/18/8 and Q/RPL 431.
60. E/R/O/, D/P 4/18/8 and Q/RPL 431.
61. Another dimension not investigated here but worthy of further consideration is the position of widows. Were their pauper inventories very different from those of male householders and, if so, in what ways? For the household context, see T. Sokoll, 'The Household Position of Elderly Widows in Poverty' in J. Henderson and R. Wall (eds), *Poor Women and Children in the European Past* (1994), pp.207–24.
62. Some of these issues are addressed for one area of expenditure in J. Styles, 'Clothing the North: The Supply of Non-elite Clothing in the Eighteenth-century North of England', *Textile History* 25 (1994), 139–66. Regional variations are discussed for better-off groups in Weatherill, *Consumer Behaviour*. If methods of quantification can be refined and more knowledge gained about where goods were obtained from, pauper inventories may also be useful in refining the debate about the growth of the home market. See, for example, D. Eversley, 'The Home Market and Economic Growth in England 1750–1780' in E. Jones and G. Mingay (eds), *Land, Labour and Population in the Industrial Revolution* (1967).
63. For an important article on an earlier period stressing the possibility that levels of poverty have been exaggerated, see J. Walter, 'The Social Economy of Dearth in Early Modern England' in J. Walter and R. Schofield (eds), *Famine, Disease and the Social Order in Early Modern Society* (Cambridge, 1989).

# 8 'An old offender tho' so young in years': The Criminal Careers of Juvenile Offenders in Middlesex in the 1830s*

Heather Shore

The growth of penal detention in the nineteenth century produced some classic accounts of prison life. Such narratives provide insights into both the multiplicity of crime and the experience of detention. There are accounts from political prisoners as well as from more reserved detainees, prisoners who anonymously relived their penal experience, such as 'one who has endured it', 'one who has suffered it' and 'one who has just left prison'.[1] However, these accounts generally start in the later nineteenth century and come largely from the hands of the more educated prisoner: they are not representative of the more commonplace offender. Nor are the gallows accounts of highwaymen, murderers or ostentatious figures like Jonathan Wild and Jack Sheppard.[2] Is it then impossible to glimpse into the lives of ordinary criminals, most of whom were working people – apprentices, servants, washerwomen, artisans – and not inclined to leave records of their activities?

Occasionally, sources do emerge which give some indication of the lives of such people. Of course, such sources are few and far between, and where they do exist should be treated with caution. One such is the subject of this chapter. In this case, a series of interviews had been conducted with juvenile offenders in 1835. The interviewer was William Augustus Miles. Miles had a rather questionable career. Whilst on the one hand he appeared as a respectable contributor to various parliamentary Select Committees, an informant of Edwin Chadwick's for the 1839 Royal Commission on Constabulary, and a one-time Commissioner for the Charity Commission, he was also viewed as somewhat of a nuisance. Rumoured to be an illegitimate son of William IV, in 1841 he gained a commission with the Sydney police, was subsequently discredited, and finally died, rather ignominiously, in New South Wales.[3]

For a time in the 1830s, Miles focused his activities on juvenile crime. Juvenile offending was of increasing concern in this period. Contemporaries perceived a worrying increase in crime, with delinquent youth being seen as a major part of the equation. Since the late 1810s, a public debate had been gathering pace, represented through the auspices of the several Select Committees on crime and policing, and through the activities of various voluntary organisations and societies, such as the Philanthropic Society, and the Prison Discipline Society.[4] In his own 1839 publication, *Poverty, Mendicity and Crime* (based, amongst other things, on the interviews collected in 1835) Miles cited the usual drumroll of causes: special emphasis was laid on the drunkenness of parents, lack of education and the corrupting effect of popular amusements.[5] Like many of his contemporaries, Miles subscribed to a subcultural view of the London criminal underworld.[6] He advocated a hardline response, recommending that juvenile delinquents be given vocational training and then sent abroad to the colonies. Paradoxically, however, Miles did at times show an emphatic understanding of his subjects. In his contributions to the 1835 Select Committee on Gaols, Miles made a thinly veiled attack on the social order and its institutions, asking:

> whether so much criminality and misery is not caused by a defect or shameful neglect in the state of society, and whether these juvenile delinquents are not the victims of a bad policy, should be a matter of serious consideration.[7]

The interviews are held amongst the Home Office papers at the Public Record Office. Filling three manuscript notebooks, as far as can be gathered they were recorded by Miles as the boys spoke or soon afterwards. The interviews are mainly in the first person, the boys referring to their own actions and experiences. He spoke to 32 boys, aged between ten and 19. There are indications in Miles' work that many more interviews took place and indeed a further set of notebooks does exist. However, these are in rough note form and lack the coherence that is found in the interviews selected for this chapter.[8] It is fairly certain that most of the interviews were conducted on the juvenile prison hulk, the *Euryalus*, moored at Chatham between 1825 and 1843. A small number of boys (five), who have proved elusive, were probably interviewed in Tothill Fields, the House of Correction for Westminster, which at that time was under the governmentship of Lieutenant A.F. Tracey, RN.[9]

All the boys were sentenced to transportation for seven years, and all were found guilty of property crimes, namely those of larceny, larceny from the person and larceny by the servant.[10] Many confessed to previous convictions. In a few cases where it was mentioned on the indictment or in the sessions papers, it was possible to trace these convictions. However, where boys had been convicted at the Westminster sessions, the lack of consistent calendars (lists of indictments) made detection of previous convictions rather speculative. Moreover, the majority of previous convictions would have been dealt with by summary jurisdiction. Since no consistent documentation survives for summary processing in this period, such convictions are untraceable. Many of the boys confessed to being in prison previously. Again, finding evidence for this was problematic, since these detentions could have been the result of summary trial or, as in one case, the boy may have been placed in the House of Correction by a parent or guardian. There is evidence to suggest that juvenile offenders accused of minor crimes, such as misdemeanours, could be informally placed in the House of Correction, or in one of the various refuges that existed at this time.[11]

For the purposes of this discussion, a small group of boys has been selected as the most fruitful cases for the illustration of models of criminal lives or biographies. From the initial interviews with Miles, the boys were traced from their appearance in the Middlesex Criminal Registers – which list the yearly indictments for the Middlesex courts (whatever the outcome) – to their original indictment, where it existed, through the records of the courts, the prisons and onto the convict ships.[12] For the 21 boys who were sent to Van Diemen's Land, further documentation exists from the various records kept from the point of disembarkation in the colony.

Many of the statements the boys made to Miles were corroborated in these records. The printed proceedings of the Old Bailey trials were particularly rich. These records, in tandem with the Miles interviews, have been used to trace the boys' 'criminal careers', and their progress through the judicial system. However, such an exercise can be misleading if it is not located in the context of debates about criminality. Consequently, the focus of this chapter will be on three areas: first, it will consider the view of juvenile offending, which emphasises the organised nature of crime and hence, the validity of descriptions of criminal networks and fraternities as evidence for 'criminal careers'. On the other hand, the view of juvenile crime as a lifecycle experience, theft that is opportunistic rather than organised, should be assessed. Second, issues of domestic and social life will be considered, assessing the relationship between a boy's residence, family, work and his offending. Third, the reformation of juvenile offenders will be evaluated through the boy's actions and their own rather pragmatic thoughts on the matter.

## SUBCULTURE VERSUS LIFECYCLE

Throughout the nineteenth century, commentators drew on lurid accounts of the criminal underworld to underline their concern over the 'nurseries of crime' which apparently existed in the metropolis. Indeed, the real extent of organised crime is impossible to gauge. However, it would probably be justified to say that it was not as pervasive as was painted by some contemporaries. Indeed, when the subject came up in contemporary Select Committees, the most usual comment was that one need look no further than the prisons for such enclaves of criminality. Some of the boys gave compelling accounts of the criminal environment and of their initiation into crime. They vitally portray the nurseries of crime and the impenetrable rookeries that were so beloved of social commentators. Moreover, it is patently obvious from Miles' work that such rich detail was integral to his description of a metropolis overrun by criminals:

> there is a youthful population in the metropolis devoted to crime, trained to it from infancy, adhering to it from education and circumstances, whose connections prevent the possibility of reformation, and whom no punishment can deter; a race *'sui generis'*, different from the rest of society, not only in thoughts, habits, and manners, but even in appearance; possessing, moreover, a language exclusively of their own.[13]

For example, 15-year-old William Cook told Miles how, after his father's death, he had been led astray by street boys:

> some boys whom I had known in the streets came and said to me 'Cook, come along with us to the Serpentine', so I went with them and they stole somebody's cloathes who was swimming and next day gave me my share of the robbery – and that was the first time I went bad.[14]

Cook had stolen 5lb of beef from a Spitalfields butcher, John Hurford, on 18 January 1835. As he told Miles:

> I was a flesh hunter when I first took to it, that is I used to steal meat of any sort. Two shillings and sixpence is a very bad day's work – hardly worth going out for – five shillings a day is more decent – I sell the meat to apple cart women and coster-mongers.[15]

William Cook was caught stealing meat valued at two shillings and fourpence – not such a good day. Cook had professed to being in prison an astonishing 15 times. However, besides the conviction in question, no others were found. In Van Diemen's Land, he admitted to previous vagrancy convictions, which would explain the lack of previous convictions in the Middlesex Criminal Registers of indictments.[16] Presumably these periods of custody, if they occurred, were the result of summary trial. Certainly, in the Van Diemen's Land conduct registers, Cook is generally portrayed as an 'incorrigible', with numerous cases of disciplining for insolence and bad conduct. However, it is a testimony to the harshness of the penal regime that this was more or less the case for many boys.[17] William had spent some time working for, and being supported by Mrs King, a mangling woman. Eventually though, he was drawn into the lodging-house culture of Whitechapel:

> I then went with them to a lodging house, Mrs Burke's in Essex street, Whitechapel where I got my bed for three pence a night and used to go out stealing in the day time – thirty or forty persons lodge in this house, all thieves and beggars, about 15 or 20 are boys .... There is a large kitchen in this house where they all meet at night – and sup and drink together in parties of three or four – the beggars come home at night, and swear, fight and, if they are cross, beat the children at a fine rate ... I have seen a beggar without money but that was only for a few minutes – they go out, sometimes come back, sit down, swear they have had no luck and then ask who will go out with them upon a thieving trip – if a child comes across them they will give it a kick and say 'damn your little eyes, go and get me some money'.[18]

A similar story was told by Samuel Holmes. Thirteen-year-old Samuel had no mother and his father, a waterman, was a drunkard who had apparently been unable to control the boy. Like Cook, Holmes had been enticed into thieving by other boys, eventually gravitating to a Stepney lodging house, east of Ratcliff Highway:

> two of these boys took me to a house in 3 Compass court in Stepney, kept by a Jew, and he agreed to board and lodge me for 2/6 a week, provided I brought and sold to him all that I might steal – he has about 13 boys in the house on the same terms – and there are four housebreakers living in the same house. They are all young men ... the landlord has also the adjoining house and there is a communication into it from every room – the back kitchen is fitted up with trap doors to help escape – and in a corner of one of the back kitchens is a sliding floor underneath

which property is hid. A coat is hung up in the kitchen or public room and boys practice how to pickpockets, the men in the House shew them how to manage – I was about a fortnight in training, and afterwards went out to assist and screen other boys when they picked pockets – in a short time I went out on my own account, as I soon saw how they did it.[19]

Holmes had stolen a tongue, three tame doves and one tame pigeon from Richard Booty Cousens on the Commercial Road, in east London.[20] He had also been convicted at the Clerkenwell Sessions the previous year with John Little, for the theft of a saucepan valued at three shillings, and a frying pan, value one shilling.[21] In this case, he had been sentenced to hard labour in the House of Correction, where he spent some time in solitary confinement, and received a good flogging before his release. Like others of the boys, he used an alias. Known as Smouchee, variously slang for a thief or a Jew, he was referred to by this alias in both his Clerkenwell indictment and in the sessions papers.[22] Richard Booty Cousens noted, in his evidence to the court, that at the house of Margaret Symonds, where Holmes had taken his goods, 'a girl came forward and said she should not go, for she would tell who she had it from – she said she received it from Smouchee'.[23] Holmes was also familiar with the metropolitan prisons, having told Miles of four previous sojourns. Incidently, Holmes expressed a dislike for the harsh regimes of the House of Correction in Coldbath Fields preferring – like many of the boys – the more relaxed environment of Tothill Fields in Westminster.[24] In Van Diemen's Land he continued an uncomfortable relationship with authority. His conduct register tells a sorry story of continual disciplining. During his stay in the colony he was disciplined several times for pilfering, insolence, using bad language, improper conduct and singing in his cell.[25]

Samuel Holmes' and William Cook's descriptions of street life and criminal networks portrayed the type of environment that was soon to be immortalised in Charles Dickens' *Oliver Twist* in 1837, and by Henry Mayhew's social observations in the 1860s.[26] In fact, descriptions of thieves' kitchens can be found as early as the sixteenth century. For example, in 1585 William Fleetwood, the Recorder of London, described 'a school house set up to learn young boys to cut purses'.[27] These descriptions may well have been informed by popular cultural images of thieves' kitchens. On the other hand, it is likely that Miles sought out those boys who were known offenders, with acknowledged criminal associations. Thus whilst these 'nurseries of crime' may well have existed, these were probably atypical of the experience of most young offenders.

The pattern of previous conviction, and former periods of detention, experienced by both Holmes and Cook, is repeated for others of the boys. It is important to emphasise that those juveniles sentenced to transportation would have been those who were considered as the more 'hardened' offenders. For many juveniles, reaching the superior courts, particularly the Old Bailey, was something of a zenith. Whilst for first offences juveniles would generally be sentenced to be whipped or to a short period of detention, 'serious' offences invariably resulted in transportation. This was particularly the case in the 1830s, which was the peak decade for transportation to Australia.[28] Moreover, this was matched by an increasing move to informal measures of compulsory emigration, effectively transportation with training. However, some boys were first offenders and these boys provide a contrast to the cases described above.

George Webster, aged 13, was found guilty of the offence 'larceny by the servant' at the May sessions in 1835. He claimed to be relatively inexperienced and, unlike many of the boys, not to have been in prison before. An orphan, Webster believed that he was about to be dismissed by his master George Weaver, a Clerkenwell cheesemonger, and had consequently decided to rob him. Webster therefore stole a box, containing nine sovereigns, 55 shillings and 13 sixpences. He absconded but was caught a few weeks later enjoying his ill-gotten gains on a Woolwich steamboat. Charles Stewart, the local superintendent, reported that:

> on the 8th of April I saw the prisoner on board a steam boat going to London – I searched him and found this pencil case on him, and 11.6s. in money – he was in company with another lad about the same age – the prisoner said he was taking the money to his master, a cap-maker, in Holborn – I said I would take him to his master – he afterwards said he lived with this person in Exmouth-street – I took him to Weaver who charged him with this.[29]

If Webster was as unfamiliar with the justice system as he maintained, the sentence of transportation he received seems unnecessarily harsh. However, the crime was a theft of substantial value, and George Webster was an orphan – exemplary material for colonial remodelling. Unfortunately, Webster was never to attain such citizenship. Transported in 1837, he served three years in the juvenile penal colony at Point Puer, dying early in 1841.[30]

Like Webster, Rowland Bassett was also indicted for 'larceny by the servant'. Bassett had previously been in court but had been found not guilty. He had been accused of stealing a fender, but as Bassett remonstrated: 'A lad asked me to carry it, and said he would give me a halfpenny.'[31] The following year he was indicted for stealing a pair of opera-glasses from his master James Gardner, the owner of the Finsbury Bazaar. Bassett had been five weeks in the service of Gardner. This time Bassett was found guilty, to be transported to Australia for seven years.[32] Whilst he confessed to Miles that he had been thieving for a year, these crimes, or potential crimes, have the mark of an opportunist thief. Rowland Bassett and George Webster had probably spent little time premeditating their crimes. There is little similarity to the world governed by organisation, hierarchy, exchange and reciprocity that was described by Holmes and Cook.

DOMESTIC/SOCIAL LIFE AND OFFENDING

Whilst evidence from the sessions and other records of the criminal justice system can tell the historian about the bare bones of an offender's 'criminal career', it is rare to find any textual evidence to cast light on an offender's domestic and/or social life. Moreover, when such evidence does exist, it has to be accepted that it is largely impossible to verify. Hence, whilst Miles' interviewees do make reference to such personal circumstances, the reliability of these statements can only be guessed at. That those facts that are verifiable do tally might be an indication; then again, home, work and residence were sensitive issues. Indeed, Miles's thesis, like that of the majority of his contemporaries, was to make conclusive links between, for example, parental negligence and offending. The work environment was also of concern. Employment, as much as unemployment, was regarded as a potential cause of crime. Critics pointed to the poor behaviour of apprentices, which they linked to the decline of living-in. Similarly, domestic servants were often under suspicion. As John Beattie points out, the crime of 'larceny from the dwelling-house' was aimed largely at pilfering servants.[33]

Like Rowland Bassett and George Webster, many of the boys seem to have spent at least some time in employment, although it is likely that much of this was short-lived. Whether this was due to the vagaries of the employment market, or to periods in custody, is unclear. There was a variety of occupations described. For example, Francis Boucher sold things from a donkey and cart his father had purchased for him. Peter Conley, an Irish boy, travelled around the country hawking books. Fourteen-year-old John Darville collected wood-shavings and sawdust and sold them for three or four pence.[34] Many of the boys described an occupational structure which could embrace the occasional (or more frequent) lapses into criminality. Moreover, as the boys were keen to point out, good money could be made from thieving. John Darville told Miles that he made a shilling a day from honest work, whereas when thieving he could make four or five shillings. A few claimed to have made their livings completely through crime. Thus, 16-year-old George Hickman commented that 'I have never worked since I began thieving.'[35]

The descriptions of familial life provided in the interviews lend considerable credence to some causal relationship between deprivation and offending. In terms of family structure the boys were not particularly atypical. Of the 32 boys interviewed by Miles, just over half (17) had both parents living, three had only a mother living, four only a father, four a parent and step-parent and four were orphans. Drink, low employment and illness seem to have been constant features of their home lives. James Edwards' mother took to drinking when her husband ran away; Peter Conley's father, a bricklayer, was described as a hard-drinking man; Francis Boucher's father, who kept a brothel in Duck Lane, was a great drunkard.[36] A few of the boys also referred to physical restraint, although this seems to have been mainly employed to stop the boys offending. Thus, Samuel Holmes described how his father:

> tried to keep me at home – has stripped me, taken away my cloathes and tied me to a bed post – because the boys used to come round the house at night and whistle and entice me to go out thieving again with them.[37]

Francis Boucher, aged 15, also attributed his deterioration to the influence of bad boys. However, since his father gave him severe beatings, he was not an altogether unwilling quarry. As Boucher told Miles, his

> Father used to pay men to bring him back, then he always beat him – severity of his father forced him to run away – Boys used to come about the house to get me out – when father went to the club boys always came for me – used to watch father out of the house because he used to beat any he could catch – boys were at last afraid to be seen in his company near home because if his father could get hold of any boy who might be in his company he was sure to get thumped.[38]

Boucher had been indicted for larceny, stealing a handkerchief from a shop door; as he told Miles, he 'used to thieve anything from shop doors'.[39] This time Boucher was caught, protesting in his defence in court:

> In the morning I was in bed – my sister took my handkerchief and pawned it – I got up, and went to get it out. I waited in the shop for ten minutes or a quarter of an hour, and in coming out I knocked down the handkerchief with my hand.[40]

## 'An old offender tho' so young in years'

The general picture that emerges from these descriptions is of a mixture of family structures, whose members balanced precariously on the fine line between poverty, drunkenness and the ups and downs of employment. A few were from 'respectable' backgrounds, but in these cases too, guardians had to engage with the task of keeping their sons from 'bad company'. Rowland Bassett came from reduced circumstances. His mother was crippled and his father, who had been a silk manufacturer, was now a milkman. The family of seven children still lived in the silk-weaving district of Shoreditch, and the majority of the siblings were either married or in service. Sixteen-year-old Rowland had initially been placed in Coldbath Fields by his father 'in order to frighten him'. This failed since immediately on his release the boy ran away and 'was induced to thieve in order to make up a sufficient sum to pay the last instalment on his trousers, which he had long purchased at the Tally shop'.[41]

A small number of boys had spurned 'normal' family life altogether. Like the youthful members of Fagin's den, they lived in the networks of thieves which in some ways provided an alternative family structure. Moreover, these could be difficult ties to break. Thomas Wade, also known as Thompson, demonstrated the obstacles to going straight:

> when a young thief comes out of prison, some of his old companions are waiting for him at the gate, and they take him away with them – if he refuses, or if his friends have got hold of him they watch the house in the evenings to entice him out and beat him if he adheres to his resolution of being honest.[42]

Wade/Thompson was an habitué of Tothill Fields. In his evidence to the 1835 Select Committee on Gaols, Lieutenant Tracey described the dangers of allowing prisoners too much association with friends and acquaintances. In doing so, he referred to the case of Thomas Wade to illustrate how well known thieves could maintain relationships with inmates. He felt that juveniles were at particular risk. William Ballard, a noted coiner, who had apparently 'figured in the public prints', had pretended to be a relation in order to gain access to the prison. Tracey said:

> I was about to discharge a boy, Thomas Wade, who had been three months in the prison, a troublesome character, though quite an urchin; a man came with an order worded thus: 'Permit William Wade to see his son Thomas Wade', this William Wade was the noted William Ballard.[43]

Ballard had promised the boy that on his release he would 'be a father to him', further enticing Thomas with the promise of a new hat. The conversation was overheard by an officer who recognised Ballard and reported to the Governor. Subsequently, Lieutenant Tracey asked the boy how he knew Ballard:

> He said, 'My sister kept company with him ... he kept a room, it is one of many that he keeps ... I have been in the habit of going there to pass bad sixpences for him.' I asked, 'Have you done it long?' He said, 'Yes, very long.' 'Do you meet any other characters there of the same description?' ... 'Yes, many little boys of my acquaintance.'[44]

Wade had also commented to Miles on this character. Wade's sister, who was then 17, had gone 'on the town' when she was 14, becoming acquainted with a group of young prostitutes. Known as 'Fair Mary Anne', she had lodged at a brothel in Coventry Street, Haymarket, with a Mrs Mendozas, a Jewess. Wade/Thompson describes his sister's 'fancy man' as 'a well known maker of bad money'. It is likely that this was William Ballard.[45] Wade/Thompson had little stable homelife. While one sister was still at home his father was away, working as a musician on a Margate steamboat. His only other family tie, his streetwalker sister, made him particularly vulnerable to the corrupting environment represented by William Ballard.

What cannot be assessed is the extent to which young criminals could opt in or out of these environments, moving between familial and criminal networks. However, the fact that boys often talk about both 'home' and 'lodging', implies that such worlds were not mutually exclusive.

Generally, the boys seem to have lodged fairly close to their original residences. Indeed, the geography of juvenile offending gives further insights into criminal lives. Few of the boys strayed far from home to commit their offences; in fact, many were known to the witnesses in court. Mobility profiles were constructed for the boys by using the original residence information in the Miles interviews, along with the indictment (for where the crime took place); the recognisances, where they were available, and other information from the prison records and from the Australian sources.[46] George Hickman told Miles that he was from Clerkenwell (to the north of the City), frequenting the Hare and Hounds in St John Street, and selling 'his plunder' to fences in Field Lane. His father was a working jeweller, confirming the Clerkenwell connection. Hickman's address in the Newgate records was given as the parish of St Andrews, bordering Clerkenwell, this included the Field Lane/Saffron Hill area.[47] This district was an infamous slum. Demolished in the 1860s, it became especially notorious in 1837 when Dickens made it the location for Fagin's den. In *Oliver Twist*, the Artful Dodger travelled with Oliver down the same roads and through neighbourhoods so frequently mentioned in George Hickman's records.[48] Like Oliver and the Dodger, Hickman and his companion Thomas Witford were apprehended locally. They were caught stealing a handkerchief from the pocket of Alfred Hole, a medical student, on Cock Lane, about five minutes' walk from Field Lane. As a 12-year-old, George, and three other boys, had been caught in Somers Town, only a mile or so to the north of Clerkenwell.

Samuel Holmes also had a fairly tightly defined patch. Holmes had two traceable previous convictions, both of which took place in the parish of St Dunstan, Stepney. This was an area to the east of the City, comprising the neighbourhood surrounding St Dunstan and the 'village' of Ratcliff. This was a particularly notorious area, home to many poor Irish emigrants. In 1811 the area was highlighted with the incident of the Ratcliff Highway murders, where on two nights in December seven people were murdered in their homes. This provoked a nationwide panic, which raised questions about both the local watch, and the development of national policing.[49] Holmes lodged in the area, thieved in the area, and fenced his goods in the area. After stealing from Richard Booty Cousens on the Commercial Road, Holmes went over to fence his goods with Margaret Symonds at Brook Street, Ratcliff. Her house was in Three Compass Court, the same court that Holmes had named as the location of the thieves' kitchen. Symonds was later accused of receiving alongside Holmes, but acquitted. Holmes denied the allegations against him, telling George Murray, the arresting police-sergeant:

> I know nothing about it; but I saw a dog running down White Horse Street with it in its mouth; I stopped him, and gave the tongue to old mother Symonds to cook.[50]

The previous examples depict a very closeknit environment. Most of the boys committed their crimes and lived their lives within fairly compact geographical areas. The majority were bunched around either the Westminster/Soho neighbourhood, or around east London and the City. Only six of the boys were apprehended more than a few miles from their residences. Peter Conley and John Murphy were two of the six. They had travelled from their homes in St Giles-in-the-Fields, east of Oxford Street, to Lawrence Lane in Cheapside in the City, and there stole the handkerchief of Thomas Boulton, a silk-dresser. Both Conley and Murphy were from Irish backgrounds. Indeed, the area surrounding St Giles had a very large Irish population at this time. Many poor emigrants coming to the City terminated their journey in St Giles, which also had a reputation as a slum and criminal rookery. Further evidence from Murphy shows that his parents lived in Buckeridge Street, which was in the heart of the slum, and was later visited as part of Henry Mayhew's survey into the criminal classes, *London Labour and the London Poor*.[51] Miles noted that 'his father and mother, two sisters and a brother inhabit the front-room second floor – for which they pay 3 shillings a week furnished'.[52] The handkerchief that Murphy and Conley stole was valued at two shillings, worth two-thirds of the amount of the weekly rent for Murphy's family – a fair prize.

It would be fair to conclude that thieving was closely tied into limited mobility. These boys stole from the streets and the shops that they were familiar with and to which they had access. Even in the case of Murphy and Conley, they stole within reasonable walking distance of home. Whilst most of the victims were of a higher social standing, they did occupy the same approximate streets and neighbourhood as these boys. It is clear that the polarisation of the poor and the middle classes should not be overplayed. A substantial number of the boys had stolen goods from shop doors and pavements, the others had picked the pockets of passers-by or stolen from their masters. Indeed, it is likely that this admixture of opportunity, occupation and residence was the experience of most juvenile offenders.

REFORMATION

From the late eighteenth century there was a steadily growing impetus to the reformation of the criminal, culminating in the great flurry of penological debate and parliamentary activity in the mid-nineteenth century. The child as criminal was frequently the focus of the debate. To contemporaries, the rise in juvenile crime seemed to indicate profound moral decay amongst the youth of the lower orders. Various solutions were considered. Prevention was debated along with cure. The means of doing this, however, was not to be by relief but rather by removing delinquent and semi-delinquent youths from the corrupting environments in which they lived. This environment, argued the reformers, included the parents who through their drunkenness and failure to socialise correctly were seen as a major cause for juvenile crime. Once the child became institutionalised, the debate revolved around ideas of reformation and retraining. Most reformers were keen to separate juveniles from the so-called 'moral contagion' of adults, and aimed to provide alternatives to the adult prisons which were seen both by offenders and reformers as training grounds for criminals. Reformation was to be by a variety of means: religious education, vocational training, rural refuge or agricultural labour in the colonies. All these were employed at one time or another. Farm schools had already been initiated in the 1830s, along with schemes of sending children to Canada, Australia and South Africa.[53] However, it is clear that none of these stratagems provided a lasting solution.

Miles believed that juvenile thieves were already irredeemably corrupted, and would be so long as they returned to their old haunts. Unlike many other reformers, he did see that criminality was part of their landscape, a necessary complement to survival. He asked several of the boys for their thoughts on reformation. For example, William Cook told Miles:

> I would not trust a thief – they can never turn right – if they get a place it would be to run away after a month or so with any thing they could get hold of – as for myself I would rather go abroad – I have no friends and if I was to get into a place I should be enticed away again.[54]

This view was echoed by Samuel Holmes who, like Cook, claimed to be an experienced thief. Both boys professed to have substantial experience of imprisonment:

> as to reforming ... I think many of the boys might get a place and wish for one, but it would only be for a day or two in order to rob their employers – they cannot reform if left in London, because they would be enticed away again.[55]

Miles felt that the boys had the capacity to change their situations but lacked correct moral training and socialisation. He cited George Laval Chesterton, Governor of Coldbath Fields House of Correction:

> Mr. Chesterton, of the House of Correction, informed me that he considers reformation among juvenile offenders to be utterly hopeless; he observed, that 'boys brought up in a low neighbourhood have no chance of being honest, because on leaving a gaol they return to their old haunts and follow the example of their parents or associates'.[56]

The boys, Miles argued, showed little respect for the majesty of the law. Reporting on the trial of George Hickman, and three other of Miles' interviewees, Charles Downes, Henry Underwood and Thomas O'Donnell, *The Times* fulminated:

> The court was literally crammed with spectators during the passing the sentences, and we regret to say that great confusion prevailed occasionally. Several of the prisoners, the majority of whom were young persons, behaved with so much levity, that the learned recorder was

compelled to recall them, and lecture them upon their indecorous and hardened behaviour. He also reminded them that transportation was not a removal to a state of comparative idleness, but a continuous course of constraint, severity and privation. Some of their friends in the gallery added to the disorder by insolent exclamations towards the learned judge of the grossest kind, and others by vehement screaming and exultations. The court however, exercised great forbearance towards those who disturbed its proceedings.[57]

Many of the boys made comments on prisons and had their own ideas about the incidence of crime. Holmes preferred Tothill Fields because the boys were under less restraint. Hickman preferred 'Newgate, in every respect except sleeping because they can see their friends, can play, talk, and do as they like'.[58] Robinson, who was a companion thief to Hickman, pointed out that a juvenile's chances often depended on where he was caught. He preferred to pick pockets in the City, where the 'officers are better to the boys and prisons are better if a fellow is caught'.[59] George Hickman also commented on the City police, who, he said:

> are frequently treated by the thieves with drink – some of the Policemen will not accept it, but very few of the City Police are so nice – There is one fellow who behaves very well to us in the city. He never cares about getting a fellow sent to prison for three months because it does him no good, but if he can make an Old Bailey case of it, he takes the Boy up, because he gets his expenses, or something, I believe, for his trouble – He sometimes stops a fellow and takes anything from him which he may have about him and lets him go again.[60]

This sort of activity had been particularly highlighted in the 1810s with the 'blood money' scandal. In 1816, six policemen were tried for conspiracy. Most notable was the Bow Street officer George Vaughan, who was known as a very effective police officer, and well known for bringing many pickpockets to justice.[61] Several of the boys also mentioned the fence, or receiver, as a protagonist. They rightly pointed out the dependent relationship between the thief and the fence. Thomas Wade/Thompson protested 'it is those "fences" who do us boys the most harm – we are only their workmen after all, and unless they are stopped you cannot stop thieving'.[62]

Ultimately, the boys seemed to have little relation to the schemes and strategies that were being deliberated on their behalf. Punishment, in one form or another, seemed something of an inevitability. Attitudes veered from apathy, as in the case of 14-year-old Philip Maine, who 'does not care much about his present situation, nor mind being transported', to the fear of 13-year-old Thomas O'Donnell, who was 'afraid of going to the bay and would prefer the House of Correction', to the resignation of 16-year-old Thompson, who concluded that

> As for transportation it is looked upon by each thief as an event which must occur some time or another, and the only point is to keep from it as long as they can.[63]

In conclusion, this chapter is just one interpretation of the words of the poor. Here, such words have been used to illustrate the possibilities of criminal lifestyles in the early nineteenth century. Moreover, they have pointed to conclusions about the duality of day-to-day existence and the more romanticised 'criminal careers' of juvenile offenders. Most importantly, the words of the boys have been used to comment on the issues, on which traditionally only the great and the good expound. The true reconstruction of past lives is an insurmountable task. We can only catch glimpses, and our interpretation of them is at best anecdotal and impressionistic – thumbnail sketches of lives that carry on before and after the juncture at which we find them. Maybe, through the findings reported in this chapter, a small group of boys have become something more than the usual one-dimensional figures that customarily represent the juvenile and other offenders. Ultimately, all of them moved on, from, and beyond the scope of historical investigation.

## NOTES

\* I would like to thank P.J. Corfield for her comments on this chapter.

1. For a general overview of criminal biography in the nineteenth century see M.P. Priestly, *Victorian Prison Lives: English Prison Biography, 1830–1914* (London: Methuen, 1985). The starting-point for any working-class biography should be J. Burnett, D. Vincent and D. Mayall (eds), *The Autobiography of the Working Class: an Annotated Critical Biography*, vol. 1: *1790–1900* (Brighton: Harvester Press, 1984), vol. 2: *1900–1945* (Brighton: Harvester Press, 1987).

2. Much of the recent work on criminal biography has been concentrated on sub-Hogarthian criminal characters: see, for example, L.B. Faller, *Turned to Account: the Forms and Functions of Criminal Biography in Late Seventeenth and Early Eighteenth-Century England* (Cambridge: Cambridge University Press, 1987); G. Howson, *Thief-Taker General: the Rise and Fall of Jonathan Wild* (London: Hutchinson, 1970); P. Rawlings, *Drunks, Whores and Idle Apprentices: Criminal Biographies of the Eighteenth Century* (London: Routledge, 1992).

3. I am indebted to David Phillips for much of the information on W.A. Miles. Phillips has conducted extensive research into Miles' activities in both England and New South Wales. See D. Phillips, 'An Uneasy Moral Entrepreneur in England and Australia: William Augustus Miles on Police, Pauperism and Crime in the 1830s and 1840s', paper presented at the Fifth Australian Modern British History Association Conference, University of Melbourne, November 1987.
4. The earliest, most significant contribution to the debate was a pamphlet published in 1816, *Report of the Committee for Investigating the Causes of the Alarming Increase of Juvenile Delinquency in the Metropolis* (London: Dove, 1816). This committee included many individuals who were to play key roles in the ensuing juvenile crime debate.
5. W.A. Miles, *Poverty, Mendicity and Crime: or, the facts, examinations, &c. upon which the Report* [on prison discipline] *was founded/presented to the House of Lords by W.A. Miles; to which is added a Dictionary of the flash or cant language, known to every thief and beggar; edited by H. Brandon* (London: Shaw and Sons, 1839), pp.41–51, 86–94.
6. This genre is most graphically represented by the work of Henry Mayhew, *London Labour and the London Poor*; more recently, derivative accounts have been written by K. Chesney, *The Victorian Underworld* (London: Maurice Temple Smith, 1970) and J.J. Tobias, *Crime and Industrial Society in the Nineteenth Century* (London: Batsford, 1967).
7. Fourth and Fifth Reports from the Select Committee of the House of Lords on the Present State of the Several Gaols and Houses of Correction in England and Wales: *Parliamentary Papers* (1835), vol. XII, p.514.
8. Public Record Office (hereafter PRO) HO 73/16, rough manuscript notebooks, vols III, IV, V.
9. Tracey was another vociferous contributor to the select committees of the time; like Miles, he made an extensive contribution to the 1835 Select Committee on Gaols.
10. The crimes for which the boys are convicted are typical of the more serious crime committed by juvenile offenders. It was rare to see juveniles convicted of violent, sexual crime, livestock theft or fraud. Only one boy, James Edwards, was found guilty of burglary.
11. Francis Hobler, the principal clerk to the Lord Mayor, referred to such a case in his contribution to the Select Committee on the State of Police of the Metropolis: *Parliamentary Papers* (1817), vol. VII, p.495.
12. PRO – HO 26/39–41, Criminal Registers – Series I, Middlesex only; PCOM 2/203, register of prisoners, Newgate, 1834–6; Home Office (hereafter HO) 9/2, registers of convict hulks, *Euryalus* at Chatham, 1825–6; HO 8/43 & 44, quarterly hulk returns; HO 11/10 & 12, convict transportation records; HO 10/51, Tasmanian muster, 1841; HO 10/32, general muster of New South Wales, 1837.
13. Miles, *Poverty, Mendicity and Crime*, p.45.
14. PRO – HO 73/16, notebook no. 3, evidence of W. Cook.
15. Ibid.
16. Archives Office of Tasmania (hereafter AOT) – CON 31/7, conduct registers, entry no. 1986.
17. Ibid.

18. PRO – HO 73/16, notebook no. 3, evidence of W. Cook.
19. PRO – HO 73/16, notebook no. 1, evidence of S. Holmes.
20. Greater London Record Office (hereafter GLRO) – CRIM 4/13, no. 81, 5 July 1835.
21. GLRO – MJ/SR 4341 SP.Clerkenwell, 12 July 1834.
22. E. Partridge, *A Dictionary of the Underworld* (London: Routledge & Kegan Paul, 1950; this edn, Ware: Wordsworth Editions, 1989), p.647.
23. *Old Bailey Sessions Papers* (hereafter OBSP), vol. 3, Ninth Session, 6 July 1835, pp.471–2, no. 1676.
24. For a full account of the Tothill Fields House of Correction in the mid-nineteenth century see H. Mayhew and J. Binny, *The Criminal Prisons of London and Scenes of Prison Life* (London: Frank Cass, 1968 edn), pp.353–486.
25. AOT – CON 31/21, conduct registers, entry no. 2078.
26. In fact, it is possible that Dickens may have had some access to Miles' work, given Dickens' involvement in parliamentary journalism in the early 1830s.
27. Cited in W.B. Sanders (ed.), *Juvenile Offenders for a Thousand Years: Selected Readings from Anglo-Saxon Times to 1900* (Chapel Hill: University of North Carolina Press, 1970), p.10.
28. L. Robson, *The Convict Settlers of Australia: An Enquiry into the Origin and Character of the Convicts Transported to New South Wales and Van Diemen's Land, 1787–1852* (Cambridge: Cambridge University Press, 1965).
29. OBSP – vol. 2, Seventh Session, 16 May 1835, pp.134–5, no. 1265.
30. AOT – CON 31/48, convict register, no. 2341; RGD 34/2, burials register, no. 164.
31. GLRO – CRIM 4/1, 11 November 1834; OBSP – First Session, 27 November 1834, p.107, no. 129.
32. GLRO – CRIM 4/5, no. 80, 2 December 1834; OBSP – vol. 2, Fifth Session, 3 March 1835, p.728, no. 704.
33. J.M. Beattie, *Crime and the Courts in England, 1660–1800* (Oxford: Clarendon Press, 1986), pp.173–5.
34. PRO – HO 73/16, notebook no. 2, the evidence of Peter Conley/Conolly and J. Darville/Darvill; notebook no. 3, the evidence of F. Boucher.
35. PRO – HO 73/16, notebook no. 1, evidence of G. Hickman.
36. PRO – HO 73/16, notebook no. 1, evidence of J. Edwards; notebook no. 2, evidence of P. Conolly; notebook no. 3, evidence of F. Boucher.
37. PRO – HO 73/16, notebook no. 1, evidence of S. Holmes.
38. PRO – HO 73/16, notebook no. 3, evidence of F. Boucher.
39. Ibid.
40. OBSP – Third Session, 6 January 1835, pp.398–9, no. 382.
41. PRO – HO 73/16, notebook no. 1, evidence of R. Bapet/Bassett.
42. PRO – HO 73/16, notebook no. 2, evidence of Thompson.
43. Select Committee on Gaols and Houses of Correction: *Parliamentary Papers* (1835), vol. XI, p.83.
44. Ibid., p.84.
45. PRO – HO 73/16, notebook no. 2, evidence of Thompson.
46. Particularly, the records of prisoners held at Newgate, post-trial but prior to being transferred to the hulks, PRO – PCOM 2/203.

47. PRO – PCOM 2/203, 28 March 1835.
48. C. Dickens, *Oliver Twist; or, the Parish Boy's Progress* (London: 1837–9).
49. See L. Radzinowicz, *A History of Criminal Law and its Administration from 1750: Volume 3, Cross-currents in the Movement for the Reform of the Police* (London: Stevens & Sons, 1956), pp.315–47.
50. OBSP – vol. 3, Ninth Session, 8 July 1835, pp.471–2, no. 1676.
51. Mayhew, *London Labour and the London Poor*. Volume IV was published in 1861–2, entitled *Those That Will Not Work, comprising Prostitutes, Thieves, Swindlers and Beggars*.
52. PRO – HO 73/16, notebook no. 2, evidence of J. Murphy.
53. The Philanthropic Society had sent numbers of their delinquent children to the colonies from the late eighteenth century. In 1849 it established its Mettray-style farm school at Redhill in Surrey. During the 1830s a similar venture was initiated by retired naval commander, Edward Pelham Brenton in Hackney Wick. The 'Society for the Suppression of Juvenile Vagrancy' (later the Children's Friend Society) sent out hundreds of children to the colonies to the extent that the Society was eventually discredited and accused of being a 'Kidnapper's Society'. See E. Bradlow, 'The Children's Friend Society at the Cape of Good Hope', *Victorian Studies* (1984), vol. 27, pp.155–77.
54. PRO – HO 73/16, notebook no. 3, evidence of W. Cook.
55. PRO – HO 73/16, notebook no. 1, evidence of S. Holmes.
56. Miles, *Poverty, Mendicity and Crime*, p.44.
57. *The Times*, 15 April 1835, p.6, c, d and e.
58. PRO – HO 73/16, notebook no. 1, evidence of G. Hickman.
59. PRO – HO 73/16, notebook no. 1, evidence of Robinson.
60. PRO – HO 73/16, notebook no. 1, evidence of G. Hickman.
61. Anon., *The Whole Four Trials of the Thief-Takers and Their Confederates ... Convicted at Hicks Hall and the Old Bailey, Sept. 1816, of a horrible Conspiracy to obtain Blood Money, and of Felony and High Treason* (London: 1816).
62. PRO – HO 73/16, notebook no. 3, evidence of Thompson.
63. PRO – HO 73/16, notebook no. 1, evidence of Mayne/Maine; notebook no. 2, evidence of J.O. Donnell, evidence of Thompson.

# 9 'The poor in blindnes': Letters from Mildenhall, Wiltshire, 1835–6
## Gregory C. Smith

> th[e] 22 November[,] mr vaisey[, who] is Church Warn and overseare put som thing upon the Church door after all the Congregation was gon in an when the servis was ended he stept out an took dit down before aney of the pepople could get out[.] i could just see that it was the poor Law[.] he took ceare that no one should not see it[.] they keep the poor in blindnes all as they can ...

This is a passage from an anonymous letter to the poor law commissioners dated 30 November 1835. It describes a blatant act of tyranny on the part of Edward Vaisey, tenant farmer and churchwarden, against the parishioners of Mildenhall, Wiltshire. The letter goes on to denounce Vaisey and the rest of 'them', the chief tenants, for the years of oppression they had inflicted on the poor of the parish. This was but the first in a series of four letters.[1] The second (to Vaisey himself) is also anonymous, but the last two (both to the poor law commissioners) provide the names and personal testimony of three agricultural labourers. The four letters are circumspect in their language and limited in their goals. Nevertheless, because the authors threw off the cloak of anonymity, the writing of these letters constitutes an act of overt defiance on the part of some of the most vulnerable members of Mildenhall society against the most powerful.

The attitudes and behaviour of the agrarian poor were a source of grave concern to the poor law commissioners. In all the vast inquiries that accompanied the preparation and implementation of the New Poor Law, however, the commissioners never sought information from labouring folk themselves. Similarly, in all the great body of modern scholarship about nineteenth-century poor relief, rural society and rural protest, the actual voices of the rural poor are seldom heard. At best, we get cryptic clues from anonymous letters and autobiographies. At worst, labouring folk are reduced to faceless components of some abstract economic model. The actual beliefs, perceptions and aspirations of the agrarian poor have remained almost a mystery.[2]

The four letters from Mildenhall have nothing like the educated prose and elegant script that characterise most of the poor law commissioners' correspondence: the handwriting is laboured, the spelling is creative and there is no punctuation whatsoever. The letters are important, however, because taken together they represent a substantial written production, one that allows a glimpse into the mental world of the labouring poor at a crucial moment in their history – the implementation of the New Poor Law. The letters are important as well because they provide enough factual detail to allow the reconstruction of the social and economic context in which they were written.

This chapter's primary concern will be to explore the significance of the authors' misconceptions about the New Poor Law. They apparently believed that Vaisey and his cronies were responsible for the reduction of poor relief in November 1835. In fact, of course, the central government was responsible – the very body from whom the authors were seeking redress. The men also expressed the belief that the New Poor Law had legislated substantial increases in their rate of pay. This again was quite simply untrue. These misapprehensions, it will be argued, are evidence both of the poor's intense localism and of their ancient belief in the paternalism of the monarch and his government. The process of discovering the truth about the New Poor Law, it will be suggested, must have given the final blow to this lingering faith.

A secondary concern of the chapter will be with the fact that Mildenhall was a 'closed' parish: a place where only one person owned most of the land and dominated the lives of the inhabitants.[3] Such places have figured large in spatial studies of rural society, but we have little idea of what it was like to live in one. The general absence of overt protest in closed parishes suggests harmonious social relations, but the Mildenhall letters pierce this surface calm and reveal a reality of hardship, suppressed rage and quiet conspiracy. By linking the letters' factual details with other sources, reasoned speculations can be made about the particular circumstances which could have empowered the three men to have made such a public demonstration of their resentment.

The chapter will begin with a synopsis of the four letters. This will be followed by a discussion of Mildenhall in the 1830s and the initial impact of the New Poor Law. We will then proceed to discuss the issues mentioned above.

## THE LETTERS

Letter 1, dated 30 November 1835, was written anonymously. It begins by informing the commissioners that the level of poor relief had recently been reduced for some families in Mildenhall and completely eliminated for others:

> this is to sertify you that Church Warnds [al]lows aman to keep awife and four small childern with 6 shellings a week[.] six shillen is Regular pay[.] some heave 5 small childern and they receve 8 pence per week in the stead of 11 pence[.] market price of bread is 11d at Marlbrough ...

The letter then relates the incident of the day before (quoted at the beginning of this chapter) when Mr Vaisey, 'Church Warn and overseare', posted what appeared to be the 'poor Law' on the church door and took it down again before anyone could read it. This was only the latest incident in a long campaign on the part of Vaisey and the rest of the chief tenants 'to keep the poor in blindnes' and to cheat them out of their rightful allowance. Incidents are described 'from 1832 or 3 or there away' proving that 'they never geave them no more then the Loves acarding to price of bread' even though repeatedly ordered to do so by higher authorities. On one occasion 'they ad aletter from the board to give them something more ... then there Loves of bread'. Instead of providing this 'they' informed the poor that 'we are under the fine of 50 pounds if wee give you aney ne[ce]ssarey what ever[,] wee deare not do it[,] wee give he to[o] much a ready'. On another occasion, Samuel Oatley (a farmer and miller) 'told me is selfe that he ad alletter from the board to giveem the price of 2 Loves an [a] alfe to coman [share] acording to there famles'. Oatley had said 'i will keep them out of that if i can[;] they wont know anything about it'. On a third occasion, the writer claims to have seen a letter requiring an increase in the level of relief. In hopes of obtaining this higher rate of relief a pauper might threaten to appeal to the local magistracy: 'if you no give it to me ill go to the magesty'. The response would be 'you go in mak your complaint me frind[.] what do you want said majesty [to do] ... give your right an more then your right[?]'

In conclusion, the letter says, 'soo it goes on now[:] ever since 1832 the[y] Been gon on like this[.] yers nothen wanten but wages rose'. With only 'six shillen to keep 5 or 6 in familey they can not get Bread enoff[,] the[y] ask for more [but] the[y] sed more likley sink another shillen a week[:] ... they will not rise the wages if the[y] can help it'. Thus, 'the poor are in destres[.] this may Be provd bey in Quierey among aney of the poor of there wages and releve ... they [are] willing to work an[d] able [–] no Loos Lay about men nor drunkards in the village[.] they are in Employ But the wages is so Low'.

Letter 2, dated 10 December, is also anonymous and is addressed to Vaisey. The letter demands that Vaisey write to the poor law commissioners himself:

> sir mr vaisey you ar desird to wright a letter to the honourbl commissioers at the bord London to certify them were you heave advanced the mens wages to the nine shellings as the poor law derect you and were you have put it upon the Church door or not during the day since november 22end or either of the following sundays.

Clearly, then, the writers were operating under the extraordinary assumption that the New Poor Law had legislated an increase in pay, and that Vaisey and the other farmers were breaking the law by withholding it. The letter finishes politely but firmly: 'the truth is required an nothing but the truth to prove my letter[.] my returne will be in the in suing week next ... i remain your humble servant'.

Letter 3, dated 9 January 1836, is again addressed to the poor law commissioners. This time, the cloak of anonymity is cast off, and the names and personal testimony of three adult male labourers are provided. The first, Charles Gregory, states: 'i ... heave five cheldern under 11 years old and here is seven of us to live out of six shelings[.] this is all as i got'. The second, James Hiscock, states that he has '5 childern seven of us in family my in com is six shelings[.] this is all as i got to live out of and maney others are in the same [situation] cease the relefing officer told us that he ad don with us'. The poor were told to look to their employers for an increase in pay, but they 'would not rise our weages because mister vaisey would not[:] if he would then we would [.]'

The third labourer, Thomas Jones, states that he has 'seven to live out of 8s 6d aweek[:] mine 6s and a boy brings in 2s 6d a week'. Jones presents a dialogue with his employer in which Vaisey is blamed for the suffering of the poor:

> my master said [']i wish they would rise the men for it tis well known that them that heave familys will be starved if the weages is not rose[.] i should give more but i must not without the rest was to [do] it[.] they never let me know aney thing about the poor law[.'] [']don't them[?'] [']no no thomas they do not[:] maney of us ob served mister vaisey put the poor law on the Church door on November the 22 after the people

were all in Church an then he taken it down be fore aney could get out so non of us codent see what it was[.']

Jones goes on to say that Mr Young (another of the chief occupiers) 'is for bring[ing] of us down to 5 shilings[.] a[h] well an[d] if they do it will be worse still[.]' Vaisey, however, is depicted as the chief villain: 'mister vaisey is Church warnd an overcear an now he is Garden of Mildenhal ... and he is the ruler in our parrish and averrey sever[e one] he as been to the poor'. Jones ends the letter by requesting the poor law commissioners to send their answer 'back derict to thomas jones at jaimes tarrants mildenhall ner Marlbrough Wilts'.

Having the identities of the three authors, the poor law commissioners initially decided to reply. A letter was drafted informing the men that the commissioners 'have no authority to interfere between the employer & the labourer as to the wages of the latter'. The letter assured them, however, that the 'Poor Law now in force in your Parish provides against a state of destitution on your part by enabling the Guardians to give the able bodied work & relief in kind'.[4] In the end, the letter was not sent. Instead, the commissioners wrote to the guardians of Marlborough Union asking them to investigate the 'application' from Gregory and Hiscock (Jones is not mentioned).[5]

On 19 January the Marlborough guardians replied, giving details of the families and earnings of Gregory and Hiscock.[6] Gregory, the report states, was 33 years old with a wife and five children, the eldest aged ten. He had been earning only the regular six shillings a week for some time, but in the last week he had earned one shilling and fourpence halfpenny per day at piecework (eight shillings and threepence per week). In earlier weeks Gregory had been offered piecework but he had refused it, claiming that he could not earn appreciably more than the regular pay: only one shilling a day and a farthing extra per week. According to his 'master', however, Gregory could not earn much at piecework because 'the man only worked a comparatively small portion of his time'. At the time of writing, it is claimed, Gregory could have made nine shillings per week 'if he will work fairly'. Gregory still had his rent paid by the parish as had been done for several years. He had not made an application to the board of guardians in the town of Marlborough, though his wife had spoken to the relieving officer.

Hiscock, the report states, was 40 years old with a wife and seven daughters. The eldest daughter (aged 18) was out at service, and his wife and the second daughter (aged 16) were both employed. His wife was earning three shillings per week. Hiscock worked with Gregory and, like him, had refused piecework. Hiscock and his wife could earn enough to support their family 'if the man chuse to exert himself'. Hiscock had not applied to the union for relief. As a final indictment, the report concludes that 'neither Gregory or Hiscock are Men of very good character'. As proof of this, a copy of the anonymous letter to Vaisey is enclosed. In acknowledging the report, the commissioners gave their 'thanks for the communication which is perfectly satisfactory'.

Letter 4, dated 27 January 1836, was written by Gregory and Jones and addressed to the poor law commissioners. On the recommendation of 'mister butler the releveng officer' the two men had at last gone to Marlborough to seek relief from the board of guardians. There they spoke to the Revd Mr Williams (magistrate and chairman of the board), who informed them 'that they was resine that theyll not giv you any thing at all'. Williams 'did not ask of us of our in Com nor he would not let us tell him ... [and did] not givus time to tell him[.] he seem to be very sharp with us'. Williams dismissed them with, 'then you might go[:] there is nothing for you'.

'So', the letter continues, 'we can get neither relef nor our weages rose an we aply to you to know whether theres any estated weags publeshed or not[.]' Gregory reiterates his financial situation: seven shillings per week and seven in the family, 'and what must I do[?]' Jones says that he has five children, and 'mister butler cut my ernings [that is, poor relief] to 1s 6d a week an that runs to 2 pence alpney aday an 1 alpney over for 7 days'. The letter closes with a final appeal: 'plese to send us ancer'. As before, no answer was sent.

## THE SETTING

### Mildenhall

The parish of Mildenhall is located on the Marlborough Downs in north-eastern Wiltshire, directly to the east of the town of Marlborough. The London–Bath road passes through the southern tip of the parish on the open downs, bypassing the parish's three villages, Mildenhall, Poulton and Stitchcombe. Mildenhall was typical of the small sheep-and-corn parishes which dominate the Wiltshire chalk country. Its 6.5 square miles (16.8 square kilometres) are open downland, covered here and there with deposits of clay and gravel. The clay and gravel had for centuries been the site of the parish's grain production; the open downs had been occupied only by sheep and a few shepherds. Early in the nineteenth century, however, the downs went under the plough. Except for a few scattered homesteads, the parish's approximately 430 inhabitants lived in the three little villages (of which Mildenhall was by far the largest), situated along the narrow banks of the rivers Ogg and Kennet.[7]

Mildenhall society was highly stratified and almost exclusively agrarian. The 1831 census tells us that out of 114 adult males, 76 were labourers (all but six of them agricultural), 12 were employed in retail, trade and handicrafts, and 17 were occupiers of the land.[8] The tithe survey (1837) provides a stark picture of the occupation of land in the parish. At the top of the social pyramid were the six great farming families (eight occupiers altogether) with holdings of 200–700 acres. These accounted for 87.5 per cent of the available land. Next there was a group of eight occupiers, holding between 1 and 150 acres, who occupied 12.3 per cent of the land in total. At the bottom there was a large group of 43 occupiers of houses and gardens or tenements and gardens (a couple also having a shop or a beerhouse). Even with the 3 acres of allotments for the poor, this large class of petty occupiers accounted for only .2 per cent of the land.[9]

Ownership was even more concentrated: the tithe survey lists nine owners, but only three of these owned 95 per cent of the land. The largest was Charles Brudenell Bruce, Marquess of Ailesbury. Ailesbury was Lord of the manors of Mildenhall, Poulton and Stitchcombe, and owned 66 per cent of the parish: four of the great occupiers and most of the tenement dwellers were his tenants. Ailesbury was the second greatest landowner in the county; his estate sprawled over much of the Marlborough Downs and the northern section of Salisbury Plain. He was the chief owner in several neighbouring places including the town of Marlborough, a pocket borough, and Great Bedwyn, a rotten borough disenfranchised in 1832.[10]

With power concentrated in so few hands, Mildenhall was not the sort of parish in which one could expect the poor to have given public expression to their grievances. Except for one incident during the Swing riots of 1830, there is no evidence of riotous disorder occurring in the parish at any time from the mid-eighteenth to the mid-nineteenth centuries. Even the single Swing incident was not perpetrated by inhabitants of Mildenhall. Rarely were Mildenhall people indicted at quarter sessions for theft or assault.[11] There is no evidence of religious nonconformity in the parish at any time after 1674. In the decades following 1815, while evangelical nonconformity was making dramatic inroads on the religious geography of the county, Mildenhall remained free of nonconformist meeting houses. (We should not, however, discount the possibility that some people attended meeting houses in neighbouring parishes.)[12] In 1842, the rector reported to the bishop that about 69 per cent of the inhabitants regularly attended the parish church on Sunday: farmers and male labourers in the morning, women mostly in the afternoon. On Census Sunday, 1851, there were 114 people at the morning service (not including the Sunday scholars), a figure large enough to encompass all the parish's farmers and male labourers. It is not unlikely that church attendance was mandatory for the labourers, a duty enforced by their employers.[13]

**'Ruler in our parrish'**

Ailesbury was the chief landowner in Mildenhall but he did not live there: his Wiltshire residence was to the south in Savernake Park. In many places on the Wiltshire Downs a single tenant took on the role of local boss.[14] Probably Letters 1 and 3 are correct in their claim that Mr Vaisey played this role, managing the place in Ailesbury's interests and enforcing discipline among the population. Edward Vaisey (70 years old in 1835) was tenant of Grove Farm and Mildenhall for most of the first half of the nineteenth century.[15] The letters are correct in describing Vaisey as *the* churchwarden: from 1801 to 1835 only Vaisey and Henry Woodman (another of Ailesbury's chief tenants) signed the bishops's transcripts as churchwarden. From 1807 Vaisey's name came first, and in many years his was the only signature.[16] Vaisey also acted as overseer in some years, but apparently far less frequently. Unfortunately, we do not know whether he did so in 1835. It is certain that in November 1835 he became Mildenhall's representative on the board of guardians for Marlborough Union.[17]

As perennial churchwarden, guardian and sometimes also as overseer, Vaisey was clearly the chief authority in the parish and in a position to dominate its social life. Together, Vaisey and the other great tenants were the 'they' that the letters complain about – a junta of grandees who controlled the vestry and through it the level of relief, the amount of pay and perhaps even the amount of information received by the rest of the poor. According to the letter-writers, Vaisey posted a document on the church door on 22 November 1835 and removed it before anyone could read it. If such an event did indeed occur, it would probably not have been a copy of the New Poor Law that he posted but rather an announcement of the election for guardian. The letter-writers, therefore, were probably wrong about the content of the notice. Nevertheless, Vaisey's control of the election would have been a clear enough indication of his dominant position.[18]

## Poverty and the New Poor Law

The New Poor Law called for the elimination of poor relief except for those willing to undergo the harsh regimen of the union workhouse. In Marlborough Union this part of the law could not at first be implemented, simply because there was not yet a workhouse. Indeed, the construction of the workhouse was not completed until 1837.[19] Parishes with poorhouses could use these as a partial substitute, but the usual strategy was to continue out-relief to the able-bodied poor at a reduced level.[20] Relief was now given purely at the discretion of the guardians and only after the poor had exhausted all other avenues to make up the shortfall: by seeking raises for the employed and work for the unemployed, or simply by working harder.

The Marlborough board of guardians held their first meeting on 26 November 1835.[21] By 30 November, according to Letter 1, the level of poor relief had already been reduced: a family of six, supported only by the father's six shillings per week, was now receiving no poor relief at all. A family of seven was still receiving eightpence per week but this was not even enough to buy a gallon loaf of bread, then elevenpence at Marlborough market.

These figures allow us to measure the precise impact of the New Poor Law on the labouring poor. Until the preceding week, the able-bodied poor in Mildenhall (as elsewhere on the Marlborough Downs) had received relief according to the Marlborough scale: a family's income was supplemented to the price of two gallon loaves for the father and one each for every other family member. Probably, the money for the father's second loaf was intended not for bread but for other necessaries, notably clothing.[22] John Bennett, MP for South Wiltshire, stated in 1814 that 'the gallon loaf per head per week is what we suppose sufficient for the maintenance of every person in the family for the week'.[23] A gallon loaf per week for each person provided about a pound of bread per day. Labouring families dependent on poor relief had little else to eat but this pound of bread and what they could grow in their cottage gardens.[24]

In November 1835, with bread selling at elevenpence per gallon, a family of six would have needed six shillings and fivepence per week – the price of seven gallon loaves – to continue at the old official level of subsistence. This would have been fivepence more than the weekly pay of the father. Under the old system, if no other family member was in employment, this fivepence would have been paid to the family out of the poor rate. Under the new system, people were simply told to exert themselves to find it. The new law, therefore, put the poor slightly below what had for years been considered the minimum income level.

The figures given in Letter 1, therefore, present us with a clear picture of immiseration as a consequence of the New Poor Law. The picture is complicated, however, by two pieces of evidence. Colonel Charles A'Court, the assistant poor law commissioner, reported on 30 October 1835, that the price of bread in Marlborough was indeed elevenpence per gallon. On the other hand, the price in Mildenhall itself was only tenpence.[25] By giving the price of bread in Marlborough rather than that obtaining in Mildenhall itself, Letter 1 is apparently misleading about the impact of the New Poor Law: at tenpence per gallon, a family of six with only the father's six shillings would still have had the price of seven loaves per week. They would not have needed poor relief (at least not at the old official subsistence level). On the other hand, the poor might well have had good reason to prefer shopping in the open, public market at Marlborough. The sale and production of bread in Mildenhall would, like everything else, have been controlled by the little circle of leading occupiers, who would have been able to subject the poor to any number of abusive practices. It is even possible that the vestry hoped to force the poor to buy bread at home, thus keeping them out of Marlborough with its unsettling political and religious influences.[26]

The guardians' report on Gregory and Hiscock of 19 January 1836 (outlined above) introduces other problems with the picture of impoverishment given in Letter 1. Gregory and Hiscock, it is claimed, refused the offer of piecework at which they could have made considerably more than their six shillings per week if they would only exert themselves fully. The men, the report says, refused the offer (until January 1836) because they said they could not in fact earn appreciably more than six shillings per week. There is no way of judging on this matter without knowing exactly when the offer was made or how hard the men would have had to 'exert' themselves to earn the full amount. What does seem clear from many sources is that piecework was not generally available in Wiltshire and that most labourers really did have to make do with their six shillings per week.[27] It may even have been that piecework was offered to Gregory and Hiscock only after the guardians learned of the men's complaint.

Hiscock's claim in Letter 3 to be supporting his family with only his six shillings per week is undermined by the revelation that his wife and two eldest daughters were in employment. On the other hand, Hiscock did not claim to support the two eldest girls, but only the remaining five. It is possible that his wife did not obtain employment until after the writing of Letter 3 on 9 January (perhaps assisted by Vaisey). This would explain why Hiscock did not contribute to Letter 4. Regardless of the particular case of Hiscock and his family, we know that in general employment was scarce for women and girls on the Wiltshire Downs and had been since the introduction of the spinning jenny in the 1790s.[28]

The guardians' report effectively introduces doubt about the men's personal economic circumstances. On the other hand, the letters' claims about the condition of the poor in general is substantiated by official reports. On 9 March 1836, Colonel A'Court, the assistant commissioner, reported that in the Marlborough Union, as elsewhere in Wiltshire:

> the moral effect of the system is stated to be extremely satisfactory. Agricultural wages are unfortunately exceedingly low – seldom amounting to more than 6/ a week, and yet at this miserable rate, manual labourers with large families are still anxious for private employment. There are in fact but few ablebodied men out of work, but owing to the lowness of wages the Guardians are sometimes compelled to assist those with large families either with provisions or by the offer of the Poor Houses for some portion of their families ...[29]

An even more extreme picture is provided by a report written in May 1836 by the Revd E.G. Williams, magistrate and chairman of the board of guardians (and the man who was 'very sharp' with Gregory and Jones):

> I do not know that we have good right to expect a very visible moral improvement in the short period of this Union's existence; but I think it must work even in this ill-paid district, in which a labourer, whatever number his family consists of, receives only 6s. a week, and no assistance at all in money or bread from the board, and he is of course found to exert every faculty of mind and body to support his family. Hence he must flee the public-house and the more noisome beer-shop: he has no time for idleness either of himself or of his children; and regular habits will lead him to seek, on the only day allotted the poor in this country, religious instruction in his church.[30]

The two reports differ regarding out-relief, but they agree that most families had only the father's six shillings per week on which to subsist. Few families' collected earnings would have amounted to more than about £20 for the year, as compared with, for example, the rector of Mildenhall's £760 or the paltry £14 000 which Ailesbury's trustees allowed him for personal and household expenses.[31] This extreme imbalance in incomes reduces to insignificance all the quibbling about the exact price of bread and the few extra shillings picked up here or there. It obscures the simple fact that the labouring poor lived at an appallingly meagre level. The gallon loaf each per week was not an adequate diet for anyone, let alone for those engaged in heavy manual labour. Even if families could afford this minimum amount of food, they can hardly have had enough for the myriad expenditures required to maintain a large household in such a way as to keep all its members healthy, let alone comfortable. In this they were hardly assisted by Ailesbury, who allowed their cottages to fall into ruinous disrepair while he endeavoured to pay the £250 000 worth of debt incurred enlarging his mansion.[32] All this lends credence to the many pathetic descriptions of Wiltshire labourers in this period. In 1826, for example, William Cobbett wrote that Wiltshire downland labourers '*look as if they are half starved ... reeling with weakness ... their poor faces present me nothing but skin and bone*'.[33] This picture is from the period when the poor law guaranteed a minimum subsistence. The reduction of relief under the New Poor Law made the situation worse. We cannot say that it made starvation imminent but it certainly made survival more difficult.

## PROTEST, RIGHTS, AND THE FAILURE OF PATERNALISM

When poor relief was withdrawn, the three labourers assumed Vaisey to be responsible and appealed to the poor law commissioners – yet the commissioners were themselves the very people most responsible. Vaisey prevented the poor from reading the notice that he posted on the church door. Not knowing what it was, the three letter-writers assumed it to be the New Poor Law, and assumed further that the new law included a mandatory increase in their pay by 50 per cent. Nothing, of course, could have been further from the truth: the commissioners perhaps had a pious hope that market forces would drive wages up, but the idea of legislating wage rates was quite contrary to the spirit of the law.

These misconceptions indicate two important elements in the labourers' thinking: that the causes of their grievances were purely local and that higher authorities were their defenders. At the heart of their thinking, therefore, was the old idea that king, parliament and magistracy were the protectors of the poor and would intercede on their behalf against the tyranny of local employers and officials. It is hardly surprising to discover that the labourers held such ideas: according to Hobsbawm and Rudé, these two 'pre-political' themes, localism and royal paternalism, dominated the thinking of protesting labourers in southern England in this period. Roger Wells, on the other hand, has recently shown that a larger number of rural labourers were influenced by unionism and radical political ideas than had previously been thought.[34] Nevertheless, as long as the magistracy continued to defend the right to relief, there would still be some poor who believed in the paternalist system. In September 1834, Revd Williams wrote to the poor law commissioners expressing his fear that 'when the Population find their natural & hereditary Protectors can no longer protect them, their allegiance will cease, of course'.[35] No doubt he was correct, but in the case of the Mildenhall letter-writers the focus of 'allegiance' was first transferred to the king and his government. This perhaps was also not surprising given that the benevolence of the king would have been a regular theme in the rector's sermons on Sunday.

The misconceptions about the nature of the New Poor Law are not the only evidence of the writers' faith in the paternalism of high authorities. In Letter 1, the authors present a series of anecdotes purporting to prove that the local elite had for years been ignoring orders from above to increase the level of relief – 'somthing more ... then there Loves of bread'. In one anecdote, a pauper threatens to appeal to the magistracy if the overseer does not provide the expected level of relief: 'if you no give it to me ill go to the magesty'. The overseer responds with contempt: 'go in mak your complaint me frind[.] what do you want said majesty ... [to do – to] give your rigt an more then your right[?]' The anecdote is interesting because it indicates that the poor, even in a closed village like Mildenhall, were not strangers to what had by the 1830s become a common form of protest.[36] The contemptuous response of the overseer in this case is probably not a reflection of Mildenhall's power structure or even of the response to be expected from the irascible Mr Williams (the only resident magistrate).[37] Rather, it reflects the simple fact that higher authorities had *not* required the Mildenhall overseers to give the poor 'more then the Loves acarding to price of bread'. The Marlborough scale by which the poor were awarded their bare subsistence was not an invention of the Mildenhall vestry, but was set by the magistracy itself. An appeal to the magistracy would have been an appeal to those who were responsible. The series of claims in Letter 1 that the vestry was cheating them out of their proper level of relief, therefore, are quite simply wrong.

The anecdotes cannot be taken as an accurate account of events, but they are important as evidence of the authors' stubborn belief that outside authorities were not responsible for the miserable condition of the poor. This faith was clung to despite the alternatives offered in the political debates erupting all around them. That the authors did have access to alternative political ideas is suggested by fragments of information which suggest connections outside of their class and beyond the boundaries of their parish.

**External influences**

In rural Wiltshire, as in the country at large, the two decades after the end of the Napoleonic Wars were ones of economic crisis, political ferment and social conflict. All over the Downs the poor expressed their resentment through arson, cattle maiming and rioting or, less dramatically, by constantly changing employers and (as was alleged of Gregory and Hiscock) by refusing to work hard. The Swing riots were but the climax of this growing wave of protest; in their aftermath, relations remained tense and sporadic outbursts of protest continued to erupt. The years 1834–6 were ones of hardship, strife and religious frenzy on the Marlborough Downs, as elsewhere in rural Wiltshire. Agriculture experienced yet another depression in which small farmers were particularly hard hit. The passing of the New Poor Law was met by protests and riots in several parishes. The Wesleyan and Primitive Methodist churches experienced revivals that convulsed much of the Marlborough Downs area.[38]

Despite the best efforts of its rulers, Mildenhall could not have remained untouched by these events. Located on the London road as it was, it may well have been visited by itinerant radicals of the sort so much complained of at the time of Swing. Even in 1833, a farmer of nearby Broad Hinton (also a closed parish) told a parliamentary committee that the agricultural labourer was still discontented: 'I fear his mind is too much occupied with politics; there are a great number of people going about the country disseminating very pernicious doctrines among the labourers and other classes, and the state of society has not been improved by them.'[39]

Directly to the west of Mildenhall was the town of Marlborough, 'a very great Thoroughfare' through which passed 'numerous paupers'.[40] If the letter-writers were concerned with the price of bread in Marlborough, it seems likely that they did their shopping there. If so, they can hardly have remained ignorant of the assault being made on Ailesbury's political domination by the Marlborough Independent Constitutional Association.[41]

Gregory and Hiscock both rented tenements directly from Ailesbury, and were thus in a particularly vulnerable position. Jones (39 years old in 1835), on the other hand, resided with his family not in Mildenhall but in neighbouring Axford, a tithing of Ramsbury.[42] He must, therefore, have been somewhat immune from Vaisey's wrath; he may also have imbibed something of the rebellious atmosphere of his parish of residence.

Ramsbury was the antithesis of Mildenhall: large, sprawling, populous, with over a hundred petty proprietors. It was a centre of Methodist revivalism, both Wesleyan and Primitive, and was one of the most riotous places during Swing. In April 1835, a local magistrate wrote that the spirit of Swing lived on among the people of Ramsbury (and neighbouring places in Berkshire): 'great concessions were made to these misguided people, and the recollection of what their own lawless efforts then gained for them is not yet extinct'.[43]

On 22 November 1830, the Swing rioters poured down the road from Ramsbury to Mildenhall and destroyed Vaisey's threshing machine. They were led by Thomas Goddard of Ramsbury, a tanner, who allegedly was a ranter and carried a tricoloured flag. Two days later the Marlborough troop of yeomanry, with Revd Williams at their head, rode from Marlborough to Ramsbury and took prisoners.[44] Two Ramsbury men were accused of smashing Vaisey's threshing machine and were imprisoned in Salisbury gaol. In December 1831, their cousin, Edward Looker of Axford, sent threatening letters to Vaisey and to Henry Woodman warning them not to testify at the upcoming assizes. Looker's father, Isaac (a man of some substance who was initially accused of writing the letters), had an old grudge against Vaisey and Woodman. Jonathon Vaisey testified in court that Isaac Looker had said he wished the rioters would go to Marlborough and cut the yeomanry's heads off.[45]

Ramsbury, therefore, was a centre of riot and radicalism with a history of conflict with Mildenhall's elite and especially with Vaisey. The Mildenhall letters have nothing like the blood-curdling threats in Looker's letters, but they may well have been inspired in part by the rebellious mood of Axford and Ramsbury more generally. That this was the case is suggested by the fact that Jones provided the largest contribution to Letter 2 and was the person to whom replies were to be addressed. This suggests in turn that Jones was the ringleader and perhaps even the person who did the actual writing.[46]

**Internal influences**

There is a clue at the end of Letters 3 and 4 which strongly suggests links between the three authors and the disgruntled among Mildenhall's petty ratepayers: 'send us anser back derict to thomas jones at jaimes tarrants mildenhall'. James Tarrant (34 years old in 1835) was the only shoemaker in the village, indeed, the entire parish of Mildenhall. Tarrant's apprentice, Joseph Greenaway, was Thomas Jones' nephew.[47] Shoemakers, of course, were the classic village radicals because of their unusually high literacy skills and their connections with the outside world. Suggestive in this respect is the fact that in 1824 Tarrant and two Ramsbury men were together convicted of riot in Marlborough. It is significant also that Tarrant rented a tenement from the rector, not from Ailesbury.[48] We can only speculate about Tarrant's role in the writing of the three letters. He could not have written them himself: his handwriting in 1841, when he was employed as a census enumerator, was incomparably superior to that of the letters. Greenaway was 12 years old in 1836 and could perhaps have been employed by Jones to do the actual writing. Even so, the fact that the commissioners' reply was to be directed to Tarrant's house suggests a degree of complicity on Tarrant's part. If Tarrant was indeed something of a village radical, it is possible to picture his house as a meeting-place for the discontented in which local grievances, national issues and radical ideas were discussed and intertwined. Tarrant was also connected with the lesser tenantry: his brother, John, was the tenant of Vicarage Farm which was only 143 acres (almost the whole of the glebe).[49] It has often been suggested that small farmers colluded with labourers in their protests against large tenants and landowners.[50] Indeed, as has been seen, the second letter presents the resentment felt by the smaller farmers against the leading oligarchy which set wages and other policy without consulting them.

Taking all these little shards of information together, we are led to the supposition that James Tarrant was the letter-writers' contact with a local oppositionist subculture. If so, this culture would not have been confined to Mildenhall but would have encompassed Marlborough, Ramsbury and all the little parishes in the neighbourhood. It would have fed upon personal animosities and appalling hardship and manifested itself in the shape of riot, radical politics and Methodism. It would also have included many ranks of local society, from the 'journeymen mechanics & Labourers in husbandry' who played the major role in Swing to tradesmen and artisans like Tarrant, Thomas Goddard of Ramsbury and the members of Marlborough's constitutional association.[51]

**'The poor in blindnes'**

If the Mildenhall letters were really the product of a radical and literate milieu, how could it be that they manifest such a complete misunderstanding of the New Poor Law? One could suppose that the faith in royal paternalism was but a ploy or stratagem masking an underlying radicalism. If that were the case, then surely the royalism would have been explicit, the accusations would have been aimed more effectively and the errors would not have been persisted in long after anything could possibly have been gained from them.[52]

There is no doubt about the three labourers' contacts outside their class and outside their parish, but these contacts do not appear to have influenced their thinking. Indeed, one can suppose that the three men (perhaps like labourers in general) remained on the outside of a group of radical artisans, tradesmen and farmers, not privy to their discussions but occasionally offered scraps of information and ideas. In the end, these were not clear enough or convincing enough to dispel the labourers' overriding assumption that the king was their protector. It could even be that their informants endeavoured to stimulate their resentment against Vaisey by wilfully offering them misinformation about the New Poor Law.[53]

The many anecdotes and conversations in the Mildenhall letters are instructive of the manner in which the poor eagerly gathered information from rumours, overheard fragments of conversation and discussions with their employers. The letters are instructive as well of the manner in which these broken bits of information were clung to for years and used to reinforce and elaborate the same old preconceptions: that Vaisey and the other great tenants were constantly endeavouring to defeat the efforts of higher authorities to improve the lot of the poor. Indeed, in Mildenhall, a place where improvement through their own efforts seemed impossible, the poor's belief in a paternalist system must have been a psychological necessity. Given this, it was only natural that the reduction of poor relief was understood as solely Vaisey's doing. Similarly, his apparent denial of information about the New Poor Law must have seemed proof that it was the poor's long-awaited deliverance from poverty and oppression. The words attributed to Samuel Oatley in Letter 1 would have seemed appropriate to Vaisey also: 'i will keep them out of that if i can they wont know anything about it'.

The one positive note in this dismal picture is that the three labourers knew they were 'in blindnes' and sought enlightenment from the Poor Law Commissioners. The letters, therefore, represent an effort to tear away the mass of ideology and misinformation which prevented them from seeing the truth. The commissioners, however, denied them the simple courtesy of writing a reply. In the end, the men's quest for knowledge – their effort to dispel their blindness – ended in failure.

## The end of 'right'

In May 1836, Colonel A'Court, the Assistant Poor Law Commissioner for most of Wiltshire, described the New Poor Law as 'a great change in the social relations of the labouring poor'.[54] Indeed, with the abolition of the magistrate's scale and magistrates' powers of intercession, the poor's 'right' to outdoor relief was eliminated. This right had long been clung to as to a lifeline; it had been a crucial weapon in the never-ending battle to avoid starvation, but late in 1835 it simply disappeared. Outdoor relief remained, but now at a much reduced level, and was given only at the discretion of the guardians. Not surprisingly, all Wiltshire unions reported in May 1836 that the poor were displaying a new submissiveness and, in some places, a desire to emigrate.[55]

On 27 January 1836, Gregory and Jones wrote to the poor law commissioners to inquire about 'whether theres any estated weags publeshed or not'. Their hope that the highest authorities would eventually intervene on their behalf had survived the failure of their other letters to obtain a response and even their rebuff at the hands of the Marlborough guardians. The deafening silence that followed this last appeal must finally have opened their eyes to the fact that the commissioners had no intention of interfering 'between the employer & the labourer as to the wages of the latter'.

In the 1840s, Thomas Mozeley, then rector of Cholderton (a small parish on Salisbury Plain), had his 'old illusion of a paternal system' shattered by the sight of workhouse paupers gnawing on rotten horse-bones before breaking them by hand.[56] Similarly, the lingering belief of Gregory and Jones in the rescue being mounted by higher authorities would have received its final blow. This would have left an enormous void in their perception of their society and the manner in which improvement was to be achieved. Perhaps this void was eventually filled with a new reliance on themselves and their class, leading perhaps to radical politics and unionism. In the meantime, however, like so many other Wiltshire labourers, they must have sought survival through submission and the renewal of deferential relationships – humiliating as this would have been. All we know is that in 1841, when the census was being taken, Gregory, Hiscock and their families were still living in the village of Mildenhall; Jones and his family were still living in Axford. They had not been forced into the workhouse; they had not migrated; they had not perished from hunger or illness.

## CONCLUSION

The four Mildenhall letters provide a fleeting moment of insight into the mental world of a few members of the labouring poor at the time of the New Poor Law. The most important conclusions are implicit in the authors' extraordinary misconceptions about the nature of that law. They did not know its content, they claimed, because Mr Vaisey, the churchwarden, had suppressed information about it. They assumed that the recent withdrawal or reduction of their poor relief was Vaisey's doing – in fact, of course, it was a central part of the New Poor Law. The three men also thought the New Poor Law had legislated a raise in their pay from six to nine shillings. In reality, once again, the law had done nothing of the sort. An explanation for these misconceptions has been sought in the labourers' experience of hardship and domination in a closed village, and the poor's desperate belief in the paternalism of king and parliament.

First, therefore, the letters are instructive about labourers' experience of social relations in closed villages. They are a corrective to the assumption that the absence of overt protest in closed villages was evidence of social harmony. In some closed villages the poor may perhaps have been patient and subservient, but in Mildenhall the appearance of calm belied a reality of hunger, fear and smouldering resentment. Overt protest in Mildenhall was clearly not a viable option: with so much power in so few hands the poor had no leverage at all. Instead, the Mildenhall poor quietly collected grievances for years on end: rumours, overheard snatches of conversation, and perhaps glimpses of official documents were remembered, shared and moulded into a single, simple demonology. Thus, the local oligarchy of great tenants and especially Edward Vaisey, the churchwarden, were perceived as responsible for the dire poverty of the labouring poor. All grievances were laid at their door: the pathetic rate of pay, the meagre subsistence level guaranteed by the Old Poor Law, and the elimination of that guarantee in the early stages of the New Poor Law.

Given their contacts with other parishes and the political excitement of the time, one could have expected the three authors to have looked beyond local causes for their complaints. After all, the miserable conditions complained of in the letters were not confined to Mildenhall but were common to rural Wiltshire and, indeed, to southern England as a whole. A share of the blame could have been meted out to Ailesbury who practically owned the parish, or to the magistracy who before 1834 had set the level of relief, or to the central government which was responsible for the New Poor Law. Instead, it was Vaisey, the tenant farmer and implementer of other people's policies who was described as 'ruler' of the parish. This extraordinary concentration on Vaisey and on local causes is perhaps the letters' central message about social relations in closed villages. It is an expression of the poor's sense of absolute domination by the local bosses: of having their entire lives scrutinised and manipulated, of the futility of trying to better their lot through their own efforts, and even of having their access to information from outside suppressed.

Overt protest was out of the question for the Mildenhall poor and they were left with no other hope than that king and parliament would eventually intervene against the tyranny of their local masters. This belief was so stubborn that influences from outside the parish and outside their social stratum (which are undeniable) could not discredit it. Unaware of the true nature of the New Poor Law, obsessed with local causes and clinging to their belief in the paternalism of the king, the three authors assumed the New Poor Law to be their long-awaited deliverance. As the truth slowly dawned on them, the tattered remnants of their faith in the paternalist system must finally have fallen away. Their eyes would at last have been opened to what the practitioners of *laissez-faire* held in store for the poor.

APPENDIX: TRANSCRIPTIONS OF THE FOUR LETTERS

**Letter 1**

Novemb 30 1835 to the honororbl from the parresh of mindenall near marlbro Wilts this is to sertify you that Church Warnds lows aman to keep awife and four small Childern with 6 shellings a week six shillen is Regular pay some heave 5 small childern and they receve 8 pence per week in the stead of 11 pence market price of bread is 11d at marlbrough th 22 Novembr mr vaisey is Church Warn and overseare put som thing upon the Church door after all the Congregation was gon in an when the servis was ended he stept out an took dit down before aney of the pepople could get out i could just see that it was the poor Law he took ceare that no one should not see it they keep the poor in blindnes all as they can they never geave them no more then the Loves acarding to price of bread when they ad aletter from the board to give them somthing more they sed then there Loves of bread they seed we are under the fine of 50 pounds if wee give you aney nessarey what ever wee deare not do it wee give he to much a redy Samuel oatley told me is selfe that he ad alletter from the board to giveem the price of 2 Loves an alfe to coman acording to there famles but i will keep them out of that if i can they wont know anything a bout it it was about 1832 or 3 or there away then another time i see alletter sined 900 pounds an then there was but verey litl poor then on the parish Book they kept 1 shilen an 2s16 26 amonth kept out of the poor if you no give it to me ill go to the magesty you go in mak your complaint me frind what do you want said majesty so an so o so so they are give your rigt an more then your right soo it goes on now ever since 1832 the Been gon on like this yers nothing wanten But wages rose six shillen to keep 5 or 6 in familey they can not get Bread enof the ask for more the

'The poor in blindnes'     231

sed more likley sink another shillen a week they expt to see the poor Law up on the Church dore novembr the 29 but he has not they will not rise the wages if the can help it the poor are in destres this may Be provd bey in Quierey among aney of the poor of there wages and releve some hav 2 pounds some 35 pounds they willing to work an able no Loos Lay about men nor drunkards in the village they are in Employ But the wages is so Low so no more from me at preasant to the Commissioners of London

*Source* PRO, MH 12/13789, Anon. to the Poor Law Commissioners, 23 November 1835.

## Letter 2

Copy of a Letter received by Mr Vaisey the Guardian of the Parish of Mildenhall supposed to be from Chas. Gregory & Jas. Hiscock.

december the 10 1835

sir mr vaisey you ar desird to wright a letter to the honourbl commissioers at the bord London to certify them were you heave advanced the mens wages to the nine shellings as the poor law derect you and were you have put it upon the Church door or not during the day since november 22end or either of the following sundays the truth is required an nothing but the truth to prove my letter my returne will be in the in suing week next so no more from me at present i remain your humbl servent

*Source* PRO, MH 12/13789, copy of Anon. to Vaisey, 10 December 1835, enclosed in Thos. Merriman to Edwin Chadwick, 19 January 1836.

## Letter 3

January the 9 pleas your honours we aply to you for to know what we are to do that heave familys our weages is six shellings aweek i Charls gregory heave five cheldern under 11 years old and here is seven of us to live out of six shelings this is all as i got James hiscock 5 childern seven of us in family my in com is six shilings this is all as i got to live out of and maney others are in the same cease the releifng officer told us that he ad don with us you must see to your masters for your an they would not rise our weages because mister vaisey would not if he would then we would me thomas Jones heave seven to live out of 8s 6d aweek mine 6s and a boy brings in 2s 6d a week this all as i heave got my master said i wish they would rise the men for it tis well known that them that heave familys will be starved if the weages is not rose i should give more but i must not without the rest was to it they never let me know aney thing about the poor law dont them no no thomas they do not maney of us ob served mister vaisey put the poor law on the Church door on november the 22 after the people were all in Church an then he taken it down be fore aney could get out so non of us codent see what it was mister young is for bring of us down to 5 shilings awell an if they do it will be worse still aman as got only himself and is wife heave six shillings as well as we mister vaisey is Church warnd an overcear an now he is Garden of mildenhal ner marlbro Wilt and he is the ruler in our parrish and averrey sever he as been to the poor if it may please your honours to send us anser back derict to thomas jones at jaimes tarrants mildenhall ner marlbrough Wilts

*Source* PRO, MH 12/13789, Gregory, Hiscock and Jones to the Poor Law Commissioners, 9 January 1836.

**Letter 4**

Jan the 27 pleas your honour we applyed to the town hall marlbro on tusday the 26 of Janary an mister Willileams the magesstret an recter at the lower Church marlbro he told us that they was resine that theyll not giv you any thing at all and he did not ask of us of our in Com nor he would not let us tell him hed not givus time to tell him he seem to be very sharp with us asked who gave he toleration to come here mister butler the releveng officer who put your ernings upon an navelleg mister butler what bisnes heave yer then you might go ther is nothing for you so we can get neither relef nor our weages rose an we aply to you to know whether theres any estated weags publeshed or not Charles gregory and thomas Jones mildenhall ner marlbrough wilts
[separate sheet of paper]
non of the gentelmen ad nothing to say about relef to us Charles gregory can ern 7s aweek an 7 of us to live out of it an what must i do an i thomas Jones heav got 5 childern mister butler cut my ernings to 1s 6d a week an that runs to 2 pence alpney aday an 1 aplney over for 7 days plese to send us ancer derect to thomas Jones at James tarrants mildenhall ner marlbrough Wilts

*Source* PRO, MH 12/13789, Gregory and Jones to the Poor Law Commissioners, 27 January 1836.

## NOTES

\*  An earlier version of this chapter was presented as a paper at a meeting of the Toronto Area Early Modern British History Working Group in February 1993. I would like to thank the members of the group for their comments and encouragement.

1. For complete references and transcripts of the four letters see the Appendix.
2. This point has been made in two important works on nineteenth-century rural protest. See J.E. Archer, *'By a Flash and a Scare': Incendiarism, Animal Maiming and Poaching in East Anglia, 1815–1870* (Oxford: Clarendon Press, 1990), p.25; and B. Reay, *The Last Rising of the Agricultural Labourers: Rural Life and Protest in Nineteenth-Century England* (Oxford: Clarendon Press, 1990), p.5. Anonymous letters by their very nature do not allow us to explore the background of their authors. They also tend to be very brief. Working-class autobiographies are longer and more detailed, but are usually written by people who have dissociated themselves from the village culture of their youth. Most are concerned more with personal spiritual development than with detailed descriptions of long-past conflicts.
3. In describing Mildenhall as a 'closed' parish, I simply mean that it was a place in which power was concentrated into very few hands. I am not implying anything whatsoever about the effect of this on population. In that respect, I am following Dennis Mills' definition: a place in which a single person owned at least half of the land and where there were fewer than 50 owners in total. See D. Mills, *Lord and Peasant in Nineteenth-Century Britain* (Croom Helm, 1980), pp.76–7.
4. Public Record Office (hereafter PRO), MH 12/13789, Poor Law Commissioners to Charles Gregory and James Hiscock, undated and marked cancelled.
5. PRO, MH 12/13789, Enclosure 2 in the letter from the Poor Law Commissioners to Thomas B. Merriman, clerk to the guardians of Marlborough Union, 13 Jan. 1836. The failure to inquire about Jones is unfortunate because he is the most interesting of the three. Perhaps the commissioners simply ignored him as unimportant because his was the last name given in Letter 3.
6. PRO, MH 12/13789, Enclosure 1 in Merriman to the Poor Law Commissioners, 19 Jan. 1836.
7. For this paragraph, see J. Freeman, 'Mildenhall', *Victoria County History of England; A History of Wiltshire* (hereafter *VCH Wilts.*), vol. XII, pp.125–38. For landholding in the chalk country in general see G.C. Smith, '"The *Knowing* Multitude". Popular Culture and the Evangelical Revival in Wiltshire, 1739–1850' (unpublished PhD thesis, University of Toronto, 1992), Chap. 1.
8. Abstract of Answers and Returns Under the Population Act, 2 Geo. IV.*cap.*30 (1823): *Parliamentary Papers* (1833), vol. XXXVII, p.148.
9. Wiltshire Record Office (hereafter WRO), Mildenhall Tithe Survey. I have excluded the 515 acres of wood and forest occupied by Ailesbury himself from the calculations and also the 45 acres of roads, river and wasteland.

The 1831 census tells us that there were 77 houses and 84 families in the parish. This suggests that the tithe survey with its 59 occupiers (including Ailesbury and the rector) should not be taken as a complete listing of poor families.

10. R. Molland, 'Agriculture, 1793–c.1870,' *VCH Wilts.*, vol. IV, pp.89–90; M. Ransome, 'Parliamentary History, 1689–1832', *VCH Wilts.*, vol. V, pp.212–14; J.H. Stevenson, 'The Borough of Marlborough', *VCH Wilts.*, vol. XII, pp.213–20; Freeman, 'Mildenhall', pp.129–32.
11. A search was made through the data collected for my PhD thesis from the following sources: PRO, ASSI 24/18, Minute Book of the Special Commission of Assize, Western Circuit, December 1830–January 1831; ASSI 23/6–10, Western Circuit Gaol Books; WRO, A1/110, Wiltshire Quarter Sessions (hereafter QS), Great Rolls; A1/125, QS Gaol Calendars; A1/145, QS Depositions; A1/150, QS Minute Books; A1/170, QS Instruction Books; A1/175, QS Recognisance Books. There were only about two people indicted for felony per decade until the 1830s, when the number jumped to seven. There were seven in the 1840s as well. All but two of these people were accused of theft.
12. Freeman, 'Mildenhall', p.137; J. Chandler (ed.), *Wiltshire Dissenters' Meeting House Certificates and Registrations, 1689–1852, Wiltshire Record Society* (hereafter *WRS*), vol. XL (1984); Smith, '"The *Knowing* Multitude"', Chap. 4.
13. WRO, D1/56/6, Bishop's Visitation Returns, 1842; PRO HO 129/255/1/8/18, Return from Church of St John the Baptist Mildenhall, 1851. The 1851 Return yields almost the same proportion of attendants (64 per cent) if one makes a simple sum of the two congregations, but making allowance for the fact that Sunday scholars attended twice. By not allowing for other double attenders, the resulting figure for the total number of churchgoers is suspiciously high. The number of communicants in 1842 was low – only 35–45. This is in rough agreement with the figures for other years: 20–30 in 1783, 60–70 in 1812, and 65 in 1864. See Ransome (ed.), *Wiltshire Returns to the Bishop's Visitation Queries, 1783, WRS*, vol. XXVII (1972), p.158; Freeman, 'Mildenhall', p.137; WRO, D1/56/7, Bishop's Visitation Returns, 1864.
14. For examples of this see Smith, '"The *Knowing* Multitude"', p.186.
15. WRO, A1/345/297, Mildenhall Land Tax Assessments.
16. WRO, Mildenhall Bishop's Transcripts. In 1783 it was reported that one churchwarden was appointed by the rector and the other by the parishioners. See Ransome (ed.), *Wiltshire Returns to the Bishop's Visitation Queries, 1783*, p.158.
17. Vaisey is described as 'the Guardian of the Parish of Mildenhall' in PRO, MH 12/13789, Merriman to the Poor Law Commissioners, 19 Jan. 1836. Except for a few miscellaneous papers, there are no overseers' accounts for the period under study. See WRO, 167/2, 3, 5, 6, 8.
18. I am indebted to Roger Wells for his suggestion that it would have been the election notice that Vaisey posted. Indeed, this was the only public notice relating to the New Poor Law that was ordered to be posted during the period. Apparently, the duty of posting the notice belonged to the tithingman, a fact that only enhances our impression of Vaisey's tyranny. For all

these points, see PRO, MH 12/13789, A'Court to the Poor Law Commissioners, 30 Oct. 1835. Unfortunately, we cannot produce any outside witnesses to confirm the letter-writers' allegation. On the other hand, the chronology is suggestive: Vaisey allegedly posted the notice on Sunday, 22 November, and the first meeting of the board of guardians took place on Thursday, 26 November (PRO, MH 12/13789, Merriman to the Poor Law Commissioners, 26 Nov. 1835). Not surprisingly, we do not know which day the 'election' occurred. If the notice was for the election, this would also explain why it was not posted on any of the following Sundays. For another example of guardian elections being undermined by posting the notice for too short a time, see PRO, MH 12/13800, John Cochrane to the Poor Law Commissioners, 28 March 1836.

19. See the correspondence for 1836–7 in PRO, MH 12/13789.
20. Mildenhall does not appear to have had a poorhouse at the time. The continuation of out-relief at least until September 1836 is clear from WRO, 167/5/2, Accounts of Marlborough Union, 1835–6. The declining level of out-relief is suggested by the substantial drop in real per capita expenditures on the poor (quarters of wheat per person): 1833–: 212, 1834–: 339, 1835–: 233, 1836–: 165, 1837–: 142, 1838–: 100. The nominal figures are found in PRO, MH 12/13789, A'Court to the Poor Law Commissioners, 30 Oct. 1835; and D.G. Ady's report to the same, 15 Oct. 1839.
21. PRO, MH 12/13789, Merriman to the Poor Law Commissioners, 26 Nov. 1835.
22. Outside of the Marlborough Downs, families were provided with sufficient income to purchase a one gallon loaf per person and have threepence left over for clothing. For the Marlborough Scale see PRO, MH 12/13789, A'Court to the Poor Law Commissioners, 30 Oct. 1835; Minutes of Evidence Taken Before Select Committee on Agriculture: *Parliamentary Papers* (1833), vol. V, p.516; Questions for Rural Districts: First Report from the Commissioners on the Poor Laws: *Parliamentary Papers* (1834), vol. XXXI, p.588. An interesting document exists from 1800 showing very clearly how the poor in Mildenhall had their incomes supplemented to the price of one loaf each. See WRO, 167/6/12, miscellaneous Mildenhall overseers' accounts.
23. Report (Communicated by the Lords) Respecting Grain, and the Corn Laws: *Parliamentary Papers* (1814–15), vol. V, p.1077.
24. WRO, Mildenhall Tithe Survey. The tithe survey shows that all houses, cottages and tenements had gardens attached. It also shows that there were about 3.5 acres of allotments for the poor, but allotments generally were confined to labourers who did not receive poor relief. Indeed, if allotments were the usual quarter-acre, there would have been enough for only 14 families. For further information on allotments and the diets of the labouring poor in Wiltshire, see Smith, '"The *Knowing* Multitude"', pp.131–44.
25. PRO, MH 12/13789, A'Court to the Poor Law Commissioners, 30 Oct. 1835.
26. In 1795, the Revd Charles Francis, rector of Mildenhall, complained to the Marquess of Ailesbury that labourers took their earnings into the nearest town (that is, Marlborough) on Sunday and thus came into contact with

radical politics and religious nonconformity. See WRO 9/35/54, Francis to Ailesbury, 29 March 1795.

27. The difficulty of obtaining piecework in Wiltshire generally is suggested by the following: Minutes of Evidence Taken before Select Committee on Agriculture: *Parliamentary Papers* (1833), vol. V, p.78; Questions for Rural Districts: First Report from the Commissioners on the Poor Laws: *Parliamentary Papers* (1834), vol. XXX, pp.578–92.

28. Questions for Rural Districts: First Report from the Commissioners on the Poor Laws: *Parliamentary Papers* (1834), vol. XXX, pp.578–92; Smith, '"The *Knowing* Multitude"', pp.125–31.

29. PRO, MH 12/13789, A'Court to the Poor Law Commissioners, 9 March 1836.

30. Second Annual Report of the Poor Law Commissioners: *Parliamentary Papers* (1836), vol. XXIX pt.1, p.281. Williams was rector of St Peter's Marlborough. See J.H. Stevenson, 'The Borough of Marlborough', *VCH Wilts.*, vol. XII, p.224.

31. Buxton's income is stated in the tithe award and in Report on Ecclesiastical Revenues: *Parliamentary Papers* (1835), vol. XXII, p.868. Ailesbury's estate had been in the hands of trustees since 1832 as a consequence of his prodigality. His gross annual income was £53 000. See F.M.L. Thompson, 'English Landownership: The Ailesbury Trust 1832–56', *Economic History Review*, 2nd ser., XI (1958), 132.

32. Thompson, 'English Landownership', 121, 128.

33. W. Cobbett, *Rural Rides* (Oxford: Oxford University Press, 1979), p.337. For other examples see Smith, '"The *Knowing* Multitude"', pp.141–4.

34. E.J. Hobsbawm and G. Rudé, *Captain Swing* (New York: Pantheon Books, 1968), p.65; R.A.E. Wells, 'Rural Rebels in Southern England in the 1830's', in C. Emsley and J. Walvin (eds), *Artisans, Peasants & Proletarians, 1760–1860: Essays Presented to Gwyn A. Williams* (Croom Helm, 1985), pp.124–7; idem, 'Tolpuddle in the Context of English Agrarian Labour History, 1780–1850', in J. Rule (ed.), *British Trade Unionism, 1750–1850: The Formative Years* (Longman, 1988), pp.112–27.

35. PRO, MH 12/13789, Williams to the Poor Law Commissioners, 6 Sept. 1834.

36. For other examples of this see Smith, '"The *Knowing* Multitude"', pp.192–4, 230–2.

37. For Williams' position as the only resident magistrate, see PRO, MH 12/234, Meyrick to Chadwick, 22 June 1835; MH 12/13789, A'Court to the Poor Law Commissioners, 1840. The A'Court letter also suggests that Williams had a bad temper. This is indeed clear from Williams' many letters to the poor law commissioners in the years after he was deposed as chairman of the Marlborough board of guardians. It should be pointed out that he played the role of defender of the poor during these years (especially if it involved irritating the guardians). Despite his initial enthusiasm for the New Poor Law, by 1845 he was referring to it as 'This horrible Poor Law'. See PRO, MH 12/12790, Williams to the Poor Law Commissioners, 22 March 1845.

38. Smith, '"The *Knowing* Multitude"', pp.230–45, 310–17; Hobsbawm and Rudé, *Captain Swing*, pp.283–4, 287; E. Billinge, 'Rural Crime and Protest in

Wiltshire, 1830–1875' (unpublished PhD thesis, University of Kent at Canterbury, 1984), Chap. 4. For the impact of the agricultural depression see Minutes of Evidence Before the Select Committee on the State of Agriculture: *Parliamentary Papers* (1837), vol. V, p.164. For the Methodist revivals see W. Pollard, 'Letter from the Hungerford Circuit', *Methodist Magazine*, LVIII (1835), 563–5; J. Ride, 'Shefford Circuit, 1834–1835', *Primitive Methodist Magazine* (1835), 301–2; G. Price, 'Farringdon Branch of Shefford Circuit', *Primitive Methodist Magazine* (1836), 467.

39. Select Committee on Agriculture: *Parliamentary Papers* (1833), vol. V, p.532.
40. PRO, MH 12/13789, Merriman to the Poor Law Commissioners, 16 Jan. 1836.
41. For Ailesbury's difficulties see Ransome, 'Parliamentary History, 1689–1832', pp.214–15; F.E. Hyde, 'Parliamentary History since 1832', *VCH Wilts.*, vol. V, p.300; Stevenson, 'The Borough of Marlborough', pp.213–20.
42. For Gregory and Hiscock's tenements see WRO, Mildenhall Tithe Award. For Jones' residence in Axford see the marriage register for 1815, the baptismal register between 1815 and 1841, and the 1841 census: WRO, Mildenhall Bishop's Transcripts; PRO, HO 107/1184, Ramsbury Census Return, 1841.
43. Information on Ramsbury was drawn from the following: Abstract of Answers and Returns Under the Population Act, 2 George IV, *cap*.30 (1823): *Parliamentary Papers* (1821), vol. XXXVII, pp.146–7; WRO, A1/344, Ramsbury land tax assessments; First Report of the Commissioners on the Poor Laws: *Parliamentary Papers* (1834), vol. XXXI, p.591; Pollard, 'Letter from the Hungerford Circuit'; J. Ride, 'Shefford Circuit', 301; 'Notes from the Circuit Reports, Brinkworth District, 1835', *Primitive Methodist Magazine* (1835), 347; PRO, ASSI 24/18/3, Minute Book of the Special Commission of Assize, Western Circuit, December 1830–January 1831. The quotation is from PRO, MH 12/234, Richard Hall to the Poor Law Commissioners, 13 April 1835. According to Hobsbawm and Rudé, Ramsbury was a 'classic "open" village'. See Hobsbawm and Rudé, *Captain Swing*, p.183.
44. *Devizes and Wiltshire Gazette*, 25 Nov., 2 Dec. 1830. It should be noted that Revd E.G. Meyrick, magistrate and rector of Ramsbury, wrote on Goddard's behalf complaining about the 'false reports so widely circulated' about him. See Gloucestershire Record Office (hereafter GRO), 1571/X/63, Meyrick to Estcourt, 2 Dec. 1830.
45. PRO, ASSI 24/18/3, Minute Book of the Special Commission of Assize, Western Circuit, 7 Jan. 1831; WRO, A1/740, Quarter Sessions files on the prosecution of the Swing rioters; *London Times* (7 January 1831), 10; GRO, 1571/X/64, testimony of Jon. Vaisey against Isaac Looker.
46. Jones was able to sign the marriage register and might, perhaps, have been able to write the letters. Neither of the other two seems a likely candidate for the writing: Gregory was unable to sign the marriage register and Hiscock, apparently, did not contribute to Letter 4. One could speculate that one of their wives did the writing, though neither Jones' nor Gregory's wife signed the marriage register. I have not been able to locate either Hiscock's or James Tarrant's marriage in the register.

47. James Tarrant is the only person described as a shoemaker in the 1841 census. Joseph Greenaway was the 'baseborn' son of Ann Greenaway of Mildenhall, labourer, born on 8 April 1822. Ann was the sister of Hannah Greenaway, who was married to Thomas Jones. The 1841 census includes Joseph Greenaway in the household of James Tarrant and describes him as an apprentice. See WRO, Mildenhall Bishop's Transcripts; PRO, HO 107/1185, Mildenhall Census Returns, 1841.
48. Hobsbawm and Rudé, *Captain Swing*, p.18; WRO, G22/1/1/6, Marlborough Quarter Sessions Indictments; WRO, Mildenhall Tithe Award. Revd Buxton, the rector, held the advowson in his own hands and, therefore, did not owe allegiance to Ailesbury. His tenants, including the brothers Tarrant, would not therefore have been directly under Ailesbury's sway. See Freeman, 'Mildenhall', p.136.
49. According to the baptismal register for 1794 and 1801, John and James Tarrant were both sons of Thomas Tarrant of Stitchcombe (described as 'miller' in 1794 and 'farmer' in 1801) and Ann Rogers. See WRO, Mildenhall Bishop's Transcripts, Mildenhall Tithe Award.
50. See, for example, Hobsbawm and Rudé, *Captain Swing*, pp.116, 230–1; Andrew Charlesworth, 'The Development of the English Rural Proletariat and Social Protest, 1700–1850: A Comment', *Journal of Peasant Studies*, VIII (October 1980), 104–6. It should be noted that Hobsbawm and Rudé considered such alliances to have been unlikely in Wiltshire.
51. The quotation is from WRO, 1553/12, Burbidge to Cobb, 25 Nov. 1830.
52. If the authors had understood the nature of the New Poor Law they would not have accused Vaisey of being solely responsible for the reduction of poor relief. They would certainly not have suggested that the New Poor Law included mandatory wage hikes. Rather, they might have argued that in the absence of a workhouse the board of guardians ought not to have reduced the level of relief – unless wage hikes were immediately put in place. They would also have complained about Vaisey's control of the election for guardian.
53. It was not uncommon for individuals to try to manipulate the labouring poor by feeding them incorrect information about the New Poor Law. See, for example, PRO, MH 12/13863, Tugwell to Nicholls, 22 and 28 Sept. 1834.
54. Second Report of the Poor Law Commissioners: *Parliamentary Papers* (1836), vol. XXIX, pt 1, p.299.
55. Ibid., pp.316–25.
56. T. Mozeley, *Reminiscences Chiefly of Oriel College and the Oxford Movement* (Boston: Houghton, Mifflin & Co., 1882), II, p.173.

# Index

A'Court, Colonel Charles, 220, 221, 227
abandonment, 157
  of children, 97
  of mother, 70, 73, 78, 92
  search for absconder, 97–8
  see also illegitimacy; illegitimate children
Adams, widow of Joshua, 180–1
adultery, 47, 57–8
  see also sex
advice literature
  for employers, 49–52
  for servants, 50–1, 54, 61
age
  at death of parishioners, 169
  of recipients of relief, 12
Ailesbury, Marquis of, see Bruce, Charles Brudenell
alcohol/drunkenness, 54, 56, 196, 200
alehouses/inns, 110–11
  as sites of courtship/sexual activity, 70; Cheshire Cheese, Chelsea, 70
  see also sex
Alexander, James, 133–4
almshouses, St Martin-in-the-Fields, 29
Amussen, Susan, 50
Anderson James, 96
apprentices, 114
  behaviour of, 199
apprenticeship
  non-parochial, 91, 93
  parochial, 75, 76; see also poor relief
Archer, Ian, 20
Ardleigh, Essex, 138
Arnold, Rev. K.A., 111
Ashdon, Essex, 166–70, 184
autobiographies
  criminal, 5, 192

working-class, 3, 128
badging the poor, 20, 34–5, 37
  see also poor relief
Bagnall, Isabel, 56
Bainbridge, Ann, 112–13, 114, 117
Bainbridge, George 112
Baisbrown, Alice, 124
Baisbrown, Matthew, 124
Ballard, William, 201–2
Banbridge, William, 33
Banton, Andrew, 70
Barrett, Elizabeth, 118
Barrett, Peter, 118
Bassett, Rowland, 198–9, 201
bastardy examinations, 5, 52, 72, 73
  see also illegitimacy; illegitimate children; settlement
bastardy rate, 71
Beardsley, Susannah, 53
Beattie, John, 199
Beck family, 115–16; Eleanor, 115; Robert, 116
bedrooms, 170, 171, 177, 184, 186
  see also inventories, pauper
begging, 32–3, 88
  see also badging the poor
Bermondsey, 99–100
Beverley, Yorkshire, 119
Bighton, Thomas, 28
Bird, Dorothy, 181
Bird, Edward, 181
Blackburn, Lancashire, 118
blackmail, 56
'blood money' scandal, 206
Board of Trade
  1695 poor relief expenditure estimates, 24
  see also poor relief
Boucher, Francis, 199, 200
Boulton, Thomas, 203
Bow Street, London, 206
Boxall, Thomas, 78

Boyer, George, 88
Braintree, Essex, 138, 140–1, 142
  level of non-resident poor, 140
  *see also* poor; poor relief
Broad Hinton, Wiltshire, 224
Brompton, Kent, 73
Brown, Rachel, 135
Browning, Robert, 123
Bruce, Charles Brudenell, Marquis of Ailesbury, 217, 218, 222, 224–5, 229
Bruton, Jane, 47
Burgh, Thomas, 171, 175, 185–6
Burke, Peter, 134
Burns, R., *The History of the Poor Law*, 157–8, 159
Burton, Ann, 33
Bussell, Elizabeth, 82

Camus, Albert, *The Plague*, 120
Carlisle, 111
celibacy, 71
census
  1831, 217
  of poor, 33, 137–8; *see also* poor
Chadwick, Edwin, 192
charity, 3, 12
  Commissioners, 7
  'Donation money', 120
  for books, 116
*charivari*, 59
  *see also* plebeian culture
Chatham, Kent, 78, 193
Cheapside, 203
Chelmsford, Essex, 89, 94, 127, 132, 134, 139, 143
Chelsea Park, 74
Cheshunt, Hertfordshire, 145
Chesterton, George Laval, 205
childbirth *see* lying-in
childhood, 6
children, burden of, 27
  *see also* illegitimacy; poor
Cholderton, Wiltshire, 228
Christ's Hospital, London, 28
church courts, 48, 49, 80
  depositions before, 48, 49, 61
  London consistory court, 53, 58
churchwardens *see* parish officers

Civil War, 178
Clare, John, 159–60, 182
Clement, Rebecca, 70, 81
Clerkenwell, 198, 202
clubs, poor's, 92, 94
  *see also* poor
Cobbett, William, 222
Cock Lane, London, 203
Colchester *see* St Botolph's, Colchester
Collingwood, R.G., 123
Colney, Peter, 199, 203–4
Commercial Road, London, 197
commonable lands/resources, 10, 12, 180, 181
Conly, Bridget, 33
constables, 33
contraception/conception, 48
  *see also* sex
Cook, William, 195–6, 197, 205
court records, 8
  depositions, 5, 7
  indictments, 7
  recognisances, 7
  *see also* church courts
courting, 70, 71–2
  *see also* illegitimacy
Cousens, Richard Booty, 197, 203
Coustos, John, 70
Covent Garden, 124
crime, 2–3, 192–210 *passim*
  against property, 194
  criminal subculture, 195–9; as alternative to domestic life, 201
criminal justice system, 80

Dales, Robert, 117
Darville, John, 199, 200
Davies, David, 139, 155–6
Dean, Mrs, 82
Dean of Westminster, 32
death
  attitude toward, 127
  confiscation of goods at, 160
  *see also* poor; poor relief
debts
  of the poor, 12, 92
  *see also* poor; poor relief
*declarations de gressesse*, 52

## Index

deference, 11
  pauper behaviour, 32
  requirement for, 33
  *see also* poor; poor relief
demography, 3, 71, 88
  urban, 79
Dickens, Charles, *Oliver Twist*, 197, 202–3
divorce/separation/family breakdown, 47, 58
  *see also* abandonment
Dobson, John, 119
doctor, role in securing relief, 122, 135
  *see also* poor relief
Dodd, William, 121
domestic service/servants, 4, 5, 70, 73, 78, 78–9, 92, 95, 120, 199
  in London, 6, 47–69 *passim*
  loss of place, 47, 48, 58, 79
  punishment of, 50, 55
  relations between, 53, 58–60
  wages for, 79
  *see also* footmen
domestic violence, 56, 57, 58–9
  against children, 200
Dormer, Diana and John, Esq., 58–60, 61
*Dormer c. Dormer*, 58–60
Downes, Charles, 205–6
Dufton, Christopher, 28

Earl, Mr, 137
economic conditions, reports of from paupers, 115, 118
economies of makeshift, 12
Eden, Sir Frederick Morton, 3, 110–11, 155-6
education
  Free Grammar School, Kirkby Lonsdale, 116
  of the poor, 114–17
  religious, 204–5
Edwards, David, 79
Edwards, Elizabeth, 74-5, 81
Edwards, Thomas, 74
elderly, 160–1
  care of by family, 135–7
  removal of, 139

role of parish in organising care of, 136
  social isolation of, 137–8
  *see also* old age; poor
elections, 118
Elers, Peter, JP, 82
Ellis, Charles, 92–3
Elvin, Mary, 136
employers, role of in relation to relief, 89, 95, 98, 103, 114, 142
  *see also* poor; poor relief
epilepsy, 56

Fairchilds, Cissie, 52, 53
fences/receivers, 206
  *see also* crime
Field Lane, London, 202
Finsbury Bazaar, London, 199
Firmin, Samuel, 82
Fleetwood, William, 197
footmen, 59
  macho culture of, 59–60
  *see also* domestic service/servants; sex
Foundling Hospital, London, 52, 71, 75
  numbers in, 76
  death rate in, 77
  *see also* illegitimacy; illegitimate children
friendly societies, 7
  *see also* clubs, poor's

game laws, 178
gaols
  accounts of, 192
  Colchester, 98
  *Euryalus*, prison hulk, 193
  Newgate, 202, 206
  Salisbury, 225
  *see also* houses of correction
Gardner, James, 199
Garnett, Stephen, 110, 111, 109–26, *passim*
Gattrell, Victor, 3, 14
Gill, John, 119
Gill, Margaret, 119
Gillis, John, 3, 80, 81
Goddard, Thomas, 225, 226

Good Easter, Essex, 173–4
Gouldon, Alice, 74
Gowlett, Sarah (née Hall), 95
Great Bedwyn, Wiltshire, 217
Great Canfield, Essex, 157
Great Hallingsbury, Essex, 47
Greenaway, Joseph, 225
Gregory, Charles, 214–16, 220, 221, 224, 228, 231–2
Grimes, Christopher, 114
Gullofson, Mary, 95

Hall, Mr, 55
Hall family, 87–108 *passim*
  decline of family fortunes, 100–1
  family tree, 90
  Elizabeth, 91, 94, 96
  Henry, 96
  John, senior, 89, 91
  John, 91, 93, 94, 95–6, 97
  Mary, 95
  religion of, 91
  reputation of, 101
  Sarah, 92–3, 94, 97–100
  settlement of, 91
  Thomas, 91, 92, 93, 94, 95, 97–100
  William, 96
Halls, Susannah, 127, 130–5, 136, 138, 143, 146
Halstead, Essex, 102
Harriage, Isaac, 145, 146
*Harrington c. Harrington*, 47
Hatfield Broad Oak, Essex, 170–1, 180–1, 184
Haymarket, 202
Haywood, Eliza, *Present for a Servant-Maid*, 50–1, 54, 61
  *see also* advice literature
Hearsum, Samuel, 139–40
hearth tax, 22
Hecht, J.J., 49
Hertford, 139
Hickman, George, 200, 202–3, 205–6, 206
Hides, John, 145
Hills, Jane, 134, 135
Himmelfarb, Gertrude, 87
Hiscock, James, 214–16, 220–1, 224, 228, 231–2

Hodgson, Jane, 121
Hogger, Alice, 58
Hole, Alfred, 203
Holmes, Samuel (Smouchee), 196–7, 200, 203, 205
houses of correction, 120, 194
  Coldbath Fields, 197, 201, 205
  preferences among young offenders, 197, 206
  Tothill Fields, 193, 197, 201, 206
  *see also* gaols
household earnings, 168

illegitimacy, 6, 47, 52, 54, 70–86 *passim*
  peer pressure in relation to, 72
  relatives, attitudes of 73
  social consequences of, 72, 77
  social position of parents, 72
  *see also* illegitimate children
illegitimate children
  abandonment by both parents, 76, 77, 81
  death of, 70, 73, 80
  enquiries into paternity of, 92
  indemnifying the parish against, 158
  numbers in metropolitan institutions, 76
  paternity of 55
  provisions for, 71, 75–6, 80, 92
  *see also* abandonment; poor relief
illness, 27, 74–5, 93, 94, 95, 96, 98–9, 112, 120, 127, 143–4, 200
  expenses of, 96
  typhus, 122
industrial revolution, 110, 123
industrial Speenhamland, 130
Ingram, Martin, 72
inventories, pauper, 5, 35–6, 114, 155–91 *passim*; for specific items, 162–5
  comparison of pauper and probate inventories, 173–7
  probate, 156, 159, 161, 162–5, 172, 173–5

James, William, 143–5
Jarvis, Thomas, 27

Johns, William and Thomas,
  fellmongers and leather
  merchants, 91, 93–4, 98, 103
  *see also* employers
Johnson, Samuel, 123
Jones, Richard, 74, 81
Jones, Thomas, 58–60, 61
Jones, Thomas, 214–15, 221, 224–5, 228, 232
Josselin, Ralph, daughters of, 49
juvenile delinquency/delinquents, 4, 9, 192–210 *passim*
  domestic life of, 199–204
  employment history of, 199–200
  geographical mobility of, 202–3
  interviews with, 193–4, 199
  reformation, attitudes towards, 204–7
  role of environment, 204–5
  role of peer group, 195–6, 196–7, 201

Keeble, Daniel, 158
Kendal, Cumbria, 111
Kendall, Mary, 120–1
Kendall, Isaac, 120
King, Mrs, mangling woman, 196
King, Susan, 116
Kirby, Essex, 173–4
Kirkby Lonsdale, Westmoreland, 109–26, *passim*
  location, 110–11
  population, 111
kitchen, 53, 170, 171, 185
  *see also* inventories

Lancaster, 121
land tax assessments, 167, 171, 180, 181
Langford (Boxall), Elizabeth, 78–9
Langford (Boxall), Mary, 78
Langford (Boxall), James, 78–9
Laslett, Peter, 87, 138
Latchingdon, Essex, 92
Lawson, Robert, 113
leisure preference, 156
Liberty of the Fleet, 78
  *see also* marriage
Lidgould, Henry, 28
Lidgould, Nicholas, 28

life-cycle, 49, 161, 166
  *see also* poor
Lillington, Jane, 53
Lincoln, Thomas, 160
Linebaugh, Peter, 3
literacy/illiteracy, 4–5, 91, 98, 102, 110, 114–17, 133–5, 212, 225–6
  role of neighbours, 89
  'scriptural power', 134, 137
  *see also* education
Little, John, 197
localism, 212, 222, 229
  *see also* poor
Lock Hospital, London, 73–4, 75
  *see also* syphilis
lodgers, 138–9, 160–1
lodging houses, 196–7
London, 9, 20, 79, 88
  *see also under specific parishes and streets*
Looker, Isaac, 225
Lowry, William, 117–18
lunacy, 82, 112
lying-in, 55, 74, 92
  *see also* midwives

Macham, Ann, 28
Macham, Thomas, 28
Magdalen Hospital, London, 75
magistrates/JPs, 11–12, 26, 29–30, 52, 87
  appeals to, 93, 97, 223
  role in verifying claims for relief, 122
  *see also* poor relief
Maine, Philip, 206–7
Malcomson, Robert, 4, 155
Manchester, 112, 113, 117, 119
Mandler, Peter, 2, 4
Margate, 202
Marlborough, Wiltshire, 217
  Independent Constitutional Association, 224, 226
  price of bread in, 219, 220
Marlborough Union
  elections to, 218
  Guardians, 215, 219, 221
  Marlborough scale (of bread), 219–20, 223

marriage, 80, 81, 95, 110, 113
  after bearing a bastard, 77
  age at, 71, 88
  clandestine, 78
  rate of, 88
  *see also* courting; illegitimacy; sex
Marton-in-Craven, West Riding, Yorkshire, 110
master, role of, 50
  single, 50–1, 54, 60
  *see also* employer
material culture, 155–91 *passim*
Mayett, Joseph, 11–12
  *see also* autobiographies
Mayhew, Henry, 197, 204
McNeill, William, 109–10
Medcalf, Mr, 47
Medick, Hans, 138
Mendozas, Mrs, 202
Merritt, David, 30
microhistory, 109–10
Middlesex Criminal Register, 194
middling sort, 178
midwives/midwifery, 47
  *see also* lying-in
migration/emigration, 7, 88, 111, 130, 228
  *see also* transportation
Milbanks, James, 97–8
Mildenhall, Wiltshire, 211–38, *passim*
  specific conditions in, 216–18
Miles, William Augustus, 192–3
minister, role in securing relief, 114, 135
  *see also* poor relief
miscarriage, 82
mistresses, role of, 50, 58, 60
  *see also* employer
Mold, Flintshire, 115
monarchy, beliefs about on the part of the poor, 212, 222, 223, 226
motherhood, attitudes towards, 80–1
Mozeley, Thomas, 228
Murphy, John, 203–4
Murray, George, 203

Namier, Lewis, 110
neighbourliness, 52, 60, 78–9

New Poor Law/Poor Law Amendment Act, 4, 9, 141, 212, 213, 214, 229
  impact of, 13, 219–20
  misconceptions about, 214, 218, 222, 223, 226–7, 228–30
New South Wales, 193
  *see also* transportation
North, John, 160
Norwich, 140, 141

Oatley, Samuel, 213
O'Donnell, Thomas, 205–6, 207
old age, 10, 27, 127–54 *passim*
  and retirement, 145
  and work, 144–5
  experience of, 143–6, 147
  *see also* elderly; poor; poor relief
Old Bailey, 198
  Sessions Papers, 194
Old Poor Law (including 43 Eliz. cap.7 and subsequent legislation), 4, 8, 9, 19–20, 26, 28, 34–5, 87, 128
  as 'multi-use-right', 102–3
  *see also* poor relief
Oldham, Lancashire, 120
overseers of the poor *see* parish officers
Owen, Jane, 35

Page, Mary Ann, 137
parenthood, 6
parish officers
  churchwardens' accounts, 120
  guardian of the poor, 110
  overseers of the poor, 20, 26–7, 31, 34, 36, 87, 88–9, 95; of Chelmsford, 127; accounts, 5, 26, 30, 122, 157, 160; of St Giles in the Fields, 53
  paid, 110
  role in applying for relief, 135
  role in confirming pauper circumstances, 114, 115–16, 122, 132
  role in distributing money to non-resident poor, 117
  *see also* poor; poor relief
parlour, 170, 171, 185
  *see also* inventories
Parminter, Widow, 142–3

Parnell, Mary, 139
paternalism, 11–12, 212, 223, 228
pauper *see* poor
pauper inventories *see* inventories, pauper
pauper letters, 5, 6, 11, 87–108 *passim*, 109–26 *passim*, 127–54 *passim*, 211–38 *passim*
  criticism of, 130–5
  institutional background to, 129–30, 146
  tone of, 93, 102, 103, 111–12, 122–3, 130–1
pauper strategies, individual, 9–10, 30–1, 33
pawnshop/tally shop, 201
Peareth, Jane, 55–6
Pearl, Valerie, 20
Pearson, John, 122
Periar, Alice, 47, 61
Prorogative Court of Canterbury, 53
Perry, Ruth, 80–1
pesthouse, 159
petitions
  models for, 115
  to quarter sessions, 89
  *see also* poor relief; pauper letters
petty sessions, 7, 11–12, 26
  *see also* magistrates/JPs
Philanthropic Society, 193
Philbrick, Elizabeth, 136
Phillips, John, 73
plebeian culture, 2, 155
  *see also* charivari
poor
  as customers, 36
  as neighbours, 36
  branding goods belonging to, 160
  disorderly behaviour by, 32–3, 34
  family relations among, 118–21, 133–4, 135–9
  fraud by, 113, 114
  household organisation of, 137–8, 146–7
  individual strategies of, 49, 57
  investigations into the circumstances of, 27, 30–1, 34, 37
  material conditions of, 91–2, 100, 119
  material possessions of, 155–91 *passim*
  non-parochial resources available to, 172–3
  political debate amongst, 224–5, 226
  social position of, 172–3
  solitary, 138
  sources of information available to, 227
  support of parish for extended families of, 136
  visibility of, 100
  *see also* poor relief; badging
Poor Law Commissioners, 141, 211, 213, 214, 215, 216, 222, 223, 227–8, 230–2
poor relief, 10, 111
  appeals to magistrates/JPs, 29–30, 36
  application for, 5, 26–9, 31–2, 32, 31–2, 88, 94, 99, 74, 114–15, 115, 121, 127, 131–1, 145; in person, 114
  belief in right to, 10–12, 13, 21, 37, 87, 89, 102, 140, 227–8
  casual/extraordinary relief, 24–5, 29, 31
  clothes, 97
  collection/distribution of, 34, 92, 117, 132, 141
  complaints about, 213
  conditions for granting, 97, 121
  discontinuance of, 34, 36, 37, 95
  funeral expenses, 94, 112
  in relation to family economy, 220–2
  inquiry into the conditions of recipients, 88–9, 94, 95, 97–8, 113–14, 117, 132, 140–1, 160
  level of, 88–9, 102, 122, 213, 215, 219
  level of expenditure, 19, 20–1, 22–6
  moving expenses, 95, 98
  non-resident, 87–108 *passim*, 109–26 *passim*, 127–54 *passim*
  number of pensioners, 31
  orders for, 28–9
  out-relief, 11
  paternalism in, 89, 103

poor relief *continued*
  pensions, 19, 20–1, 22–6, 29, 95, 97, 112, 119, 132, 141, 142, 167
  relinquishment of goods in exchange for, 35–6, 37, 159, 182
  rent, 115
  to able-bodied, 219
  work for, 95, 97
  *see also* badging; poor; workhouse
poorhouse, 159
postage, 117
Powell, Ann, 33
Pratt, Isabella, 121
Preston, Lancashire, 117
Prison Discipline Society, 193
Proctor, Mary Ann, 119–20
prosopography, pauper, 111
prostitution, 202
punishment, attitudes towards, 206–7

quantitative analysis, 2–3
Quarter Sessions
  Clerkenwell, 197
  Westminster, 194

Ramsbury, Wiltshire, 224–5
rape, 7, 54, 55–6, 82
Ratcliff Highway murders, 203
rate-payers, 225–6
  numbers, 23, 27
  overlap with recipients of poor relief, 10–11, 92, 182
Red Lion Square, London, 70
reformation of manners, 9, 82
Reilly, Elizabeth, 135
religion
  non-conformity, 217–18, 225
  Old Meeting House, Chelmsford, 91, minutes of, 93
  revivals, 224
rent, 144
reputation, 53–5, 72, 73, 79–80, 101, 120
  claims to respectability, 89, 100, 201
  of household, 56
Rhodes, Henry, bookseller, 53
Richardson, Samuel, *Pamela*, 51
Rising, Daniel, 102
Roberts, Michael, 52–3

Robinson, Thomas, 116–17
Rogers, Nicholas, 71, 72
Royal Commission on Constabulary, 192
Rudé, George, 222
Rumbold, Joan, 73–4, 81
rural protest, 212, 217, 222–3, 224–5

Saunders, Mr (Bermondsey builder), 98
Schofield, Roger, 102
Scott, James, 5
seduction, 52
Select Committee on Gaols, 193, 201
Seleski, Patricia, 59
'servant class', 49
  *see also* domestic service/servant
settlement, 55, 87, 88, 91, 110, 127, 130, 140
  examinations, 3, 5, 73, 94, 95, 128
  laws, 4, 129
  legal cases to determine, 120
  removal to, 95–6, 97, 99, 123, 129, 139–43, 147, cost of, 99, 140, 142
  *see also* vagrancy
Seward, Mrs (St Botolph's workhouse keeper), 97
sex, 48, 74
  and pleasure, 81
  as courtship, 71, 73, 78, 79, 80
  boasting about, 56, 59
  consensual, 81–2
  female servant with master, 49–57
  male attitudes towards, 81
  male servant with mistress, 57–60
  repelling sexual advances from masters, 50–1, 53, 54
  servant-employer, 48
  sexual harassment, 55
  *see also* illegitimacy
Sharp, Rev. Joseph, 112
Shepherd, Jack, 192
Sheppey, John, 89
Shoreditch, 201
Shorter, Edward, 52
Sill, Edward, 120
Sill, Thomas, 120
Slack, Paul, 9, 19, 20–1, 137, 181

# Index

sleeping arrangements, 56
Smith, Joseph, 166–70, 171, 180, 184
Snell, Keith, 128
social capital, 12, 19–20
social control, 2, 19–21, 37
Sokoll, Thomas (excluding Chapter 6), 157
Speenhamland system, 88
Spooner, Susan, 140, 141
Spooner, Elizabeth, 141
Spufford, Margaret, 3
St Botolph's, Colchester, 88, 91, 94, 95
St Botolph's Aldgate, London, 47
St Clement Danes, London, 82
St Giles in the Fields, London, 54, 55, 136, 203–4
St James Westminster, 22, 55
St Luke's Chelsea, 70–86 *passim*
St Margaret's Westminster
  death of children in workhouse, 77
St Martin-in-the-Fields, 19–46 *passim*
  almshouse, 29
  population, 22
  number of pensioners, 22–4
  ratepayers, 23
St Marylebone, 139
St Nicholas, Ipswich, 127
St Osyth, Essex, 158
St Paul, Covent Garden, 22, 30
St Paul's, Shadwell, London, 78–9
St Peter, Colchester, 143
St Anne Soho, 22
Stammers, Mr, 82
standard of living debate, 3
Stanley, Isabella, 33
Steeple Bumpstead, Essex, 137
Stepney, 196, 203
Stewart, Charles, 198
Stone, Lawrence, 57
Sturges Bourne's Act (58 George III, cap. 69), 89
Styles, John, 8
Swing riots, *see* rural protest
Sydney police, 192
Symonds, Margaret, 197, 203
syphilis/venereal disease (various), 56, 73
  *see also* Lock Hospital, London

Tadgell, John, 170–1, 175, 180, 184–5
Tadgell, Widow, 170, 175
Tarrant, John, 226
Tarrant, James, 215, 225–6
Taylor, James Stephen (not including Chapter 5), 128, 130
tea-drinking, 177–8
Teabay, Betty, 109, 110
theft, 8, 101
  *see also* crime
Theydon Garnon, Essex, 160, 171, 185
thieves' kitchen, 197, 202–3
Thistlewaite, John, 114–15
Thomas, Keith, 143
Thompson, Edward, 2, 4
Thornton-in-Lonsdale, Westmoreland, 110
Thorpe, Essex, 173–4
threatening letters, 4, 128
Thudgett, Ann, 136
Thurtle, John, 102
*Times, The*, 205–6
tithe survey, 217
Tracy R.N., Lieutenant A.F., 193, 201
transportation, 193, 194, 198, 199
  as reformation, 205
  attitudes towards, 207
  behaviour in colonies, 196
  Point Puer, 198; subsequent death, 198
  Van Dieman's Land, 194, 196, 197
  *see also* migration/emigration.

Underwood, Henry, 205–6
unemployment/underemployment, 6
Upminster, Essex, 139

vagrancy, convictions for, 196
  examinations, 6
Vaisey, Edward, 211, 212, 213, 214, 218, 220, 222, 224, 225, 227, 228–9, 230–2
Vaughan, George, 206
Vesey, Mr, 55
vestries, 11, 27, 30
  Braintree, 141
  decisions of, 87, 94, 97
  meetings, 114
  minutes of, 26–7

vestries *continued*
  orders of, 33, 120
  reports to, 34
  select, 9, 94, 141
  *see also* parish officers
Vincent, David, 102
vocational training, 193, 205
  *see also* apprenticeship
Vose, Martha, 54–5, 61

Wade, Elizabeth, spinster, 53
Wade, Thomas (Thompson), 201–2, 207
Walton, Essex, 173–4
Warner, Thomas, 182
washhouse, 171, 186
Weatherill, Lorna, 156, 174, 183
Weaver, George, 198
Webster, George, 198
Webster, James, 59
Wells, Roger, 222–3
Wells, Sarah, 33
Westminster, 72
Wethersfield, Essex, 160, 180
whipping, public, 101
White, Samuel, 102
Whitechapel, 96, 196
Whitehaven, 122
widowhood, 160

Wigan, 120
Wild, Jonathan, 192
Williams, Rev. Mr, 216, 221, 223, 225
Wilson, Adrian, 71
Wilson, James, 114, 116, 117
Wilson, Widow, 160
Witford, Thomas, 203
Woodman, Henry, 218, 225
Woolwich, 198
work, 6
workhouse, 49, 75, 76, 158, 159, 172, 219, 228
  Braintree, 141, 142
  Chelmsford, 140
  Chelsea, 70, 73, 74–5, 78–9, 82
  goods delivered into, 158
  Kirkby Lonsdale, 123
  mortality rate of children in, 77
  St Botolphs, Colchester, 96, 97
  St Osyth, Essex, 158
  *see also* poor relief
Wright, Ann, 30
Wright, George, 157
Wrightson, Keith, 19–20
Writtle, Essex, 173–4

Yeareley, Susannah, 56
Young, Mr, 215